Current Debates on Public Finance

M. Erkan Üyümez / Canatay Hacıköylü (eds.)

Current Debates on Public Finance

Theory and Practice

PETER LANG
Lausanne • Berlin • Bruxelles • Chennai • New York • Oxford

Library of Congress Cataloging-in-Publication Data
A CIP catalog record for this book has been applied for at the Library of Congress.

Bibliographic Information published by the Deutsche Nationalbibliothek
The Deutsche Nationalbibliothek lists this publication in the Deutsche Nationalbibliografie; detailed bibliographic data is available online at http://dnb.d-nb.de.

ISBN 978-3-631-89686-0 (Print)
E-ISBN 978-3-631-90196-0 (E-PDF)
E-ISBN 978-3-631-90197-7 (E-PUB)
10.3726/b20820

Published by Peter Lang GmbH, Berlin, Deutschland

info@peterlang.com - www.peterlang.com

This publication has been peer reviewed.

Table of Contents

List of Contributors

Şebnem Tosunoğlu
Ph.D., Professor, Anadolu University, FEAS, Department of Public Finance, ssel@anadolu.edu.tr, ORCID ID: 0000-0002-5591-4403

Süleyman Kasal
Ph.D., Assistant Professor, Anadolu University, FEAS, Department of Public Finance, skasal@anadolu.edu.tr, ORCID ID: 0000-0001-8409-1090

Özlem Genç
Ph.D., Research Assistant, Ankara University, Faculty of Political Sciences, Department of Public Finance, ogenc@law.ankara.edu.tr ORCID: 0000-0001-6253-1120

Özlem Atay
Ph.D., Professor, Ankara University Faculty of Political Sciences, Department of Management, ozkanli@politics.ankara.edu.tr, ORCID: 0000-0002-2563-825X

M. Oğuz Arslan
Ph.D., Professor, Anadolu University, FEAS, Department of Public Finance, moarslan@anadolu.edu.tr, ORCID: 0000-0001-6011-4331

Hatice Altınok
Ph.D., Research Assistant, Anadolu University, FEAS, Department of Public Finance, haltinok@anadolu.edu.tr, ORCID: 0000-0002-1093-403X

Y. Tamer Ergül
Ph.D., Assistant Professor, Anadolu University, FEAS, Department of Public Finance, ytergul@anadolu.edu.tr, ORCID: 0000-0002-0180-2553

Sedef Oluklulu
Ph.D., Assistant Professor, Anadolu University, FEAS, Department of Public Finance, sedefcelik@anadolu.edu.tr, ORCID: 0000-0002-1335-7880

B. Tuğberk Tosunoğlu
Ph.D., Assistant Professor, Anadolu University, FEAS, Department of Economics, ttosunoglu@anadolu.edu.tr, ORCID: 0000-0001-9377-5136

Zeynep Karal Önder
Ph.D., Assistant Professor, Anadolu University, Faculty of Economics, Department of Public Finance, zkaral@anadolu.edu.tr, ORCID: 0000-0002-7032-9448

Ceran Arslan Olcay
Ph.D., Assistant Professor, Ankara University, Faculty of Political Sciences, Department of Economics, colcay@ankara.edu.tr, ORCID: 0000-0002-2114-4076

Bora Azamet Korkmaz
Research Assistant, Anadolu University, FEAS, Department of Public Finance, bakrkmz@gmail.com, ORCID: 0000-0001-5273-2893

Celali Yilmaz
Ph.D., Professor, Istanbul Medeniyet University, Faculty of Political Sciences, Department of Public Finance, celali.yilmaz@medeniyet.edu.tr, ORCID: 0000-0003-2767-1149

Burçin Bozdoğanoğlu
Ph.D., Professor, Bandırma Onyedi Eylül University, FEAS, Public Finance Department, bbozdoganoglu@bandirma.edu.tr, ORCID: 0000-0002-9337-2895

Kadir Yasin Eryiğit
Ph.D., Professor, Bursa Uludağ University, FEAS, Econometrics Department, kyeryigit@uludag.edu.tr, ORCID: 0000-0001-6857-7402

Adnan Gerçek
Ph.D., Professor, Bursa Uludağ University, FEAS, Public Finance Department, agercek@uludag.edu.tr, ORCID: 0000-0002-9495-2429

Esra Uygun
Ph.D., Lecturer, Tokat Gaziosmanpaşa University, Zile Vocational Scholl, Public Finance Department, esra.uygun@gop.edu.tr, ORCID: 0000-0001-5332-0831

Müslüm Gümüş
Ph.D., Assistant Professor, Hakkari University, FEAS, Department of Public Finance, muslumgumus@hakkari.edu.tr, ORCID:0000-0001-9790-7028

Mustafa Erkan Üyümez
Ph.D., Professor, Anadolu University, FEAS, Department of Public Finance, meuyumez@anadolu.edu.tr, ORCID:0000-0001-7567-3486

Ayşegül Yücel
Research Assistant, Bandırma Onyedi Eylül University, FEAS, Department of Public Finance, ayucel@bandirma.edu.tr, ORCID: 0000-0001-9577-4348

Ali Osman Yılmaz
Ph.D., Assistant Professor, Karabük University, Safranbolu Ş.Y.D. Vocational School, Department of Accounting and Tax, aliyilmaz@karabuk.edu.tr, ORCID: 0000-0001-7758-1323

Süleyman Kasal[1] & Şebnem Tosunoğlu[2]

Fiscal Stance and Inflation Expectations in Turkey: A Markov Regime Switching Analysis[3]

1. Introduction

One major issue that closely concerns both fiscal policy and monetary policymakers is expectations. The economic actors' expectations play an important role to decision-makers. Because policymakers make decisions according to the economic actors' expectations. Especially, inflation expectations are a guide for policy makers.

With the broad adoption of inflation targeting within the context of monetary policy, the idea of expectations has received increased attention (Kara & Küçük-Tuğer, 2010: 2725). For example, Turkey's new monetary policy following the 2001 crisis stresses the need of managing public expectations in order to eliminate inertia in inflation dynamics by moving economic actors' inflation expectations to a forward-looking perspective (Oral et al., 2011: 6). On the other hand, as is known that the inflation expectations are also shaped according to fiscal policy. According to the traditional view, monetary policy alone is not enough to ensure price stability, and an suitable fiscal policy is also necessary to control inflation (Lyziak & Mackiewicz-Lyziak, 2020: 296).

The first study emphasizing the importance of fiscal policy in ensuring price stability was conducted by Sargent and Wallace (1981). The authors developed their studies on the assumptions that monetary and fiscal policy dominate each other. In their studies, Sargent and Wallace (1981) argue that the monetary authority cannot control the monetary base and inflation forever under the assumption that fiscal policy dominates monetary policy. Indeed, the fact that budget deficits cannot be financed forever by borrowing causes principal and

---

1 Anadolu University, FEAS, Department of Public Finance, skasal@anadolu.edu.tr, ORCID ID: 0000-0001-8409-1090

2 Anadolu University, FEAS, Department of Public Finance, ssel@anadolu.edu.tr, ORCID ID: 0000-0002-5591-4403

3 This article presented as an "abstract (not full paper)" at the 36th International Public Finance Conference to be held on 27–30 October 2022 in Antalya, Turkey.

interest payments on bonds already sold to combat inflation to be financed, at least in part, by seigniorage, which requires the creation of an additional monetary base. According to the authors, in a monetizing economy, this practice sooner or later results in additional inflation (unpleasant monetarist arithmetic). In later years, this view was examined by many academics within the framework of the fiscal theory of the price level (Leeper (1991); Sims (1994); Woodford (1994); Cochrane (2001); Leeper and Yun (2006); Davig and Leeper (2007); Bajo-Rubio et al. (2009)). Within the framework of the fiscal theory of the price level, two different policy regimes have been put forward in the literature: the Ricardian regime (monetary dominant) and the non-Ricardian regime (fiscal dominance).[4] In the Ricardian regime, the price level is determined by monetary policy, while in non-Ricardian regimes, the price level is determined by the government budget constraint (Oktayer, 2013: 54). For any given price level, the intertemporal government budget constraint under the Ricardian regime is satisfied by primary surpluses (Lyziak & Mackiewicz-Lyziak, 2020: 297). Monetary policy becomes passive and fiscal policy active in non-Ricardian regimes. Consequently, in the fiscal dominant regime, fiscal policies influence the price level (budget deficits and debt). As a result, it is critical to consider how the fiscal stance affects the level of prices.

The fiscal stance also affects inflation expectations. In their studies, Leeper and Leith (2016: 2314), when economic agents are aware that policymakers may favor inflation surprises in order to ease the debt burden, they boost inflation expectations as debt levels grow until this motivation is no longer present. Despite this, little is known about the connection between fiscal policy and inflation expectations, and this relationship is unclear. In his study, Webb (1986) concluded that inflation expectations depend on fiscal news for Germany. Celasun et al. (2004) found that an improvement in the primary balance significantly reduced inflation expectations for emerging countries. In their study, Cerisola and Gelos (2009) concluded that fiscal stance (proxied by the ratio of primary surplus to GDP) is effective in shaping inflation expectations for Brasil. In their weekly survey of inflation expectations, Galati et al. (2011) concluded that the government debt concerns triggered by the Greek financial crisis had some effect on short- and medium-term inflation expectations, albeit slightly, long-term expectations. Lyziak and Mackiewicz-Lyziak (2020) found that fiscal stance

4 While Leeper (1991) distinguishes between active and passive authority, this separation is brought by Woodford (1994) in subsequent studies to bring the distinction between fiscal policy dominance and monetary policy dominance regime (Saçkan, 2006: 7).

(proxied by the general government debt to GDP ratio) in 22 European countries affected the inflation expectations of consumer and professional forecasters.

Our aim is to analyze how government debt (as an indicator of fiscal stance) affects inflation expectations in periods when the economic actors' expectations are different. The main purpose of this study is to better understand the dynamics of inflation expectations for fiscal policymakers. As is known, Turkey had low inflation and inflation expectations between 2006 and 2016. However, inflation increased and expectations deteriorated in the post-2017 period. Therefore, we can be divide inflation periods into two periods as single-digit and double-digit periods. Figure 1 presents box-plot graphs of the arithmetic averages of the expectation of 12 months ahead annual CPI (consumer price index) obtained from the Central Bank of the Republic of Turkey (CBRT) Market Participants Survey for two sub-periods.

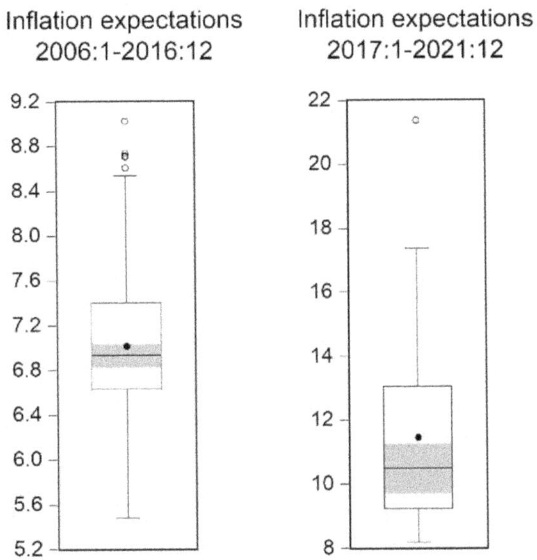

Fig. 1: *Box-plot charts of 12-month ahead inflation expectations in Turkey*

As seen in Fig. 1, the expectation of 12 months ahead annual CPI in Turkey differ for two different periods. While economic actors had single-digit inflation expectations between 2006 and 2016, they had double-digit inflation expectations as of 2017. Therefore, it is necessary to analyze inflation expectations dynamics in terms of different periods. For this purpose, the questions about the effects of the fiscal stance on inflation expectations in Turkey were examined with the Markov regime switching model for the period 2006:1-2021:12. The results showed that the fiscal stance affects inflation expectations differently in low and high inflation expectation regimes. These results indicate that the fiscal stance should be differentiated according to inflation expectation regimes.

The remainder of the research is structured as follows: Section 2 covers the study's data, while Section 3 discusses the method. Section 4 discusses the empirical findings. The final section is the conclusion.

2. Data

Our model is based on the study of Lyziak and Mackiewicz-Lyziak (2020). The authors analyze the impact of fiscal sustainability on the setting of inflation expectations in 22 European countries at a quarterly frequency between 2000 and 2017. In their study, inflation expectations beyond 1 and 2 years, change in 12-month consumer price index, short-term interest rate, nominal exchange rate index, output deficit and growth rate of oil prices were used. The authors used the ratio of general government debt to GDP as an indicator of fiscal stance. Similar to the Lyziak and Mackiewicz-Lyziak (2020) study, we used the exchange rate volatility predicted by the EGARCH(1, 1) method, the deviation of the logarithmic industrial production index from the trend (with HP filtered-output gap), the logarithmic percentage change in the total central government debt stock as an indicator of the fiscal stance, the CBRT policy interest rate, the annual inflation rate (π_t) and the arithmetic averages of the expectation of 12 months ahead annual CPI $\left(\pi^f_{t+12}\right)$ obtained from the CBRT in our study. The forecast period begins in January 2006 and ends in December 2021. The variables were obtained from IMF-IFS and CBRT-EDDS. Figure 2 presents the scatter plots between inflation expectations and variables.

As seen in Fig. 2, it is understood that the variables have a positive relationship with inflation expectations. According to Fig. 2, the direction of change in inflation expectations is the same as the direction of change in other variables. For instance, the correlation coefficient between the government debt and inflation expectations is 0.24 at 1 % significance level. However, we need to an econometric analysis to determine the exact direction of the relationship between the variables.

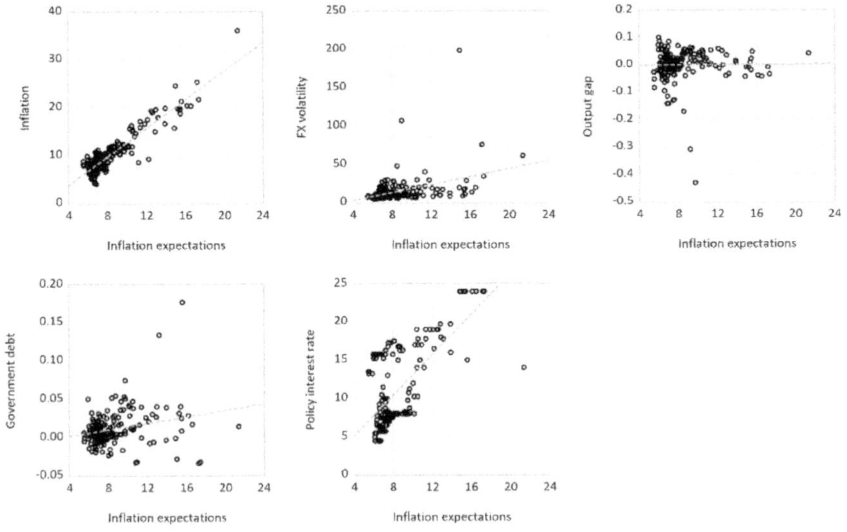

Fig. 2: *The scatter plots between 12-month ahead inflation expectations and the variables*

3. Methodology

The relationship between the variables will be analyzed by the Markov regime switching model. The Markov regime switching model is a nonlinear method introduced to the literature by Hamilton (1989). In this method, the variables switch to a new structure with the changing regime. This method offers the opportunity to evaluate periods with different characteristics in a different way. For example; the periods of expansion and contraction of the economy are determined according to s_t state variable, which is random variable and cannot be directly observed (Barışık et al., 2010: 93). For this purpose, the Markov regime switching model was used in our study to determine the periods when inflation expectations were low and high. Because while the average inflation in Turkey was single digits between 2006 and 2016, the inflation increased to double digits in the 2017–2021 period. The transition to double-digit inflation after 2017 has had distorting effects on inflation expectations. Since the transition to the regime of high inflation expectation affects economic actors, so is appropriate to analyze the effect of the change in fiscal stance on inflation expectations with the Markov regime switching model.

In the Markov regime switching model, variables should not have a unit root and should not be linear. Therefore, unit root test and linearity tests should be performed on the variables before analyzing the relationship between the variables. We first test for the stationarity of the variables by using Ng and Perron (2001) unit root test. We used linearity tests developed by Keenan (1985), Brock et al. (1987), Tsay (1986), Harvey et al. (2008).

4. Empirical Results

The unit root test developed by Ng and Perron (2001) was applied to the variables before analyzing the relationship between the variables. In their study, the authors aimed to improve the power of many tests that show a small size distortion problem when the moving average polynomials of the first-order differences of the series have a wide negative root. Also with this unit root test, the authors aimed to provide an improved procedure for selecting truncation lag. Therefore, Ng and Perron (2001) unit root test provides high power gains and size performance. The authors developed three test statistics in their work. In our study, we used MZ_a test statistics among these three tests. The lag length was chosen by the AIC. The maximum lag length is set at 12. In addition, the variance estimation method is based on the study of Sul et al. (2005). The unit root test results are presented in Tab. 1.

Tab. 1: Unit root test results (with constant model)

Variables	MZ_a
fx volatility	-76.496*** (0)
output gap	-27.023*** (2)
debt	-77.680*** (7)
policy interest rate	-11.939** (5)
π_t	-6.443* (12)
π^f_{t+12}	-91.304** (6)

Notes: 1 %, 5 % and 10 % critical values for *Ng – Perron* (MZ_a) unit root test are -13.800, -8.10, and -5.70 respectively. The AIC is used to choose for lag order with the maximum lag set at 12. (…) indicates lag length. Long-run consistent variance estimation method is based on Sul et al., (2005)'s study. ***, ** and * represent at 1 %, 5 % and 10 % significance levels.

According to the results presented in Tab. 1, the variables are stationary in their level values. The results in Tab. 1 indicate that the null hypothesis of a unit root is rejected for five variables at the 1 %, 5 %, and 10 % significance levels.

After the unit root tests, the linearity tests were performed. Whether the variables are linear or not is determined by tests developed by Keenan (1985), Brock et al. (1987), Tsay (1986), Harvey et al. (2008). The tests developed by Keenan (1985) and Tsay (1986) are based on the assumption that the variables are stationary. However, the Harvey et al. (2008) test does not make an assumption about the stationary of the variables and has better finite sample size and power characteristics (Yılancı & Tıraşoğlu, 2016: 5). The test developed by Brock et al. (1987) is applied to the error terms obtained after the series are delineated from their linear structure (Barışık et al., 2010: 95). In these linearity tests, the null hypothesis of the linearity is tested against the alternative hypothesis of the nonlinearity. The linearity test results are presented in Tab. 2.

Tab. 2: The linearity test results for variables

Variables	BDS	Harvey et al. (2008)	Tsay (1986)	Keenan (1985)
fx volatility	11.731*** [0.000]	6.27*	4.146**(1) [0.043]	30.670***(1) [0.000]
output gap	18.537*** [0.000]	7.17**	4.289***(3) [0.000]	0.386 (3) [0.534]
debt	7.541*** [0.000]	17.16***	11.79***(1) [0.000]	16.362***(1) [0.000]
policy interest rate	40.777*** [0.000]	1.46	2.10*(3) [0.054]	0.123 (3) [0.725]
π_t	7.828*** [0.000]	3.60	0.885 (2) [0.450]	0.230 (1) [0.631]
π^f_{t+12}	19.955*** [0.000]	13.06***	2.351*(2) [0.07]	0.242 (2) [0.622]

Notes: Table critical values for the Harvey et al. (2008) unit root test at 1 %, 5 % and 10 % significance levels are 9.210, 5.991, 4.605. (…) indicates the order length. […] indicates the probability values. ***, ** and * represent 1 %, 5 % and 10 % significance levels, respectively. BDS: Brock et al. (1987).

As seen in Tab. 2, the linearity tests indicate that all variables are not linear according to Brock et al. (1987)'s test. Therefore, there is not a problem in investigating the variables with the Markov regime switching model. Table 3 presents the results of a Markov regime switching model with two regimes, taking into account periods of low and high inflation expectation. The lagged values of the variables were used in the model. The reason is that inflation expectations are based on the realizations of the previous period. For instance, inflation expectations in the next period will be renewed as a result of a change in fiscal stance or the change in the output gap. Furthermore, the proposed variables are suitably lagged such that they are compatible with the data set used to create the expectations (Kara & Küçük-Tuğer, 2010: 2734).

Tab. 3: Markov regime switching model results

Dependent variable π^{f}_{t+12}	**Regime 1**	**Prob.**	**Regime 2**	**Prob.**
π_{t-1}	0.217***	0.000	0.663***	0.000
$fx\ volatility_{t-1}$	0.029***	0.000	0.014***	0.000
$output\ gap_{t-1}$	1.890*	0.056	5.604***	0.008
$debt_{t-1}$	14.778***	0.009	24.879***	0.000
$policy\ interest\ rate_{t-1}$	0.311***	0.000	-0.136***	0.000
c	2.981***	0.000	2.502***	0.000
$\log(\sigma)$		[-0.701***]		
AIC		1.817		
Log likelihood		-157.65		
$\begin{bmatrix} p_{11} & p_{12} \\ p_{21} & p_{22} \end{bmatrix}$		$\begin{bmatrix} 0.966 & 0.034 \\ 0.035 & 0.965 \end{bmatrix}$		
$1/1-p_{11}$		~29		
$1/1-p_{22}$		~28		

***, ** and * represent at 1 %, 5 % and 10 % significance levels.

The results obtained from Tab. 3 indicate that the results have changed in two different inflation expectation regimes. The results show that inflation, output gap, government debt and policy interest rate affect inflation expectations to different magnitudes in two different regimes. Inflation inertia (coefficient of past inflation) was found to be statistically significant in both regimes. However, the inflation inertia coefficient is higher in the high inflation expectation regime than in the low inflation expectation regime. This result indicates that inertia is strong in the high inflation expectation regime. The results are different in the two regimes for monetary policy. In the low inflation expectation regime, monetary policy and inflation expectations move in the same direction. This situation is called the “price puzzle” in the literature. The concept of the price puzzle introduced by the Sims (1992) study and labeled by Eichenbaum (1992), is defined as the positive reaction of prices to positive monetary policy shocks (Castelnuovo & Surico, 2010: 1262). In the regime of high inflation expectation, the opposite is the case. Inflation expectations fall in response to an increase in the policy interest rate. Therefore, in the regime of high inflation expectation, the central bank has the opportunity to reduce inflation expectations with the policy interest rate tool.

A change in fiscal policy stance affects inflation expectations differently in the low and high inflation expectation regimes. A change in fiscal policy stance in the low inflation expectation regime is less distorting inflation expectations. However, the fiscal policy stance has a more distorting effect on expectations in the high inflation expectation regime. As Lyziak and Mackiewicz-Lyziak (2020) emphasize, in the case of high fiscal risk, economic actors react to the increase in government debt by increasing inflation expectations.

Another conclusion from Tab. 3 relates to regime transition possibilities. The results indicate that the transition between regimes is rigid. To put it more precisely, the diagonals of the transition matrices showing regime probabilities were found to be more than 90 % for both regimes. This result supports the studies of Çatık and Önder (2011) and Çatık and Karaçuka (2012). In addition, the results indicate that the average duration in the regimes is very close to each other. More specifically, the average duration in both regimes is about 29 months. Therefore, regimes are permanent. Succinctly, high inflation expectation regime takes a long time.

Another of the conclusions drawn from the Markov regime switching model relates to the transition probability between regimes. The smoothed probabilities are shown in Fig. 3. The first panel in Fig. 3 represents the transition probabilities to a low inflation expectation regime, and the second panel represents the transition probabilities to a high inflation expectation regime.

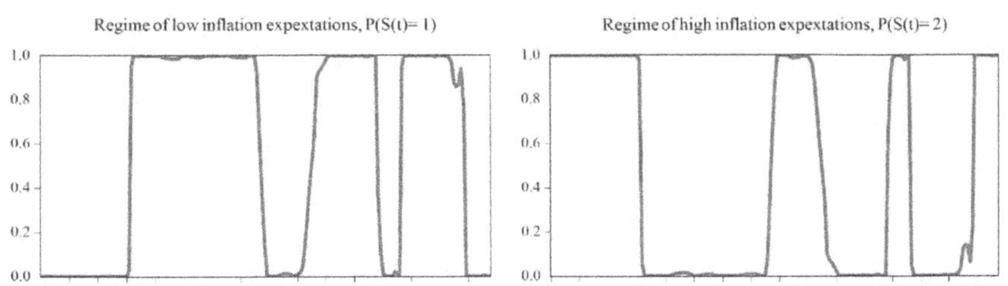

Fig. 3: *Smoothed probabilities for regimes*

As can be seen in Fig. 3, the high inflation expectation regime coincides with vital fiscal, economic and political incidents in Turkey. According to these results, the periods between March 2006 and March 2009, August 2013 and April 2016, December 2017 and December 2018, and the period after June 2020, indicate a high inflation expectation regime in Turkey.

5. Conclusion

High inflation in Turkey has recently become one of the most important problems. In periods of high inflation, there are widespread discourses on the issues of high budget deficits and government debts, the deficit financing and inflation relationship in Turkey. It is important to examine the effects of the fiscal policy stance on inflation. Additionally, it is necessary to analyze the effects of the fiscal stance on inflation expectations. This study examines the role of government debt on inflation expectations in Turkey between the periods 2006:1-2021:12 with the Markov regime switching model. The main objective of the study is to analyze in a nonlinear way how government debt affects expectations during periods of low and high inflation expectations. For this reason, Markov regime switching model which is one of the nonlinear methods was used in the study.

We analyzed the reactions of the variables in the low and high inflation expectation regime through the Markov regime switching model. The results indicate that economic actors increase inflation expectations in response to an increase in government debt. Moreover, economic actors worsen their inflation expectations more in the high inflation expectation regime than in the low inflation expectation regime. The results also show that the transition probabilities between the regimes are rigid. This result indicates that the deterioration in expectations has a high rigidity. When the results are evaluated within the policy framework, they indicate the significance of fiscal stance and demonstrate that inflation and inflation expectations cannot be solely influenced by monetary policy. Therefore, contrary to the traditional view that inflation is only a monetary phenomenon, it can be said that fiscal policy is an important policy in managing expectations. Therefore, government debt sustainability is a more critical issue in the regime of high inflation expectation. It is vital that the government provides intertemporal budget constraint.

References

Bajo-Rubio, O., Diaz-Roldan, C., & Esteve, V. (2009). Deficit Sustainability and Inflation in EMU: An Analysis from The Fiscal Theory of The Price Level.

European Journal of Political Economy, 25(4), pp. 525–539. https://doi.org/10.1016/j.ejpoleco.2009.04.001

Barışık, S., Çevik, E. İ., & Kırcı Çevik, N. (2010). Türkiye'de Okun Yasası, Asimetri İlişkisi ve İstihdam Yaratmayan Büyüme: Markov-Switching Yaklaşımı. *Maliye Dergisi, 159*(Temmuz-Aralık), 88–102.

Brock, W. A., Dechert, W. D., & Scheinkman, J. A. (1987). *A Test for Independence Based on the Correlation Dimension*. Department of Economics, University of Wisconsin at Madison, University of Houston, University of Chicago.

Castelnuovo, E., & Surico, P. (2010). Monetary Policy, Inflation Expectations and the Price Puzzle. *Economic Journal, 120*(549), 1262–1283. https://doi.org/10.1111/j.1468-0297.2010.02368.x

Çatık, A. N., & Karaçuka, M. (2012). Oil Pass-Through to Domestic Prices in Turkey: Does the Change in Inflation Regime Matter? *Ekonomska Istrazivanja, 25*(2), 277–296. https://doi.org/10.1080/1331677X.2012.11517508

Çatık, A. N., & Önder, A. Ö. (2011). Inflationary Effects of Oil Prices in Turkey: A Regime-Switching Approach. *Emerging Markets Finance & Trade, 47*(5), 125–140. https://doi.org/10.2753/REE1

Celasun, O., Gelos, R. G., & Prati, A. (2004). Obstacles to Disinflation: What Is the Role of Fiscal Expectations?, IMF Working Paper, WP/04/111. IMF.

Cerisola, M., & Gelos, G. (2009). What Drives Inflation Expectations in Brazil? An Empirical Analysis. *Applied Economics, 41*(10), 1215–1227. https://doi.org/10.1080/00036840601166892

Cochrane, J. H. (2001). Long-Term Debt and Optimal Policy in the Fiscal Theory of the Price Level. *Econometrica, 69*(1). https://www.jstor.org/stable/2692186

Davig, T., & Leeper, E. M. (2007). Fluctuating Macro Policies and the Fiscal Theory. *NBER Macroeconomics Annual, Volume 21*, pp. 247–315.

Eichenbaum, M. (1992). Comment on Interpreting the Macroeconomic Time Series Facts: The Effects of Monetary Policy by C.A. Sims, *European Economic Review, 36*(5), pp. 1001–11. https://doi.org/10.1016/0014-2921(92)90042-U

Galati, G., Heemeijer, P., & Moessner, R. (2011). *How Do Inflation Expectations Form? New Insights from a High-Frequency Survey*. DNB Working Paper, No. 283, March 2011. http://ssrn.com/abstract=1861066

Hamilton, J. D. (1989). A New Approach to the Economic Analysis of Nonstationary Time Series and the Business Cycle. *Econometrica, 57*(2), pp. 357–384. https://www.jstor.org/stable/1912559

Harvey, D. I., Leybourne, S. J., & Xiao, B. (2008). A Powerful Test for Linearity When the Order of Integration is Unknown. *Studies in Nonlinear Dynamics & Econometrics, 12*(3), pp. 1–22. https://doi.org/10.2202/1558-3708.1582

Kara, H., & Küçük-Tuğer, H. (2010). Inflation expectations in Turkey: Learning to be rational, *Applied Economics, 42*(21), pp. 2725–2742. https://doi.org/10.1080/00036840801964559

Keenan, D. M. (1985). A Tukey Nonadditivity-Type Test for Time Series Nonlinearity, *Biometrika, 72*, pp. 39–44. https://doi.org/10.2307/2336333

Leeper, E. M. (1991). Equilibria Under "Active" and "Passive" Monetary and Fiscal Policies. *Journal of Monetary Economics, 27*(1), pp. 129–147. https://doi.org/10.1016/0304-3932(91)90007-B

Leeper, E. M., & Leith, C. (2016). "Understanding Inflation as a Joint Monetary—Fiscal Phenomenon". In: J. Taylor, H. Uhlig (Eds.), *Handbook of Macroeconomics*, vol. 2B. Elsevier, Amsterdam, Netherlands, pp. 2305–2415.

Leeper, E. M., & Yun, T. (2006). Monetary-Fiscal Policy Interactions and the Price Level: Background and Beyond. *International Tax and Public Finance, 13*(4), pp. 373–409. https://doi.org/10.1007/s10797-006-8599-2

Łyziak, T., & Mackiewicz-Łyziak, J. (2020). Does Fiscal Stance Affect Inflation Expectations? Evidence for European Economies. *Economic Analysis and Policy, 68*, pp. 296–310. https://doi.org/10.1016/j.eap.2020.09.010

Ng, S., & Perron, P. (2001). Lag Length Selection and the Construction of Unit Root Tests with Good Size, *Econometrica, 69*(6), pp. 1519–1554. https://doi.org/10.1111/1468-0262.00256

Oktayer, A. (2013). Fiyat Düzeyi Mali Teorisinin Türkiye Açısından Geçerliliği: Ampirik Bir Analiz, *İktisat Fakültesi Mecmuası, 63*(1), pp. 51–79.

Oral, E., Saygılı, H., Saygılı, M., Tuncel, S. Özge. (2011), "Inflation Expectations in Turkey: Evidence from Panel Data", *OECD Journal: Journal of Business Cycle Measurement and Analysis*, vol. 2011/1, https://doi.org/10.1787/jbcma-2011-5kgg5k53np7c.

Saçkan, O. (2006). *Genel Fiyat Düzeyinin Belirlenmesinde Para ve Maliye Politikası Dominant Rejimler: Türkiye Örneği, 1988–2005* (Unpublished thesis). Türkiye Cumhuriyet Merkez Bankası, Ankara.

Sargent, T. J., & Wallace, N. (1981). Some Unpleasant Monetarist Arithmetic District Conditions, *Federal Reserve Bank of Minneapolis Quarterly Review, 5*(3), pp. 1–18. http://www.minneapolisfed.org/research/QR/QR531.pdf

Sims, C. A. (1992). Interpreting the Macroeconomic Time Series Facts, the Effects of Monetary Policy, *European Economic Review, 36*(5), pp. 975–1000. https://doi.org/10.1016/0014-2921(92)90041-T

Sims, C. A. (1994). A Simple Model for Study of the Determination of the Price Level and the Interaction of Monetary and Fiscal Policy, *Economic Theory, 4*(3), pp. 381–399. https://www.jstor.org/stable/25054771

Sul, D., Phillips, P. C. B., & Choi, C.-Y. (2005). Prewhitening Bias in HAC Estimation, *Oxford Bulletin of Economics and Statistics, 67*(4), pp. 517–546. https://doi.org/10.1111/j.1468-0084.2005.00130.x

Tsay, R. S. (1986). Nonlinearity Tests for Time Series, *Biometrika, 73*(2), pp. 461–466. https://www.jstor.org/stable/2336223

Webb, S. B. (1986). Fiscal News and Inflationary Expectations in Germany After World War I, *The Journal of Economic History*, *46*(3), pp. 769–794. https://www.jstor.org/stable/212148

Woodford, M. (1994). Monetary Policy and Price Level Determinacy in a Cash-in-Advance Economy, *Economic Theory, 4*(3), pp. 345–380. https://www.jstor.org/stable/25054770

Yılancı, V., & Tıraşoğlu, M. (2016). Türkiye'nin Makroekonomik Zaman Serilerinin Doğrusallığının Testi, *Çankırı Karatekin Üniversitesi İktisadi ve İdari Bilimler Fakültesi Dergisi,* 6(2), pp. 1–16.

Özlem Genç[1] & Özlem Atay[2]

EU Anchor, Turkish Governance and Economic Performance

1. Introduction

Institutions play a crucial role in economic growth and development of a country. Inclusive and extractive institutions approach developed by Acemoğlu and Robinson (2012) states that while inclusive institutions contribute to economic growth positively, extractive ones have damaging effects on the economy. In this context, governance emerges as the main element, wide-ranging repercussions of which affect the economy and well-being of citizens positively. Common aspects of governance are maintaining rule of law and democracy, establishing a participatory and inclusive governance approach and combatting corruption. Transparency, accountability, equitability and responsibility are prerequisites for good governance.

International organisations such as International Monetary Fund, the World Bank and the European Union have attached great significance at the concept of governance. Particularly, the European Union, by exerting great influence on its partnership relations makes effort to impose good governance. The model based on Copenhagen criteria in the process of admitting a new country to the Union, entails the country in question to comply with rule of law, free market economy, and the ability to take on obligations of membership.

Outcomes of Turkey–European Union relationship have been the establishment of customs union and negotiation process, both entailing regulatory requirements. In terms of Turkey's expectation to become a member, the status of affairs has been unsatisfactory, somehow had transformative effects on its institutional structure and governance.

The main hypothesis of this research is that the period in which Turkey has had close relationship with the European Union has contributed to economic performance through governance; on the other hand, derailing from the

1 Ph.D., Research Assistant, Ankara University, Faculty of Political Sciences, Department of Public Finance, ogenc@law.ankara.edu.tr, ORCID: 0000-0001-6253-1120

2 Ph.D., Professor, Ankara University Faculty of Political Sciences, Department of Management, ozkanli@politics.ankara.edu.tr, ORCID: 0000-0002-2563-825X

European Union process has had negative impacts. Apparently, the European Union process together with agreements with International Monetary Fund and World Bank have been instrumental as double anchors. Implementing rule-based decision making by founding autonomous authorities independent from political pressure, enacting disciplining laws have been consequences of the process, culminating in high growth and attracting foreign direct investments. Setbacks from reform process, conversely, have given rise to decadence of governance and economic performance. Quality of growth has deteriorated and foreign direct investments have contracted.

In the context of this research, literature on governance and economic performance is analysed, the effect of the relationship between Turkey and the European Union on Turkey's economic performance is evaluated by analysing European Commission's Progress Reports on Turkey and World Governance Indicators data released by the World Bank.

2. Literature Review

Institutions are known as "the rules of the game" as put forth by North. Within this prominent framework, institutions are distinguished as formal and informal institutions. When political, economic and legal rules are the instances of formal institutions; concepts such as norms of behavior, codes of conduct and culture compose informal institutions (North, 1999/2010: 9–13). Works of Acemoğlu and Robinson on institutions that have been mostly debated and assumptions of which are commonly accepted distinguish institutions as inclusive and extractive. While inclusive institutions reflect positively on economic performance and human development, extractive ones pave the way for a poor nation (Acemoğlu & Robinson, 2012). Repercussions of institutions on economic performance bring about the concepts of institutional quality and level of institutional development that lead to the concept of governance. Although there is not a generally accepted definition of governance, common aspects of different definitions that form governance or the elements that are associated with are, rule of law, democracy, and anti-corruption approach, inclusive and participatory governance approach. The basic principles of governance are stated as equitability, accountability, transparency and responsibility. The adoption of those principles are of great significance in the process of establishing inclusive institutions. As revealed by North in a historical perspective, it takes a long historical process for institutions to be established and is affected by cultural, economic, social and legal factors. It is obvious that adoption of those principles in governance has a transforming effect (North, 1999/2010: 97–136). Through establishment of inclusive institutions, governance encourages democratic and human development as well as economic development. Furthermore, positive effect of governance on human capital and capital investments lays the groundwork for innovation and technology transfer, investment and economic development. In this way, governance capacity of the country is led to translate economic and social resources into development (Hall & Jones, 1999: 83–84). Good governance and high quality institutions ensuring particularly rule of law, accountability and transparency are of great significance to combat corruption, rent-seeking behavior and socially unfair privileges enjoyed by specific groups (Masuch et al., 2018: 15).

International organisations such as World Bank and International Monetary Fund (IMF) have also contemplated governance as a guiding principle in policy making while their own role and transformation have been debated. Kaufmann of Brookings Institution, Kraay and Mastruzzi of World Bank have defined governance as the traditions and institutions determining how authority has been exercised (Kauffman et al., 2010: 1–4). Their research based on data sources starting from 1996 has been mainstreamed in the literature and come up with widely used indicators. We used these indicators in this research to evaluate governance in Turkey. Three areas of governance have been defined concerning the process ensuring the election, monitoring and replacement of governments, the capacity of the government to formulate and implement effective policies, the respect of governments and citizens for the institutions determining their economic and social relations surrounding them. World Governance Indicators (WGI) based on those areas have thus been formulated. Two indicators corresponding to three governance areas have paved the way for six interrelated indicators: voice and accountability, political stability and absence of violence/terrorism, government effectiveness, regulatory quality, rule of law, control of corruption (The World Bank, 2022b).

3. EU Anchor and Governance

Among the organisations or communities of Western states, the European Union (EU) as a regional integration has the leading role to emphasize governance, human rights, democracy, and the rule of law as the main elements of its external partnerships (Börzel et al., 2008: 4).

The EU defines its objective as promoting peace, its values and wellbeing of people. To reach those goals, the Union has established a single market and prioritised sustainable development based on balanced economic growth, price stability, full employment, a highly competitive social market economy, a high level of protection of the environment. (Treaty on EU art. 2–3) From the Union's point of view, those goals can be reached through good governance. Rule of law that is undeniably an element of good governance is the primary condition that needs to be fulfilled for a country to be admitted to the EU.

Among various external relationships, the EU has set with the outer world such as enlargement, neighbourhood and trade, enlargement is the one thatthe EU exerts the most influence and exercises transformative power (Öniş &Kutlay, 2019: 230, Yalman & Göksel, 2017). In this respect, enlargement process is the instrument of institutional transformation. The EU has formulated the enlargement process based on Copenhagen criteria that stipulate a country to ensure rule of law and democracy along with a functioning free market economy and the ability to take on the obligations of membership (EUR-LEX, 2022).

3.1. A Brief Review of EU Turkey Relations

Turkey-EU relations can be traced back to the year 1959 when Turkey applied for partnership with the European Economic Community. The most concrete outcomes of this inconclusive relationship with difficulties have been customs union and negotiation process. By signing the Ankara Agreement in 1963, a customs union has been planned to be established between Turkey and the European Economic Community. In case Turkey fulfilled its commitments arising from the agreement, the Community would consider Turkey's membership. Notwithstanding, expansion of the Community's trade relations, Turkey's incapacity to fulfil its commitments that were incompatible with its import substitution development model and derailing from democracy as a result of 1980 coup have ceased the relations. Revival of the relations has been the consequence of Turkey's inclining to free market economy in the aftermath of 1980 coup. Aiming at opening to international markets, attracting foreign direct investment and receiving loans from European countries have been the motives of Turkey to apply for full membership in 1987 (Akman & Çekin, 2021; 300) To this end, tariff cuts that were not made earlier were carried out and customs union was accomplished by the end of 1995. The establishment of the customs union between Turkey and the EU has been the initial step for subsequent developments that have transformed Turkey's governance and economic performance. After Turkey was acknowledged as a candidate country in 1999, the decision to start negotiations was taken in 2004 and negotiations have commenced in 2005. The negotiation process is related to the terms and conditions under which the candidate country will be admitted to the Union. The negotiation process necessitates the candidate country to fulfil obligations of the EU membership and adopt the EU acquis. The EU carries out this process through the model based on Copenhagen criteria that has been formulated in the Central and Eastern Europe enlargement.

3.2. The Effect of Negotiation Process on Turkish Governance

Turkey's negotiation process has started with conditionality under 35 chapters in the context of adopting the EU acquis. From the outset, when Turkey was acknowledged as a candidate country by the end of 1999, the state of affairs can be examined in two periods. The first period which has lasted until 2008 global crisis, corresponds to vivid negotiation process helping to transforming institutional structure and building good governance. On the contrary, the second period beginning thereafter overlaps with the deterioration of the relations, stalling of the negotiation process and institutional decadence. In the first period, institutional transformation has yielded high quality growth; "EU anchor" has attracted foreign direct investments. In the second period, however, decadence of institutions has generated low quality growth and the volume of foreign direct investments has decreased.

3.2.1. The Process from Customs Union to Global Crisis of 2008

In the context of customs union and negotiation process, Turkey has made a great number of institutional arrangements and regulations that have contributed to its institutional capacity. To start with, in the framework of customs union, Turkey had to align with the EU's execution of customs, technical standards, preferential trade regimes, intellectual property rights, competition and state aid policies. Furthermore, regulatory institutions in those areas such as Competition Authority, Turkish Patent and Trademark Office, Turkish Accreditation Agency were established within this framework. Customs union with the EU has meant more than cutting tariffs and applying common customs tariff for the third parties. It has required regulations and establishment of regulatory authorities (Akman & Çekin, 2021: 307).

Along with trade regulations, the structure of the economy has been subject to transformation according to the principles of free market economy. The EU monitors developments in candidate countries through its progress reports that are launched regularly. The first progress report for Turkey was launched in 1998 which stated that Turkey had institutional structure of a free market economy, expressing the need to diminish the size of the public sector in the economy (T.C. Dışişleri Bakanlığı AB Başkanlığı, 2022a: 20). In this context, Turkey has started privatization practices and privatized the sectors of electricity, petrol, tobacco and sugar, established regulatory authorities in the privatized sectors such as

Energy Market Regulatory Authority, Tobacco and Alcohol Market Regulatory Authority (Morgil, 2006: 94–95).

Preparing for the EU membership process has also coincided with the recovery period after two consequent crises of 1999 and 2001. Strong Economy Programme launched in the wake of 2001 crisis under the agreement signed with IMF was prepared in order to restructure banking system, discipline public finance and sustain financial stability. Establishment of Banking Regulation and Supervision Agency, Central Bank independence and amendment of Capital Market Law have been the regulatory reforms implemented in this respect (Acemoğlu & Üçer, 2015: 12–13). Therefore, this process was backed up by double anchors of Bretton Woods institutions-World Bank – IMF, and the EU.

Central Bank independence which came into force in 2001 has explicitly stated that primary objective of the Central Bank of the Republic of Turkey was price stability and prohibited to finance government by transacting in the primary market (The Law on the Central Bank of Republic of Turkey, art. 56). Two important laws regarding public finance were enacted. The Public Finance and Debt Management Law of 2002 and the Public Financial Management and Control Law of 2003. The Law of 2002 has targeted preventing non-transparent borrowing, providing financial accountability, bringing government borrowing, assurances under strict rules, and the obligation to report. The latter has set the framework for financial management. Principles and merits, multiyear budgeting, scope and execution of the budget, performance management, strategic planning and internal control, accounting, monitoring and reporting have been introduced within this framework (Atiyas, 2012: 12–13).

The most significant development came with the enactment of Public Procurement Law of 2002 under the surveillance of World Bank. The aim of this law was assuring effectiveness, transparency and competitiveness in public procurement (Acemoğlu & Üçer, 2015: 13).

Along with regulation in the monetary, fiscal and public procurement areas, by adopting "European model" in the public management area, autonomous authorities have been established in the sectors that have been liberated. Through rule based policy making, as is the case of Competition Authority, power to make decision has been left to autonomous authorities, unlimited power of the executive has been restricted and providing autonomous authorities independent from government influence has been targeted in these terms (Atiyas, 2012: 22).

Autonomous authorities are as follows:

Competition Authority (founded in 1994 and came into operation in 1997 under the customs union.), Banking Regulation and Supervision Agency (founded in 1999 and came into operation in 2000), Telecommunication

Authority (founded in 2000 and renamed to Information Technologies and Communication Authority in 2008), Energy Market Regulatory Authority (2001), Tobacco and Alcohol Market Regulatory Authority (founded in 2002, dissolved and transferred to Ministry of Agriculture and Forestry in 2017), Public Procurement Authority (2002). Revision of Capital Market Board established in 1981. (Yalman & Göksel, 2017: 27).

The reforms and institutional structuring in question played significant role in disciplining public finance and stabilizing financial system. The infamous duty losses have been swept away to a great degree and the rate of inflation has been decreased to one digit number as of 2004 (Akman & Çekin, 2021: 300). Based on Acemoğlu and Üçer's works of 2015 and 2019, Turkey's economy for the period between 2002 and 2006 can be compared to a rising star, with the annual growth rate of %7,6 (see Fig. 1) and the total factor productivity rate around %5.2 for this period. When Gini coefficient for the year 2003 was 42 %, it has fallen to 38 % in 2008 (Acemoğlu & Üçer, 2019: 10–11). It has again risen to 41.9 % in 2019 (The World Bank, 2022a). Recovery in the distribution of income has been supported with the distribution of public services such as education, healthcare and infrastructure. Income has been distributed geographically giving rise to the so-called Anatolian tigers (Acemoğlu & Üçer; 2015: 6).

Fig. 1: GDP growth (%) (1960–2018)

Source: Acemoğlu and Üçer, 2019 based on TURKSTAT data.

The decision of 2004 to start negotiations and the commencement of negotiations in 2005 have contributed to inflow of foreign direct investments from European countries. As of 2004, inflow of FDI from European countries has risen drastically and maintained high until the adverse of effects of global crisis have hit European countries (see Fig.2) (Akman & Çekin, 2021: 301).

Fig. 2: Value and share of inflows of FDI in Turkey originating from the EU (2002–2019) (in million Dollars and %)
Source: Akman & Çekin, 2021; 301.

3.2.2. The Collapse of the EU Anchor

Reform process in the wake of the crisis of 2001 and EU membership perspective have contributed to Turkey's economy, effects of which have reflected to economic indicators positively. However, the positive atmosphere has started to alleviate due to EU's attitude to design negotiation process in an open-ended framework and declare that the termination of the process could not be assured. Membership of Southern Cyprus without unification and obligation of Turkey to open its ports to Southern Cyprus ships under customs union brought about the issue of declaration by Turkey and counter declaration by the EU. Suspension of negotiations under eight chapters associated with customs union has been the consequence of the developments taking place. Ambivalent nature of the negotiation process as well as blockages coming from EU countries have exacerbated trust (Yalman & Göksel, 2017: 31).

The first signs of the process that can be called de-Europeanisation have appeared in the course of 2008 global crisis and 2010 Sovereign Debt Crisis thereafter. The economic slowdown in EU has reflected to Turkey's economy as narrowing of the market. Deceleration of the enlargement process because of the crisis has also had adverse effects. Stalling of the negotiation process has eventually destroyed EU anchor and EU advantage has lost its impact. Post crisis period has introduced BRICS as new alliances for Turkey and moved away from former allies of the West as EU, World Bank and IMF. In the process of de-Europeanisation, relations with Russia, China and Qatar have gained importance (Akman & Çekin, 2021: 302, Öniş & Kutlay, 2019: 234).

The post crisis period has witnessed not only deterioration of Turkey-EU relations but also the decline of the institutional reform process. Allegations of corruption against four ministers in 2013 have risen perception of risk on Turkey that has reflected to progress report as allegations of political influence on public tenders. A state of emergency has been declared in Turkey after the coup attempt in 2016. It has been criticized in the progress report by emphasizing the worsening of investment environment and warning against setback from economic reforms (Acemoğlu & Üçer, 2019: 31–32).

Modernisation of customs union to rejuvenate relations which came to fore with a declaration by the Commission and Turkey gained approval from the European Parliament on the condition to bring a clause on human rights and fundamental freedoms, however has been subject to objections of some member states led by Germany. Modernisation of customs union has thus been shelved and remained inconclusive (Ülgen, 2017). The latest chapter opened in the negotiation process has been the financial and budgetary provisions in 2016 (T.C. Dışişleri Bakanlığı Avrupa Birliği Başkanlığı, 2022b). From then on, relations have developed in the axes of refugee crisis and security (İktisadi Kalkınma Vakfı, 2017: 41).

EU anchor has been functional in terms of Turkey's economy. Yet, this functionality has served beginning from 1999 until 2008. From this point of view, it can be concluded that negotiation process has been beneficial until negotiations have started. Adverse effects of the Europeanisation and losing of anchors have come into existence in governance, particularly in the field of public tenders. Alterations to the public procurement law and increasing number of exemptions are incompatible with principles of transparency and accountability. Therefore, they are subject to be criticized in progress reports of the EU. Some of the instances of criticisms elaborated are as follows: Turkey has not made progress in the field of public procurement, Public Procurement Authority is not autonomous and local government and infrastructure tenders are open to corruption (European Commission, 2019: 66–68). Another crucial aspect of public procurement practices is that negotiation procedure (Public Procurement Law Article 21/b) rather than open procedure has turned out to be ordinary procedure although specified in the circumstances of natural disasters and unforeseen situations requiring emergency action (Toker, 2019: 43–45). As for fight against corruption, not setting up anti-corruption bodies and not implementing recommendations of Council of Europe's Group of States against Corruption (GRECO) have been repeatedly covered in progress reports (European Commission, 2022: 70–72).

3.3. Evaluation of World Governance Indicators (WGI) for Turkey

WGI developed by World Bank are widely used in the literature to measure governance quality of a country. Data collected for 200 countries and territories, for the period starting from 1996, indicate a country's rank, 0 corresponding to the lowest and 100 corresponding to the highest. Table 1 displays WGI for Turkey for the period 1996–2021. A glance at Tab. 1 shows a trend of increase in a positive way corresponding to rising quality of governance at the beginning of the table and a decrease at the end of the table corresponding to a setback of governance quality. Considering all indicators, all have evolved differently showing different levels of development; however, there is a similar trend for all indicators staying below where they started. Rising trends generally overlap with the period of institutional and governance reforms. On the contrary, low ranks coincide with the period when institutional reform process has dwindled.

Tab. 1: WGI for Turkey (1996–2021)

Years	Voice and Accountability	Political Stability and Absence of Violence/ Terrorism	Government Effectiveness	Regulatory Quality	Rule of Law	Control of Corruption
1996	45,5	10,64	55,74	59,24	47,24	51,61
1998	31,84	12,23	46,11	68,39	48	45,36
2000	40,3	21,16	56,92	64,62	50,5	49,75
2002	42,29	21,69	60,71	58,67	52,48	34,85
2003	45,77	25,13	60,71	56,12	59,41	52,02
2004	49,52	20,87	57,64	56,65	58,37	51,71

Tab. 1: Continued

Years	Voice and Accountability	Political Stability and Absence of Violence/ Terrorism	Government Effectiveness	Regulatory Quality	Rule of Law	Control of Corruption
2005	50,96	27,67	58,82	60,78	58,37	56,1
2006	45,67	27,05	59,02	59,31	55,5	58,05
2007	46,15	19,81	64,08	62,14	54,07	59,71
2008	46,15	18,75	63,59	59,22	56,73	60,68
2009	45,5	15,64	63,16	59,81	57,82	60,29
2010	44,55	18,96	64,11	59,81	58,77	58,57
2011	44,13	18,48	65,4	62,09	57,75	58,29
2012	41,78	12,8	65,4	64,93	57,28	62,56
2013	40,85	10,9	64,45	64,93	55,87	61,14
2014	36,45	11,9	67,79	66,35	57,21	52,88
2015	35,47	9,05	62,02	62,5	53,37	53,37
2016	30,05	4,76	54,81	61,06	46,63	50,48
2017	27,59	7,14	55,29	57,21	45,19	49,52
2018	25,12	10	53,85	52,4	42,31	43,75
2019	24,63	10	54,33	54,81	44,71	44,71
2020	24,15	12,74	47,60	50,48	38,46	43,27
2021	23,67	12,26	49,52	49,04	36,54	40,38

Source: (Worldbank, 2022c) WGI, https://info.worldbank.org/governance/wgi/Home/Reports (15.10.2022)

4. Conclusion

The most recent approach on the relationship between institutions and economic performance is that of Acemoğlu and Robinson distinguishing institutions as inclusive and extractive ones and emphasizing the role of inclusive institutions on growth and development of a country. The questions of how a country is governed in terms of election, monitoring and replacement of governments, the government's ability to formulate sound policies and both governments and citizens' respect for institutions have paved the way for indicators mainstreamed in the literature to gauge governance in a country. Rule of law, democracy, anti-corruption approach and participatory governance are of great significance for a country to reach its full potential. International institutions have designed their role emphasizing the significance of governance. The EU as a regional integration has transformative power on countries which it exerts influence on. Enlargement is an instrument of transformative power of the EU. Through Copenhagen criteria, a country is motivated to ensure rule of law and democracy along with a functioning free market economy and the ability to take on the obligations of membership. In addition, practices of good governance are imposed on candidate country.

Turkey and EU have maintained a partnership relationship since 1959 and negotiations have commenced in 2005 in the pursuit of the EU's acknowledging Turkey as a candidate country in 1999. EU candidacy status has accelerated the institutional reform process that had already begun with IMF and World Bank in the wake of two consecutive crises of 1999 and 2001. Double anchors of EU, IMF and World Bank have contributed to the transformation of Turkey's economy and institutional structure. By setting up autonomous authorities and rule-based decision-making, main principles of governance-transparency and accountability have been achieved. Good governance has reflected to economic performance as well. Due to cyclical developments taking place in both the EU and Turkey as well as global crisis of 2008, negotiation process has stalled and institutional transformation has lost pace and collapsed. The negotiation process has been functional until the negotiations have been interrupted. Losing EU anchor has had repercussions on decadence of institutional quality and economic performance verified by the evaluation of WGI on Turkey.

References

Acemoglu, D., & Robinson J. (2012). *Why Nations Fail: The Origins of Power, Prosperity and Poverty*, London, Profile Books.

Acemoğlu, D., & Üçer, M. (2015). "The Ups and Downs of Turkish Growth, 2002–2015 Political Dynamics, The European Union and the Institutional Slide", NBER Working Paper 21608.

Acemoğlu, D., & Üçer, M. (2019). "High-Quality Versus Low-Quality Growth in Turkey-Causes and Consequences", CEPR Press Discussion Paper 14070.

Akman, M. S., & Çekin, S. E. (2021). "The EU as an Anchor for Turkey's Macroeconomic and Trade Policy", *EU-Turkey Relations: Theories, Institutions and Policies*, (Ed.) Reiners, W. & Turhan, E., Cham, Palgrave Macmillan, pp. 2955–322.

Atiyas, İ. (2012). "Economic Institutions and Institutional Change in Turkey During the Neoliberal Era". https://research.sabanciuniv.edu/id/eprint/20470/1/economic_institutions_npt.pdf, (10.10.2022).

Börzel, T. A., Pamuk, Y., & Stahn, A. (2008). "Good Governance in the European Union", Freie Universitat Berlin, Berlin Working Paper on European Integration, No.7.

EUR-LEX, European Union. (2022). Accession Criteria (Copenhagen Criteria), https://eur-lex.europa.eu/EN/legal-content/glossary/accession-criteria-copenhagen-criteria.html, (15.11.2022).

European Commission. (2019). Turkey 2019 Report, Brussels. https://neighbourhood-enlargement.ec.europa.eu/turkiye-report-2019_en, (10.10.2022).

European Commission. (2022). Türkiye 2022 Report, Brussels, https://neighbourhood-enlargement.ec.europa.eu/turkiye-report-2022_en, (13.10.2022).

Hall, R. E., & Jones, C. I. (1999). "Why Do Some Countries Produce So Much More Output Per Worker Than Others?", *The Quarterly Journal of Economics,* February 1999, pp. 83–116.

İktisadi Kalkınma Vakfı. (2017). İKV Report on Turkey-EU Relations: Keeping Together in the Face of Multiple Challenges, İstanbul, Publication No.288.

Kaufmann,D., Kraay, A., & Mastruzzi, M. (2010). "The Worldwide Governance Indicators: Methodology and Analytical Issues", World Bank Draft Policy Research Paper.

Masuch, K., Anderton, R. S., & Benalal, N. (2018). "Structural Policies in the Euro Area", Occasional Paper Series, No. 210.

Morgil, O. (2006). "Kopenhag Ekonomik Kriterleri ve Türkiye'nin Uyum Süreci", *Ankara Avrupa Çalışmaları Dergisi: Prof. Dr. Ahmet Gökdere'ye Armağan, 5*(2), pp. 91–102.

North, D. C. (2010). *Kurumlar, Kurumsal Değişim ve Ekonomik Performans* (G. Ç. Güven,Trans.) Cambridge, Cambridge University Press (Original Work Published-1999).

Öniş, Z., & Kutlay, M. (2019). "Global Shifts and the Limits of the EU's Transformative Power in the European Periphery: Comparative Perspectives from Hungary and Turkey", *Government and Opposition, 54*(2), pp. 226–253.

T.C. Dışişleri Bakanlığı AB Başkanlığı. (2022a). Türkiye'nin Katılım Yönünde İlerlemesi Üzerine Komisyon'un 1998 Düzenli Raporu, https://www.ab.gov.tr/files/AB_Iliskileri/AdaylikSureci/IlerlemeRaporlari/Turkiye_Ilerleme_Rap_1998.pdf, (15.10.2022).

T.C. Dışişleri Bakanlığı AB Başkanlığı. (2022b). Katılım Müzakerelerinde Mevcut Durum, https://www.ab.gov.tr/katilim-muzakerelerinde-mevcut-durum_65.html, (15.11.2022)

The World Bank. (2022a). World Development Indicators: Distribution of Income or Consumption, http://wdi.worldbank.org/table/1.3, (15.11.2022)

The World Bank. (2022b). World Governance Indicators, https://info.worldbank.org/governance/wgi/, (15.11.2022).

The World Bank. (2022c). World Governance Indicators: Türkiye, https://info.worldbank.org/governance/wgi/Home/Reports (15.10.2022)

Toker, Ç. (2019). Kamu İhalelerinde Olağan İşler, Tekin Yayınevi: 765, ISBN: 978-9944-61-276-0.

Ülgen, S. (2017). "Trade as Turkey's EU Anchor", https://carnegieeurope.eu/2017/12/13/trade-as-turkey-s-eu-anchor-pub-75002, (10.10.2022).

Yalman, G. L., & Göksel, A. (2017). "Transforming Turkey? Putting the Turkey-European Union Relations into a Historical Perspective", *Uluslararası İlişkiler, 14*(56), pp. 23–37.

M. Oğuz Arslan[1] & Hatice Altinok[2]

Forecasting Business Cycles with System Dynamics

1. Introduction

Goodwin's growth model is one of the main macroeconomic system dynamics models. The predator-prey (Lotka-Volterra) model, a mathematical ecology model, is used in Goodwin's model to analyze the fluctuation of income distribution between labor and capital in an economy. Furthermore, Goodwin argues that the competition between labor and capital for a larger share of GDP has exhibited a cyclical feature. In this study, we test Goodwin's model to see if an income conflict between labor and capital is conjunctural for the economies of Turkey, Spain, and Greece from 1970 to 2021.

There are four sections to this study. The system dynamics technique is summarily explained in the first section. The second section then provides Goodwin's growth model structure. The third section, which is the main focus of the investigation, applies Goodwin's growth model to analyze the dynamics of income distribution in Turkey, Spain, and Greece. The conclusion is in the fourth.

2. System Dynamics in Summary

System dynamics is an approach that focuses on the changing character of problems and a method by which different aspects of systems interact and evolve through time to generate complex systems, according to the definition by Sterman (2000). Jay M. Forrester created system dynamics to analyze fluctuations of an industrial procedure and to pinpoint common causes of failure in previous processes (Forrester, 1961).

Typical components of a simple system dynamics model include certain stocks, flows, and connections acting as feedback loops. In general, stocks represent information or material that enters or exits a system, flows reflect rates of change that affect stocks, and feedbacks represent information loops (Ford, 2009).

---

1 Anadolu University, FEAS, Department of Public Finance, moarslan@anadolu.edu.tr, ORCID: 0000-0001-6011-4331

2 Anadolu University, FEAS, Department of Public Finance, haltinok@anadolu.edu.tr, ORCID: 0000-0002-1093-403X

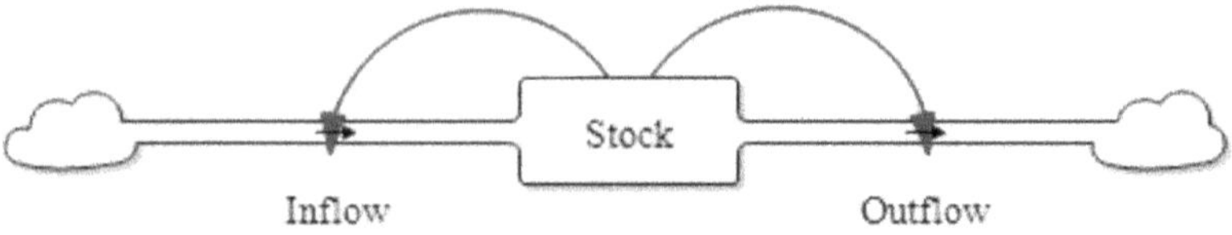

Fig. 1: *Stock and flow variables*

Figure 1 depicts the connections between the variables of stock and flows in the methodology of system dynamics. The stock variable in this image can be viewed to represent the difference between flows. The taps decide on operations that control systemic flow. In a system dynamics model, we mathematically define the relationship between the stock and inflow-outflow variables as follows (Barlas, 2007; Sterman, 2000):

$$\frac{d(Stock)}{dt} = Net\ Change\ in\ Stock = Inflow(t) - Outflow(t)$$
$$\Rightarrow Stock(t) = Stock(t_0) + \int_{t_0}^{t} (Inflow(s) - Outflow(s))\,ds \tag{1}$$

3. Goodwin's Growth Model

Richard M. Goodwin was among the most well-known economists who were enthusiastic about applying the system dynamics framework to economics. Goodwin did probably the most important studies on this topic between 1940 and 1970. The growth model proposed by Goodwin (1967) is particularly significant among them. Goodwin's model directly references the predator-prey model as an ecological forerunner. According to Goodwin's theory, workers play the role of predators in wage demands because their wage demands lead to the reversal of investment-led capitalist development (Rosser, 2009).

According to Goodwin (1967), it is helpful to comprehend the dynamical paradoxes of an economy by looking at the symbiotic relationships between two populations that are partially complementary and partially unfriendly. In the model of Goodwin, the GDP share of labor, represented by u, is the predator, while the GDP share of capital, represented by v (the employment rate), is the prey. The following two differential equations provide Goodwin's growth model:

$$\frac{dx}{dt} = x(+a - by) \Rightarrow \frac{dv}{dt} = \left\{\frac{1}{\sigma} - (\alpha + \beta) - \frac{u}{\sigma}\right\} v \tag{2}$$

$$\frac{dy}{dt} = y(-c + dx) \Rightarrow \frac{du}{dt} = \{-(\alpha + \gamma) + \rho v\}\ u \tag{3}$$

The following definitions apply to the variables in the differential equations: σ is the capital-output ratio, α is the growth rate of population, β is the growth rate of labor productivity, γ is the intersection of Phillips curve, and ρ is the slope of Phillips curve. Besides, $\frac{dv}{dt}$ provides the net employment rate, and $\frac{du}{dt}$ provides the net labor's share. Also, the variables are defined as; a, the natural growth rate of employment, b, the density of employment rate, c, the natural growth rate of employment's rate, and d, the density of labor's share.

4. The Analysis of the Dynamics of Income Distribution for Turkey, Spain, and Greece Employing Goodwin's Growth Model

4.1. The Equations and the Structure of the Goodwin's Growth Model

We described stock and flow equations in Goodwin's growth model applied to the Turkish, Spanish, and Greek economies as demonstrated by Goodwin (1967), Harvie (2000), and Utama (2012) as below:

Tab. 1: *Stock and flow variables of the model*

Stock and Flow Variables	Equations	Explanations
The level of the growth rate of labor productivity, $\frac{da}{dt}$	$\frac{da}{dt} = \alpha a$	a, the labor productivity; α, the growth rate of labor productivity ($\alpha > 0$)
The growth rate of population-level, $\frac{dN}{dt}$	$\frac{dN}{dt} = \beta N$	N, the labor supply; β the growth rate of population ($\beta > 0$)
The change rate of capital stock level, $\frac{dK}{dt}$	$\frac{dK}{dt} = I - \delta K$	I, the investment; δ, the depreciation rate; K, the capital stock
The change rate of real wage, $\frac{dw}{dt}$	$\frac{dw}{dt} = (-\gamma + \rho v)w$	γ, ρ, the coefficients of the linear Phillips curve; v the employment rate; w, the real wages

Again, we described auxiliary variables to make our model's stock variables more explanatory as shown by Goodwin (1967), Harvie (2000), and Utama (2012) as below:

Tab. 2: *Auxiliary variables of the model*

Auxiliary Variables	Equations	Explanations
The output, **Y**	$Y = \frac{K}{\sigma}$	K, the capital; σ, the accelerator
The investment, **I**	$I = \pi$	π, The profits
The profits, $\boldsymbol{\pi}$	$\pi = Y - wL$	wL, the wages bill
The labor, **L**	$L = \frac{Y}{a}$	Y, the output; a, the labor productivity
The wages' share, **u**	$u = \frac{w}{a}$	w, the real wages; a, the labor productivity
The employment rate, **v**	$v = \frac{L}{N}$	L, the labor; N, the labor supply

The equations given in Tab. 1 and Tab. 2 are shown in the structure of the system dynamics model in Fig. 2.

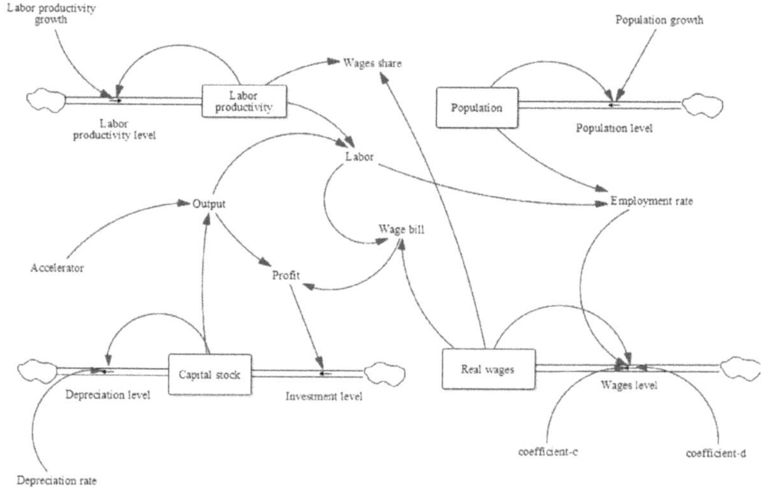

Fig. 2: *The system dynamics model of Goodwin's growth model*

4.2. Econometric Estimate for Variables in the Model

We used the data from various sources (e.g. https://stats.oecd.org; www.knoema.com; https://ec.europa.eu; https://data.worldbank.org) for the 1970–2021 period for those economies. We remove six zeros from population and capital stock values to become close to the original Goodwin's model. The removal of zeros did not alter the time interval of the orbit of the system and the overall features of the system.

For running our application, the default values of each stock variable must be certain. The coefficient of the accelerator and the depreciation rate are calculated as the mean values of the 1970–2021 term for each country. Besides, a, K, N, and w are accepted as the default values of 1970 for each country. We found the coefficients α, β, γ and ρ using some econometric methods:

- Productivity growth, α

We use exponential productivity growth equation which is calculated by taking logs of equation: $\ln a = e \ln a_0 + \alpha t + \varepsilon_{1t}$. The parameter α is estimated for Turkey and Spain using ordinary least squares (OLS) regression. Estimated outcomes are given in Appendix-Tab. A1.

- Labor force growth, β

An alike exponential function by taking the log of the equation is again employed to model the growth of the labor force: $\ln N = f \ln N_0 + \beta t + \varepsilon_{2t}$. The parameter β is estimated for Turkey and Spain using ordinary last squares (OLS) regression. Estimated results are given in Appendix-Tab. A2.

- Intersection and slope coefficients of Phillips curve,γ and ρ,

Goodwin asserts that the growth rate of real wage increase in the neighborhood of full employment. According to Harvie (2000, p. 356), the differential equation $\left(\frac{dw}{dt} = (-\gamma + \rho v) w\right)$ should be replaced with its difference equation because the data is discrete. So, difference equation $\frac{\Delta w_{t+1}}{w_t \Delta t} = -\gamma + \rho v_t$ should be used instead of differential equations which are $\frac{\dot{w}}{w} \sim \frac{\Delta w_{t+1}}{w_t \Delta t}$ and $\Delta w_{t+1} = w_{t+1} - w_t$. The correlation between the real wage and employment rate is analyzed in long-run. As seen in Appendix, there are structural breaks in variables. The Bai-Perron test (Bai & Perron, 2003) test is used for determining the multiple structural breaks of variables. According to the results of the test, the structural break years for Turkey are found as 2010; the structural break years for Spain are found as 1979,

1988, 2000, and 2010; and the structural break years for Greece are found as 1980, 1994, 2008, and 2015. The parameters γ and ρ *are* estimated for Turkey and Spain by using two-stage least squares (TSLS). Also, the connection between real wage and employment rate is estimated in long-run using TSLS. The coefficients obtained from this estimation are used in our system dynamics model. Estimated results will be given in Appendix-Tab. A3–A4. The coefficients obtained from this estimation are used in our system dynamics model.

The periods of the system for Turkey, Spain, and Greece are calculated according to the formula:

$$T = \frac{2\pi}{\sqrt{(\alpha+\gamma)\left(\frac{1}{\sigma}-(\alpha+\beta)\right)}} \tag{4}$$

4.3. The Default Values of the Variables of the Model

We employed the data between 1970 and 2021 for the Turkish, Spanish, and Greek economies in our model. The default values of the variables of the systems are given below.

Tab. 3: *The default values of the variables of the systems for Turkey, Spain, and Greece*

Variables	Turkey	Spain	Greece
Labor productivity, a	1.6	3.4	3.6
Capital stock, K	348	1432	244
Population, N	35	34	9
Real wages, w	0.919	0.9428	0.9209
The depreciation rate, δ	0.057022	0.0806	0.12
The coefficient of accelerator, σ	2.66	3.13	3.575
The growth rate of the labor productivity, α	0.026510	0.013928	0.010723
The growth rate of the population, β	0.016037	0.014755	0.009516
The coefficient-c of Phillips curve, γ	-1.623605	-5.617011	-9.602538
The coefficient-d of Phillips curve, ρ	8.830119	10.64376	25.72504
Period	8.08	4.68	3.79
dt	0.001	0.001	0.001

4.4. The Results of the Model

The factual orbits of the rates of the shares of employment and workers for the Turkish, Spanish, and Greek economies between 1970 and 2021 are depicted in Fig. 3.

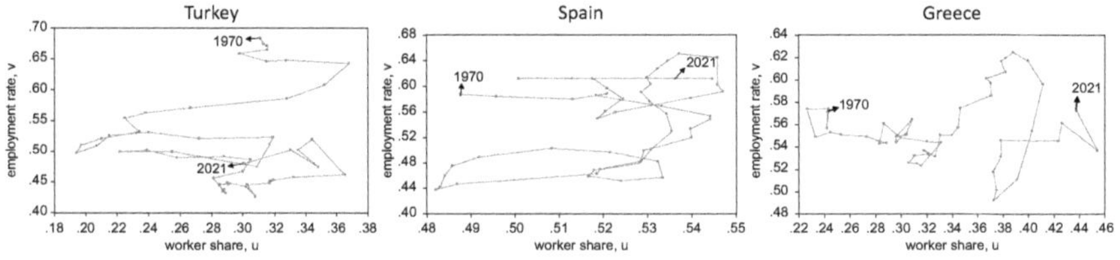

Fig. 3: *Goodwin's growth model for the Turkish, Spanish, and Greek economies in the long run*

Source: Authors' own calculations.

We also generated the conjunctural pattern of Goodwin's model for Turkey, Spain, and Greece for the 1970–2021 term by employing Vensim software as seen in Fig. 4.

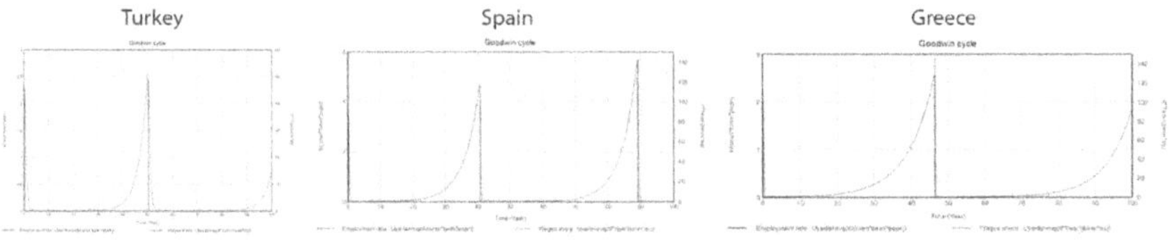

Fig. 4: *Goodwin-type cyclical behavior of the Turkish, Spanish, and Greek economies between 1970–2021*

In Fig. 4, the employment rates and wage shares tend toward zero but never reach zero. For Turkey, Spain, and Greece, the cycles at the start of the periods repeat with a frequency of 8.08, 4.68, and 3.79 years, respectively.

Also, Goodwin-type growth cycles of our model for Turkey, Spain, and Greece are shown in Fig. 5.

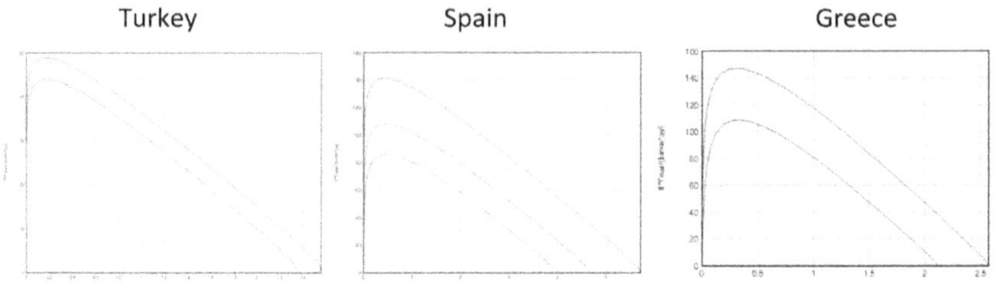

Fig. 5: *Goodwin-type growth cycle of the Turkish, Spanish, and Greek economies between 1970–2021*

We produced slightly different cycle figures, as shown in Fig. 5, although the original Goodwin's growth model has an ellipse-formed conjuncture. We accepted that this discord was caused by a discrepancy between a mathematical model's (the original Goodwin's model) predictions and its actual use. Though our model obtains u and v values greater than 1, Goodwin's growth model obtains these values between 0 and 1 with perfect precision. However, our findings show that the conflict over the distribution of income between labor and capital has a dynamic conjunctural feature in the economies of Turkey, Spain, and Greece between 1970 and 2021.

4.5. The Explanation of the Results of the Model for the Turkish, Spanish, and Greek Economies

The growth cycle frequencies of the Turkish, Spanish, and Greek economies generated different cycle years for these economies after the starting year 1970. For the Turkish economy, the cycle years are 1978, 1986, 1994, 2002, 2010, 2018, 2026, 2034, and so on. For the Spanish economy, the cycle years are 1974, 1979, 1983, 1988, 1992, 1997, 2001, 2006, 2010, 2015, 2019, 2024, 2028, and so on. For the Greek economy, the cycle years are numerous since it has the lowest frequency. The cycle years of the Greek economy are 1973, 1977, 1980, 1984, 1987, 1991, 1994, 1998, 2001, 2005, 2008, 2012, 2015, 2019, 2022, 2026, 2029, and so on.

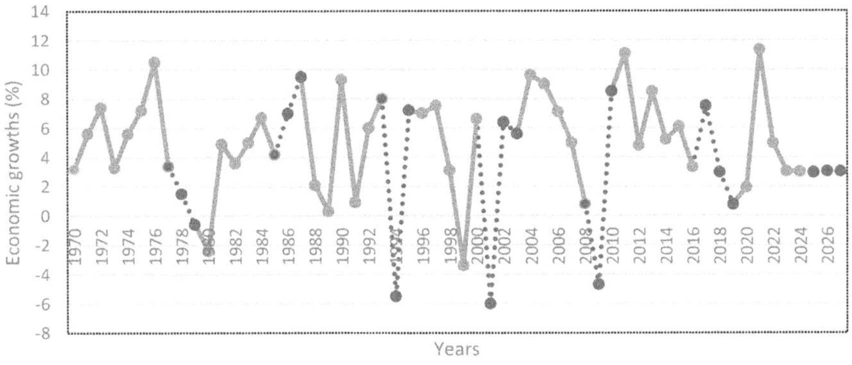

Fig. 6: *The growth rates of the Turkish economy over time*
Source: https://www.imf.org/en/data

As seen in Fig.6, the major economic crises that occurred in the Turkish economy between 1970-2021 generally came across the terms of Goodwin-type conjunctural shifts in shares of national income between labor and capital. When we look at Fig.6, we can notice that the economy of Turkey becomes quite vulnerable throughout periods of conjunctural shifts in income distribution conflict between labor and capital as depicted in the dotted line. In these time intervals, we can conclude that economic turmoil happens if some important elements (political and external) are also present. To a certain extent, our Goodwin model built for Turkey explains previous economic crises. Moreover, the outcomes of our model can be utilized to forecast Turkey's future economic situation. In accordance with the model, the possibility of an economic emergency in future cyclical shifting periods will be greater than in ordinary years. To the model, for example, the risk of happening an economic crisis developing around 2026 is larger than it is during normal times for the Turkish economy. In this regard, our research clearly shows that Goodwin's growth model clarifies historical fluctuations of growth and has a high capacity for forecasting future growth fluctuations.

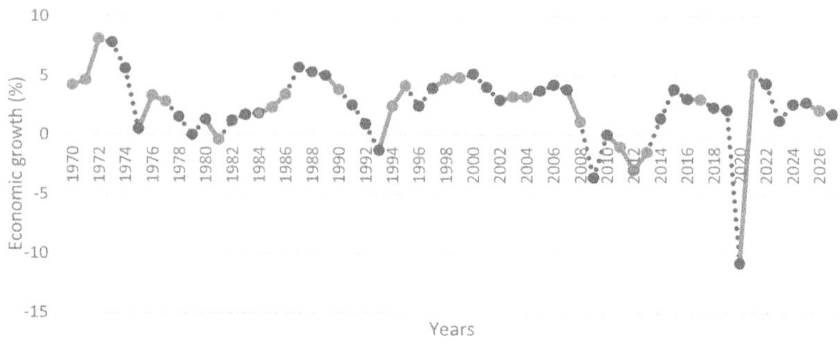

Fig. 7: *The growth rates of the Spanish economy over time*
Source: https://www.imf.org/en/data

According to Fig.7, there was no severe economic crisis in the Spanish economy from 1970 until the 2008 Global Financial Crisis. The repercussions of the 2008 Global Financial Crisis pushed the Spanish economy into an economic crisis in 2009, which coincided with a Goodwin-type cyclical shift in sharing national income between labor and capital. When we look at Fig.7, we can see that the Spanish economy becomes vulnerable in times of conjunctural fluctuations in income competition between labor and capital, as represented by the dotted line. This model can potentially be used to forecast potential economic crises in Spain in the future. According to the model, the risk of happening an economic crisis emerging around 2024 is higher than normal times for the Spanish economy.

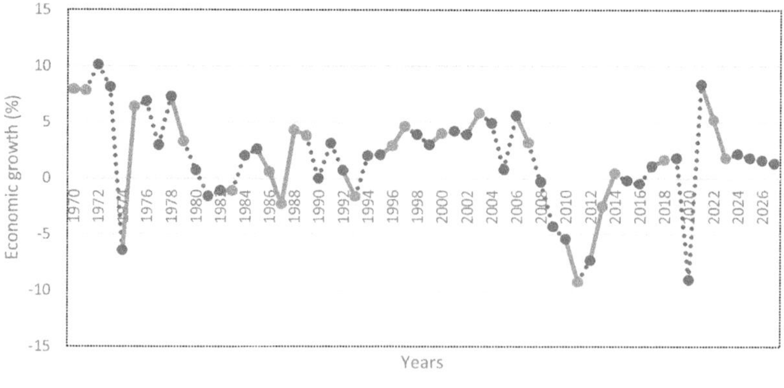

Fig. 8: *The growth rates of the Greek economy over time*
Source: https://www.imf.org/en/data

According to the model, similar consequences might be drawn for Greece. The Greek economic depressions and crises that occurred between 1970 and 2021 also come across the periods of Goodwin-type conjunctural shifts in shares of national income between labor and capital, as seen in Fig. 8. Also, we can see that the Greek economy becomes vulnerable in times of conjunctural fluctuation periods in the income conflict between labor and capital, as shown by the dotted line in Fig. 8. This model can potentially be used to forecast potential economic problems in Greece in the future. According to the model, the risk of an economic crisis emerging around 2025 is higher than the normal times for the Greek economy.

5. Conclusion

According to Goodwin's growth model, the income distribution battle between labor and capital has displayed a dynamic conjunctural nature in the Turkish, Spanish, and Greek economies between 1970 and 2021. When we interpret this circumstance for these countries, we get startling findings. The biggest economic crises that happened in these economies during these 51 years often corresponded with periods of Goodwin-type cyclical fluctuations in shares of national income between labor and capital. To put it differently, at the time of conjunctural period shifts in the competition between labor and capital for increased national income, these economies became quite vulnerable. During these times, an economic crisis happened in these economies while other variables (political, global, etc.) were also at play. As a result, our Goodwin model partially explains the recent economic crises of Turkey, Spain, and Greece. Furthermore, the model's results can be utilized to forecast future economic turmoil and crises in these economies.

References

Bai, J., & Perron, P. (2003). Computation and Analysis of Multiple Structural Change Models. *Journal of Applied Econometrics*, *18*(1), pp. 1–22.

Barlas, Y. (2007). System Dynamics: Systemic Feedback Modeling for Policy Analysis. *System 1,* 59, pp. 1131–1175.

Ford, D. N. (2009). *Modeling the Environment.* 2nd ed., Washington, DC: Island Press.

Forrester, J. W. (1961). *Industrial Dynamics.* Cambridge, MA: MIT Press.

Goodwin, R. M. (1967). A Growth Cycle. In C. H. Feinstein (Ed.), *Socialism, Capitalism, and Economic Growth.* Cambridge, MA: Cambridge University Press, pp. 54–58.

Harvie, D. (2000). Testing Goodwin: Growth Cycles in Ten OECD Countries. *Cambridge Journal of Economics, 24*, pp. 349–376.

Rosser, J. B. (2009). Theoretical and Policy Issues in Complex Post Keynesian Ecological Economics. In P. F. Holt, S. Pressman, & C. L. Spash (Eds.), *Post Keynesian and Ecological Economics: Confronting Environmental Issues*, Cheltenham: Edward Elgar, pp. 221–236.

Sterman, J. D. (2000). *Business Dynamics: Systems Thinking and Modeling for a Complex World*. New York: McGraw-Hill.

Utama, G. (2012). *A New System Dynamics Modeling Framework for the Financial System (with a Case Study of the Keen-Minsky Model)*. Unpublished doctoral dissertation. Rotterdam: Erasmus University.

https://stats.oecd.org, (03.01.2023).

www.knoema.com, (03.01.2023).

https://ec.europa.eu, (03.01.2023).

https://data.worldbank.org, (03.01.2023).

https://www.imf.org/en/data, (03.01.2023).

Appendix

Tab. A1

	Turkey	**Spain**	**Greece**
Constant	-42.88199* (0.00000)	-18.05265* (0.0000)	3.780527* (0.00000)
Time trend	0.026510* (0.00000)	0.013928* (0.0000)	0.010723* (0.00000)
R-squared	0.965155	0.860369	0.857766
R-bar-sq	0.964458	0.857266	0.854673
Normality of errors, $\chi^2(2)$	0.480156	3.208118*	3.155250*
Heteroscedasticity, $\chi^2(1)$	21.86589*	9.078715*	2.495540
Serial correlation, $\chi^2(1)$	23.86299*	37.87527*	58.76140*

Note: * shows that the test statistics is significant at the 5 % level. The critical values at 5 % level of significance are $\chi^2(1) = 3.841$ and $\chi^2(2) = 5.991$.

Tab. A2

	Turkey	Spain	Greece
Constant	-15.13649* (0.00000)	-19.69032* (0.00000)	-17.56143* (0.00000)
Time trend	0.016037* (0.0000)	0.014755* (0.0000)	0.009516* (0.00000)
R-squared	0.966537	0.946171	0.882549
R-bar-sq	0.965867	0.945094	0.880200
Normality of errors, $\chi^2(2)$	7.210726*	5.581235*	1.631600
Heteroscedasticity, $\chi^2(1)$	10.88479*	2.693905	20.32748*
Serial correlation, $\chi^2(1)$	64.78877*	264.5877*	320.2160*

Note: * shows that the test statistics is significant at the 5 % level. The critical values at 5 % level of significance are $\chi^2(1) = 3.841$ and $\chi^2(2) = 5.991$.

Tab. A3

The results for Bai and Perron (2003) test of multiple break points						
Country/Variable	**F Stat**	**Break 1**	**Break 2**	**Break 3**	**Break 4**	**Break 5**
Turkey						
w	3.868936	2010	-	-	-	-
v	24.36679*	1978	1985	2000	2015	-
Spain						
w	1.755851	1979	1988	2000	2010	-
v	81.57163*	1979	2000	-	-	-
Greece						
w	0.542812	1980	1994	2008	2015	-
v	66.80449*	2002	2011	-	-	-

Note: * shows that the test statistics is significant at the 5 % level.

Tab. A4

2SLS – Two-stage least squares results igital long-term			
	Turkey	**Spain**	**Greece**
Constant	-1.623605 (0.9402)	-5.617011 (0.9238)	-9.602538 (0.9257)
v	8.830119 (0.8213)	10.64376 (0.9200)	25.72504 (0.8902)
Dum1979	-	-4.231171 (0.8099)	-
Dum1980	-	-	27.40464 (0.3284)
Dum1988	-	8.777572 (0.1828)	-
Dum1994	-	-	29.13308 (0.3168)
Dum2000	-	1.763011 (0.7386)	-
Dum2008	-	-	24.00682 (0.2644)
Dum2010	13.87114 (0.1697)	1.663291 (0.8373)	-
Dum2015	-	-	8.383475 (0.6558)
R-squared	0.024738	-0.846094	-0.348361
R-bar-sq	-0.017665	-1.065867	-0.516906
F-stat	1.469732	1.637037	0.628524
Prob(F-stat)	0.013091	0.171300	0.678964

Note: * shows that the test statistics is significant at the 5 % level.

Y. Tamer Ergül[1] & Sedef Oluklulu[2]

Household Borrowing and Economic Stability[3]

1. Introduction

This study draws attention to the issue of household indebtedness observed with financialization and globalization. As it is known, financialization is a phenomenon that has been extensively analyzed with its economic and even social aspects. However, household borrowing is another aspect of financialization that has not been emphasized much. With the financialization process, regulations in the financial system have been reduced. Thus, financial institutions have gained the opportunity to lend to households, which they could not reach before, and thus increase their profits. Through borrowing, households have had the opportunity to consume in accordance with the norms of the social group to which they feel they belong. In addition to these developments, it has been observed that income distribution in many economies of the world has deteriorated to the detriment of wage incomes. In the face of this situation, households have tried to protect their consumption standards by borrowing again. As a result, the rate of household debt has started to increase in many countries of the world.

Household borrowing is not only a phenomenon that concerns households at the micro level. The income constraint on households' consumption has been loosened through borrowing. Although this situation is welcomed by the governments as it provides economic vitality in the short run, it may reduce the effectiveness of these policies when stabilization policies are needed. In addition, the decline in consumption based on excessive borrowing over time may also be unfavorable for economic stability and employment. Therefore, while analyzing the functioning of the financial system today, the tendency of consumers, in other words, households, to consume by borrowing should also be taken into account.

---

1 Ph.D., Assistant Professor, Anadolu University, Faculty of Economics and Administrative Sciences, Department of Public Finance, ytergul@anadolu.edu.tr, ORCID: 0000-0002-0180-2553

2 Ph.D., Assistant Professor, Anadolu University, Faculty of Economics and Administrative Sciences, Department of Public Finance, sedefcelik@anadolu.edu.tr, ORCID: 0000-0002-1335-7880

3 This article was developed from the paper titled "Financialization of Consumer Loans and Aggregate Demand Management" presented as "abstract (not full text)" at the 36th International Public Finance Conference held in Antalya, Turkey on 27-30 October 2022.

2. The concept of financialization

There are various definitions of the concept of financialization. Epstein defines it as "the increasing role of financial motives, financial markets, financial actors and financial institutions in the operations of the domestic and international economies" (Epstein, 2005: 3). According to Krippner, financialization is a model of accumulation in which profits are generated through financial channels rather than through trade or production of goods (Krippner, 2005: 174). Stockhammer defines financialization in a narrow sense and emphasizes the increased activity of non-financial enterprises in financial markets. This level of activity can be seen in the source of income flows (Stockhammer, 2004: 720)[4] Another aspect of financialization, especially in developed countries, is the prominence of the concept of shareholder value. According to this concept, the aim of firms is to prioritize the interests of their shareholders (Ertürk, 2020: 43). At this point, financialization also stands out as a new growth model alternative. In this system, financial institutions take the central position (Boyer, 2010: 112).

Ferreiro and Gómez summarize the common points of these definitions as follows: "(i) the rising weight and size of financial activities, sectors, institutions and products, in modern market economies; (ii) the rising size of indebtedness of private agents (families and non-financial corporations); and (iii) the rising influence of financial variables on the non-financial private agents' decisions on their resources allocation processes" (Ferreiro & Gómez, 2016: 89).

What is decisive in financialization is not the existence of financial institutions and instruments. They have existed at least since the beginning of capitalism. However, as can be seen from the definition, with the financialization process, the weight of financial institutions in the economy has increased, and financial instruments have become very diversified and have reached a level that can determine the decisions of non-financial sectors. In other words, in this process, financial institutions are not only neutral institutions that act as intermediaries between savers and investors as suggested by textbooks.[5] With financialization, the

---

4 Lapavitsas defines the increase in the profitability of the financial sector as "Profiting without producing" in the title of his book and draws attention to the increase in the proportion of the financial sector in total profits, especially in developed countries (2013: 213)

5 It should not be forgotten that financial institutions, especially banks, are profit-oriented enterprises. These enterprises aim to increase their profitability like those in the real sector. Especially in post-Keynesian economics, banks are considered as institutions that create credit and purchasing power. Banks can increase their assets and liabilities by lending and issuing new financial instruments. This also boosts aggregate

intermediation functions of financial institutions receded into the background, while debt and asset trading and the transformation of receivables into tradable assets, defined as securitization, came to the fore (Montgomerie, 2006: 304).

The theoretical basis behind financialization is often traced back to the work of McKinnon and Shaw. Both authors argue that in economies where financial constraints are imposed and interest rates are administratively constrained by ceilings, savings growth will be limited. Because of the low-interest rates offered by banks on deposits, savers will direct their savings to non-productive areas such as land purchases rather than utilizing them within the banking system. Therefore, investment and growth will also be limited. At the same time, high reserve requirement ratios limit the amount of debt that banks can lend to investors. On the other hand, financial liberalization will lead to an increase in interest rates by liberalizing them. High-interest rates will encourage savings and the amount of savings will increase. The question may arise whether rising interest rates will have negative effects on investments. According to the authors, high-interest rates will encourage productive investments. Since investments that yield higher returns than high-interest rates will be made, efficiency in resource allocation in the economy will be ensured (Arestis, 2006: 349, 351).

Vercelli states that historically, financialization emerged in two waves. The first wave started in the mid-19th century and lasted until the Great Depression. The second wave started in 1971 with the end of the Bretton Woods era and is still ongoing (2013, p. 25). This period also corresponds to the period when Keynesian full employment policies began to be abandoned and neo-liberal policies began to take their place. It should also be noted that historically, the trend of financialization has gone along with globalization. Of course, these phenomena did not occur simultaneously and at the same scale in every economy. Figure 1 shows the share of debt to the private sector in GDP as a measure of financialization.

---

demand (Lavoie, 2022, 199). In addition, rapid developments in communication and information technologies have expanded banks' traditional operations, reduced the importance of revenues from loans to industrial and commercial firms, and facilitated their orientation toward households (Lapavitsas & Dos Santos, 2008: 32).

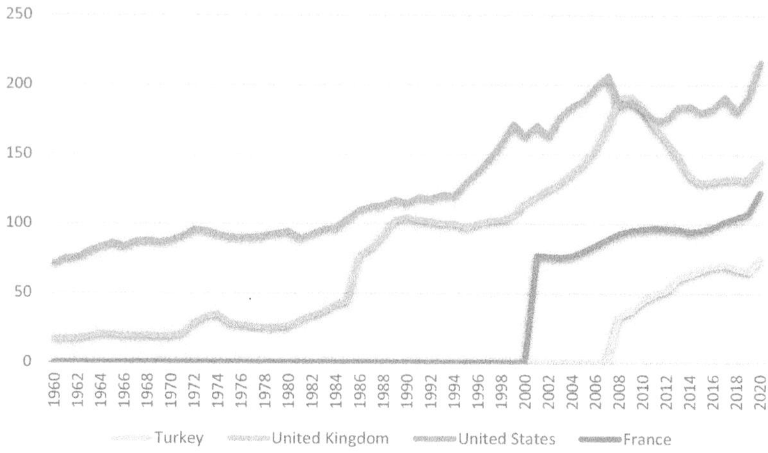

Fig. 1. Domestic credit to the private sector for selected countries (% of GDP)
Source: World Development Indicators[6] (WDI), World Bank (15.10.2022)

The beginning of financial liberalization policies in the Turkish economy was the January 24th Decisions, which were implemented in 1980 within the framework of a stand-by agreement with the IMF. Until this period, the Turkish economy was a planned economy adopting the import substitution development model. These decisions mainly aimed to reduce the weight of the public sector in the economy and to realize an export-oriented development model. Within this framework, measures were also taken to freely determine interest rates and exchange rates in the market, but the full implementation of these measures was not realized until the late 1980s. Nevertheless, the Turkish economy also made progress toward financialization. An important date in this regard is 1989. This year, the convertibility of the Turkish lira was achieved, making it possible for the private sector to borrow from abroad.

3. Financialization, Consumption Behavior and Household Indebtedness

Financialization in an economy affects all economic agents (households and firms). In this way, financialization also creates macroeconomic effects. The consequences of financialization on economic agents can be summarized as follows in Table 1:

6 Data for pre-2001 France and pre-2008 Turkey are not available.

Tab. 1. The consequences of financialization on economic agents

Consequences of Financialisation	**Households**	Intense dependence of credit Intense indebtedness Unfeasible levels of consumption Owners of financial assets
	Non-financial partnership	Engagement in financial activities Lower confinement ratios Supplying of financial services
	Financial partnership	Boost of the shadow banking system Direct credit to households Commercial banks alternate as investment banks
	Policy makers	Free trade Privatizations Payroll taxes and taxes from capital Leaving of full employment goals Centralization of inflation targeting policies Elasticity of employment

Source: Barradas, 2015:20

The impact on households is through their ability to consume beyond what their current income allows through borrowing. Before analyzing this situation, it is necessary to address the consumption functions of households, the smallest consumer unit in the economy.

As it is known, consumption is explained by Keynes as a function of current income. Accordingly, as consumers' income increases, their consumption will increase to the extent determined by the marginal rate of consumption. In case of a decrease in income, consumption will decrease again depending on the marginal rate of consumption. However, studies have indeed shown that consumers' consumption increases when their incomes increase but does not decrease at the same rate when their incomes decrease. In other words, the Keynesian consumption function is unidirectional. The first explanation of this situation came from Duesenberry. According to this explanation, known as the "relative income hypothesis", current income alone is not sufficient to explain consumption behavior. Consumption is also influenced by the existing habits of consumers and the "superior" goods consumed by the social environment they are related to. Duesenberry calls the situation where consumption is influenced by the social environment, independent of income and price, the "demonstration effect".[7] In fact, Veblen's concept of "conspicuous consumption" also shows that consumption may not always be linked to income (Mason, 2000: 555). This model is consistent with the main empirical findings on consumer behavior. It can also explain the effect of changes in income distribution on consumption and saving decisions. It explains why consumption inequality is lower than income inequality. At the same time, if consumers are driven by relative consumption motives, they will not increase their leisure preferences even in the event of wage increases (Stiglitz, 2008: 54).

In the following period, Duesenberry's "relative income hypothesis" was stripped of its sociological elements and tried to be placed in a more economic framework. In this context, Modigliani defined consumption as a function of current income and the highest income in the past. Brown, on the other hand, brought another change to Duesenberry's model and introduced the concept of "highest previous consumption" instead of "highest previous income" and in overtime, the model turned into the Duesenberry-Modigliani-Brown hypothesis (Mason, 2000: 559).

On the other hand, it is also known that Duesenberry's consumption model has not gained much ground in mainstream economics.[8] One of the reasons for

7 This situation is also defined as "keeping up with Joneses effect" (Albayrak, 2020: 6). A similar approach to this issue comes from the field of evolutionary psychology; "Humans evolved in small social groups in which image and status were all-important… Today we ornament ourselves with goods and services to make an impression on other people's minds… Many products are signals first and material objects second. Our vast social-primate brains evolved to pursue one central social goal: to look good in the eyes of others. Buying impressive products in a money-based economy is just the most recent way to fulfill that goal" (Miller, 2010: 1).

8 Especially in the 1970s, the views adopted in mainstream economics were Modigliani and Brumberg's "the life cycle theory of consumption" and Friedman's "permanent income hypothesis". In these models, consumers are considered far-sighted and rational. Depending on their expected lifetime income, they aim to maintain their consumption without fluctuations through intemporal planning. They are indifferent to the income and consumption of other consumers. Borrowing is undertaken only to compensate for temporary deviations in their incomes (Albayrak, 2020: 5). On the other hand, the indicators regarding the increase in household indebtedness do not confirm the claim that borrowing is a rarely used option.

this is that the model is not suitable for making policy recommendations and clear inferences and is not developed within an analyzable framework. With this structure, it is not easily taught in economics courses (Palley, 2010: 53).

However, Duesenberry's and his followers' approach seems to be more appropriate to explain the phenomenon of household indebtedness, which has emerged especially with financialization. The fact that consumers make consumption decisions by taking into account the social environment to which they belong has become even more evident due to continuous technological innovations. The modern business world is based on attracting consumers by constantly introducing new products to the market. Marketing techniques also influence consumers' consumption standards. Moreover, goods and services such as internet access or computers, which were not considered essential before, or even did not exist before a certain date, have started to be perceived as essential consumption goods. Consumers have started to see the consumption of new goods and services as a necessity to keep up with the changing society. Each consumer's consumption creates an externality for others. Households that strain their budgets to consume newly launched goods set an example for others to follow suit. Moreover, advertisements delivered by the mass media compare consumers not only with their social circles and neighbors, but also with an imaginary group of consumers. In a sense, the media has expanded people's definition of "neighborliness". Advertisements reach everyone, not just the target audience. This leads consumers to increase the portion of their disposable income that they allocate to consumption. If this is not possible, they resort to borrowing (Cynamon & Fazzari, 2013: 141–142).

Akerlof (2007: 15) also draws attention to the sociological perspective on consumption. Sociologists argue that consumption is largely determined by norms about what individuals should consume. These norms in turn depend on the position of the individual and their ideas about who they are.

4. Financialization, Income Distribution and Debt

Another factor that should be emphasized with respect to household borrowing is the deterioration in income distribution observed in various countries. This situation causes the consumption tendency described above to result in borrowing. The deterioration in income distribution can be observed beyond income distribution indicators, as real wages remain below productivity. In this sense, borrowing becomes a way to protect the consumption standards of lower and middle-income groups against the deteriorating income distribution in favor of upper-income groups. Thus, households' consumption will tend to be inelastic even if real incomes fall (Barba & Pivetti, 2009: 122). Such a relationship leads to a buoyant aggregate demand in the economy even if real wages do not increase, thanks to consumption financed by borrowing. Thus, at least in some economies, there will be no significant increase in unemployment. Moreover, the incentive to consume more may also lead to a decline in household savings.

Households' tendency to consume by borrowing would not have had a macroeconomic impact without the financialization phenomenon mentioned above. In both developed and developing countries, households' access to credit has been limited for many years due to government regulations on financial markets. The deregulation of these regulations was realized in developed countries in the early 1980s. Although this trend emerged in the same period in Turkey, its main effects were observed especially in the 2000s. Thus, banks started to view the income of individuals and households as a source of profit. Households became increasingly dependent on the financial system to access goods and services in basic areas such as housing, health, education, and transportation (Lapavitsas, 2013: 794). Of course, this is linked to the neoliberal policies implemented in many countries along with financialization, which envisage the withdrawal of the public sector from areas such as education and health, leaving these areas to the private sector.

Stockhammer (2015: 493) argues that the deterioration in income distribution affects economic stability through four channels. The first of these is that increasing inequality stagnates aggregate demand. Since wage earners have a higher marginal propensity to consume, a decline in their incomes will have a negative impact on consumption. Secondly, in countries with a debt-based growth model, current account deficits and consumption increase due to financial liberalization. The third source of instability, as discussed below, is that rising inequality increases household borrowing. Finally, the deterioration in income distribution increases the tendency to speculate in the economy. When income distribution shifts in favor of higher income groups, they have more resources to allocate to risky investments, which in turn increases speculative investments (Stockhammer, 2015: 945–8).

The relationship between increasing inequality in income distribution, household consumption and indebtedness has been the subject of various studies in recent years. These studies are generally focused on the US economy. For example, Barba and Pivetti (2009) find that in the US case, increasing income inequality in the 1980–2006 period did not lead to a similar inequality in consumption. This was achieved through increased borrowing on a large scale. Bousney and Weller (2006) also find that the deterioration in income distribution against wages in the US economy has increased credit card debt in this segment. Christen and Morgan (2005), who analyze the 1980–2003 period of the US economy, also find that increasing income inequality has a significant impact on the increase in household borrowing. On the other hand, relatively low-interest rates in the US and other advanced economies after 2000 have been another factor encouraging borrowing.

5. Household Borrowing and Economic Stability

The effects of financialization on economic stability have been widely discussed. Especially after the 2007 crisis, the relationship between financialization and economic stability has been discussed in various dimensions. However, there are relatively fewer studies on the impact of increased household borrowing on economic stability. One of the pioneers of these studies is Brown (2007). Brown especially emphasis on the post-1987 growth of markets for securities backed by credit card, installment, student loan, and home equity receivables in the US economy. Here, Brown extends Minsky's cash flow-debt principle for firms to households. If households hold significant amounts of debt or finance a significant portion of their purchases through borrowing, this principle would be valid. Accordingly, economic agents in an economy are divided into three categories according to their financing status:

1. Hedge units: Cash receipts (or income) are sufficient to repay interest and principal.
2. Speculative units: Cash receipts (or income) are adequate to repay interest but not principal. These units must roll over existing debts.
3. Ponzi Units: Cash receipts (or income) are insufficient to repay interest or principal. Ponzi units must add debts (or sell assets) merely to pay interest on existing debt obligations.

According to Minsky, the operation of the economy directs economic units from hedge to speculative units and from speculative to Ponzi units. (1992: 7) A debt-deflation situation adversely affects the economy in two ways. First, it makes it more difficult for funds to be spent on the consumption of physical goods (such as producer and consumer durables), and second, income flows are diverted from consumer markets and used to pay down debt. Whether households borrow to maintain consumption as predicted by the relative income hypothesis or to compensate for the deterioration in income distribution, at some point they will face the problem of repaying their growing debt. This would have a negative impact on aggregate demand. Because some of the income that could be used to purchase goods and services will be allocated to debt repayment (Brown,

2007: 438–51). As a result, the factors affecting the sustainability of borrowing in the long run, even for households, are similar to those of public debt. What matters for households is the difference between the increase in the interest rate and the increase in income. If the increase in the interest rate is greater than the increase in the income rate, the debt/income ratio of households will also increase (Barba & Pivetti, 2009: 127).

One of the first studies to draw attention to the link between the deterioration in income distribution and the increase in household borrowing belongs to Rajan (2010). Rajan points out that the deterioration in income distribution will lead to stagnation in aggregate demand. Economies that adopt a debt-based growth model, such as the US, consciously or unconsciously support households to maintain their consumption through borrowing. Thus, aggregate demand will not decline (Rajan, 2010: 8–9). As mentioned above, the fact that financial institutions are ultimately for-profit organizations leads them to circumvent regulations and lend to segments that cannot easily borrow under normal conditions. This situation, which negatively affects economic stability, is also considered among the causes of the 2008 crisis (Kapeller & Schütz, 2014: 785).

Mian and Sufi (2018) are among the authors who argue that household borrowing can cause economic fluctuations. Financial liberalization leads to an increase in capital inflows into the country. Thus, it becomes possible for households to borrow more, and the economy starts to boost. This situation will continue as firms increase their production capacity. However the downturn is driven initially by a decline in aggregate demand which is further amplified by nominal rigidities, constraints on monetary policy, possible banking sector disruptions, and legacy distortions from the boom (Mian & Sufi, 2018: 52).

Heterodox economists are not the only ones to warn about this issue. In its 2017 Global Financial Stability Report, the IMF also emphasized that increased household borrowing may stimulate demand in the short run but may lead to economic instability in the medium term. If aggregate demand determines the level of output, the economy may enter a recession after a certain point as over-indebted households reduce their consumption. At this stage, consumption expenditures of less indebted households may not be enough to compensate for the reduced consumption expenditures. At the same time, the possibility of borrowing may also create behavioral distortions in households; consumers may pay more attention to their current consumption and continuously postpone their savings. Excessive optimism may lead to a significant increase in consumer debt (IMF, 2017: 56–7).

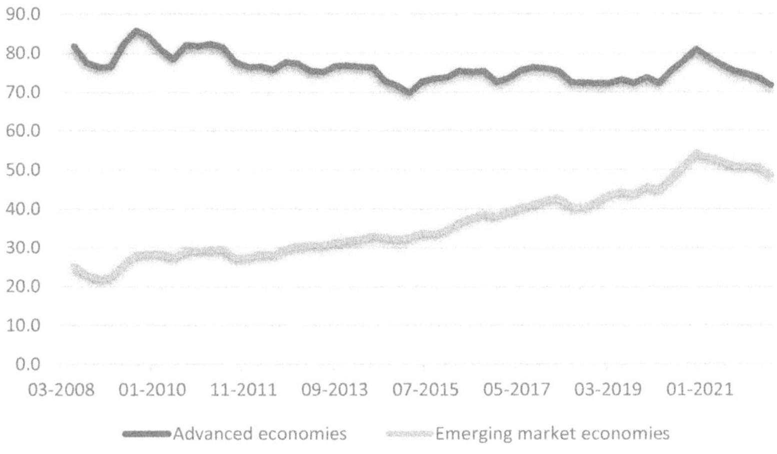

Fig. 2: Household borrowing to GDP
Source: IMF, 2017: 56

The Fig. 2 shows the ratio of household borrowing to GDP over time. This ratio is lower in emerging economies than in advanced economies. This difference can be explained by the fact that consumers have less access to credit in these economies and the prevalence of mortgage loans in developed countries. Nevertheless, this ratio tends to increase gradually in developing countries.

Using data from 80 countries, the IMF found that household borrowing is positively associated with macroeconomic indicators such as GDP growth, consumption and employment in the short run and negatively in the medium term. The model also predicted a decline in GDP growth and banking risk. However, these relationships vary according to the level of household borrowing in economies. For example, short-term effects are stronger in emerging economies, while medium-term effects are weaker (IMF, 2017, p. 63).

6. Conclusion

The economic and social effects of globalization and synchronized financialization have been addressed in numerous studies. However, studies on the effects of household borrowing, which is one of the phenomena observed with financialization, are relatively new and fewer. One of the reasons for this situation is that the increase in households' access to credit, especially in developing countries, is a relatively new emerging phenomenon. On the other hand, it is not surprising that this issue is becoming increasingly important, as consumers in both developed and developing countries tend to resort to more sources of credit. Duesenberry's relative income hypothesis suggests that consumers take into account not only their income but also their social environment when making consumption decisions. However, developments in advertising and marketing add new dimensions to the relative income hypothesis. Namely, even if a product is not consumed in the social environment with which the consumer is physically in contact, advertising and marketing make it possible for a person to think that he/she has a certain status by consuming that product. In any case, marketing tactics enable consumers to consume certain products, sometimes resorting to borrowing. This situation is much more complex than the consumption relations in the first half of the 20th century that Duesenberry analyzed. In addition, the stagnation in wage incomes observed in many economies, or at least the fact that wage increases remain below productivity increases, is another reason why households resort to borrowing in order to maintain their consumption levels. Financial institutions, which did not pay much attention to households until the 1980s for developed countries and somewhat more recently for developing countries, now see them as a serious source of profit and strive to market appropriate products to these segments.

Household borrowing is an issue that should be taken into account in terms of economic policies. This issue is closely related to the stability of aggregate demand. As is known, after the Second World War, especially developed countries focused on aggregate demand management through monetary and fiscal policies. Accordingly, if the economy is heading towards stagnation, expansionary monetary and fiscal policies can revive aggregate demand. On the contrary, in periods of excessive expansion, the inflationary pressure of aggregate demand can be alleviated by contractionary policies. Underlying this approach is the fact that consumption is a function of income as envisaged by Keynes. However, if the current income constraint on consumption is relaxed due to easier access to credit, policymakers may fail to control inflationary pressures with conventional instruments. While increased borrowing is not seen as a problem by policymakers as it helps sustain economic vitality in the short run, over-indebted households are likely to threaten economic stability in the medium and long run. Indeed, one of the pillars of the 2008 crisis was borrowers who were unable to repay their debts.

Another dimension of the issue is related to the trade balances of economies. According to Brown (2007, 452), one of the reasons for the US trade deficits in the late 1990s and early 2000s was consumption expansion financed by borrowing.

In Turkey, it can be assumed that concerns about the balance of trade were behind the restriction on credit card installments for some electronic goods.

The issue of borrowing raises new issues for economic policies. First of all, it is difficult to manage aggregate demand and thus ensure economic stability through traditional monetary and fiscal policies. Moreover, excessive borrowing by firms and households may lead to a deterioration in economic stability, a decline in the growth rate, and an increase in unemployment. One of the causes of economic crises in developing countries was the excessive borrowing of the public sector, in other words, unhealthy public finances. However, at this point, it is seen that the borrowing levels of economic agents other than the state may pose a threat to economic stability. In order to overcome this problem, the functioning of the financial system should be analyzed more carefully and regulations should be made in these areas if necessary.

References

Journals/Periodicals:

Akerlof, G. A. (2007). "The missing motivation in macroeconomics". *American Economic Review, 97*(1), pp 5–36.

Barba, A., & Pivetti, M. (2009). "Rising household debt: Its causes and macroeconomic implications—A long-period analysis". *Cambridge Journal of Economics, 33*(1), pp. 113–137.

Boyer, R. (2010). "Is a finance-led growth regime a viable alternative to Fordism? A preliminary analysis". *Economy and Society, 29*(1), pp. 111–145.

Brown, C. (2007). "Financial engineering, consumer credit, and the stability of effective demand". *Journal of Post Keynesian Economics, 29*(3), pp. 427–453.

Christen, M., & Morgan, R. M. (2005). "Keeping up with the Joneses: Analyzing the effect of income inequality on consumer borrowing". *Quantitative Marketing and Economics, 3*(2), pp. 145–173.

Ferreiro J., & Gomez, G. (2016). "Bank rescues and fiscal policy in the European Union during the great recession". *Panoeconomicus, 63*(2), pp. 211–230.

Kapeller, J., & Schütz, B. (2014). Debt, boom, bust: A theory of Minsky-Veblen cycles. *Journal of Post Keynesian Economics, 36*(4), pp. 781–814.

Krippner, G. R. (2005). "The financialization of the American Economy". *Socio-Economic Review, 3*(2), pp. 173–208.

Lapavistsas, C. (2013). "The financialization of capitalism 'Profiting without producing". *City, 17*(6), pp. 792–805.

Lapavitsas, C., & Dos Santos, P. (2008). "Globalization and contemporary baning: On the impact of new technology". *Contributions to Political Economy, 27*(1), pp. 31–56.

Mason, R. (2000). "The social significance of consumption: James Duesenberry's contribution to consumer theory". *Journal of Economic Issues, 34*(3), pp. 553–572.

Mian, A., & Sufi, A. (2018). "Finance and business cycles: The credit-driven household demand channel". *The Journal of Economic Perspectives, 32*(3), pp. 31–58.

Montgomerie, J. (2006). "Giving credit where it's due: Public policy and household Dept in the United States, the United Kingdom and Canada". *Policy and Society, 25*(3), pp. 109–144.

Palley, T. (2010). "The Relative Permanent Income Theory of Consumption: A synthetic Keynes-Duesenberry-Friedman Model", *Review of Political Economy, 22*(1), pp 41–56.

Stockhammer, E. (2004). "Financialization and the slowdown of accumulation". *Cambridge Journal of Economics, 28*(5), pp. 719–741.

Stockhammer, E. (2015). "Rising inequality as a cause of the present crisis". *Cambridge Journal of Economics, 39*(3), pp. 935–958.

Vercelli A. (2013). "Financialization in a long-run perspective", *International Journal of Political Economy, 42*(4), pp. 19–46.

Books:

Epstein, G. (2005). Financialization and the World Economy, US, Edward Elgar Publishing.

Lavoie, M. (2022). Post-Keynesian Economics New Foundations, US, Edward Elgar Publishing.

Miller, G. (2010). *Spent: Sex, evolution, and consumer behaviour*, New York, Penguin Books.

Rajan, R. G. (2010). *Fault lines: How hidden fractures still threaten the world economy*, New Jersey, Princeton University Press.

Edited Books:

Arestis, P. (2006). "Financial liberalization and the between finance and growth", *"A handbook of alternative monetary economics"*, (Ed.) Arestis P., & Sawyer M., Cheltenham, UK, Edward Elgar Publishing, pp. 346–364.

Cynamon, B. Z., & Fazzari, S. M. (2013). "The end of the consumer age", "*After the great recession: The struggle for economic recovery and growth*", (Eds.) Cynamon, B. Z., Fazzari, S. M., & Kuttner, R., Cambridge, Cambridge University Press.

Ertürk, I. (2020). "Shareholder primacy and corporate financialization", "*The Routledge international handbook of financialization*", (Ed.) Mader, P., Mertens, D., & Zwan N., London, Routledge, pp. 40–53.

Stiglitz, J. E. (2008). "Toward a general theory of consumerism: Reflections on Keynes's economic possibilities for our grandchildren", "*Revisiting Keynes: Economic Possibilities for Our Grandchildren*", (Ed.) Pecchi, L., & Piga G., USA, MIT Press, pp. 40–85.

Papers:

Albayrak, Ö. (2020). "Household consumption, household indebtness, and inequality in Turkey". Working Paper No. 954, Levy Economics Institute of Bard College.

Boushey, H., & Weller, C. E. (2006). "Inequality and household economic hardship in the United States of America". Working Paper No. 18, United Nations Department of Economic and Social Affairs.

Minsky, H. (1992). "The financial instability hypothesis", Working Paper No.74. In: The Jerome Levy Economics Institute of Bard College.

Internet Sources:

International Monetary Fund. (2017). Global financial stability report: Is growth at risk? Washington, DC. https://www.imf.org/en/Publications/GFSR/Issues/2017/09/27/global-financial-stability-report-october-2017 (01.12.2022).

B. Tuğberk Tosunoğlu[1]

Financial Stability and Economic Growth in Turkey[2]

1. Introduction

Financial stability became an important issue in academic and political economics after the 2008 Global Financial Crisis. According to the International Monetary Fund (IMF) estimations, in the last 20 years, financial instabilities in several countries caused costs of up to 10 % of the GDP. Research in this field mostly focused on macroeconomic stability and economic growth because of the close interaction between these variables. However, the relationship between financial stability and economic growth has been neglected.

This study aims to survey the relationship between financial stability and economic growth in Turkey as a developing country. After the liberalization policies of the 1980s, Turkey faced serious financial crises in 1987, 1994, 1997, 2001, and 2008. While some of these crises were reflections of the international economic crises (1987, 1997, and 2008), others were domestic crises caused by financial instabilities (1994 and 2001). Thus, such dynamics make Turkey a country worth analyzing.

A financial system is a structure comprised of economic actors that demand and supply funds, regulatory bodies, and tools. This structure functions within regulatory laws and administrative rules. The financial system allocates savings to investments through fund transfers. Thus, social welfare is maintained along with the increase in economic growth and income level. It could be suggested that an effective financial system contributes to economic growth (Kunt & Levine, 2008a: 5; Beck, 2012: 5). In the last 30 years, due to the rapid developments of financial markets, new financial instruments have been introduced and the volume of transactions have reached to high levels. The 2008 Global Financial

1 Anadolu University, FEAS, Department of Economics, ttosunoglu@anadolu.edu.tr, ORCID: 0000-0001-9377-5136

2 This chapter is the revised and developed version of the study that was presented as an "abstract (not full paper)" at the IISES, 35th International Academic Conference, Barcelona, 15 – 18 May 2018.

crisis showed that any abnormalities in these markets can lead to huge economic and social costs. These possibilities prove the importance of financial stability while making central banks and market regulating bodies worldwide reconsider their policies.

There is no clear consensus on the definition of financial stability in the economics literature. The difficulty in predicting the developments in the financial system, the dynamic structure of the system, and differences between countries are among the factors that make it difficult to provide a definition. Financial stability is generally referred as "the resilience of the economy against unexpected developments that may disrupt balances in the financial system" (Schinasi, 2004: 6). In this study, financial instability is defined as the sudden and extreme fluctuations in asset prices, the failure to fulfill the functions of the financial institutions, and deterioration of the functioning of the national or international credit system (Mishkin, 1999: 6).

This study aims to demonstrate the relative importance of financial stability in Turkey's economic growth process. In the second part of the study, the concept of financial stability and its importance in the process of economic growth are discussed. In the third part, a financial stability measure for Turkey is suggested. The fourth part of the study examines the adopted economic growth model to assess the relationship between financial stability and economic growth.

2. Financial Stability and Economic Growth

Theoretical debates on the relationship between an effective financial system and economic growth date back to Bagehot (1873) and Schumpeter (1912). These economists acknowledged that financial intermediaries play an important role in allocating resources to the most efficient production areas (Levine, 1997). In the 1960s and 1970s Goldsmith (1969), McKinnon (1973), and Shaw (1973) stressed that constraints such as interest rate restrictions and required reserve practices detract the financial system from efficiency and threaten economic growth. The existence of an effective financial system for economic growth and stability in the financial system was proved to be a prerequisite for economic stability and stable economic growth (Bernanke & Gertler, 1989, 1990). Later studies were aimed at proving that a stable, effective financial system has a positive impact on economic growth (King & Levine, 1993; Obstfeld, 1994; Bencivenga et al., 1995; Greenwood & Smith, 1997; Levine, 1997; Levine & Demirgüç-Kunt, 2008b). In these studies, three channels are considered to affect the economic performance of financial stability: (1) Effective financial intermediaries in the efficiency of investments. (2) An efficient financial system increases savings by reducing transaction costs. (3) An effective financial system strengthens the resource flow to the country by reducing the risk and thus, supports economic growth.

While pre-crisis literature in 2008 mostly focused on the interaction of financial stability and economic growth with the volatility in asset prices (Bernanke & Gertler, 1999, 2001; Gilchrist & Leahy, 2002), recent literature has established this interaction through monetary policy. Smets (2014) and Loisel (2014) summarize the studies conducted within this framework. The general trend is to examine the problem within the framework of dynamic stochastic general equilibrium (DSGE) models. The main advantages of this approach are the possibility of introducing various problems in the financial system to the model, better identification of externalities caused by these problems, and the introduction of financial crisis possibilities (For example Woodford, 2012; Ajello et al., 2015). On the other hand, in some models, macroprudential policies have been included in the monetary policy, economic instability, and growth interaction (Angeloni et al., 2015 Siklar & Akça, 2018).

3. Measurement of Financial Stability

In addition to the lack of a widely accepted definition, there is no consensus on the measurement of financial stability. For this reason, it is necessary to show how financial stability will be measured before modeling the financial stability and economic growth relationship. It is clear that this measure must bring together the various components of the financial system and take into account the structural characteristics of the country's financial system.

In many middle-income countries like Turkey, commercial banks are the most important actors in the financial system. Although the countries in the group have recently seen significant improvements in capital markets, the size of these markets is limited. On the other hand, high inflation rates in the past led to the continuation of a strong dollarization trend. Thus, this section of the study considers the development of the measure called the Financial Stability Indicator (FSI) for Turkey.

The financial stability indicator is the weighted average of the indicators on which financial system components (FSC) are represented. In this context, FSC for Turkey will be studied in four blocks. Each of these blocks will be represented by two components. The blocks and the components are given below:

Block 1: Banking Sector Block

- 1.1. Return on Assets
- 1.2. Leverage Ratio

Block 2: Credit Market Block
- 2.1. Consumer Loans Interest Rate
- 2.2. Commercial Loans Volume

Block 3: Capital Market Block
- 3.1. Istanbul Stock Exchange (BIST) 100 Index
- 3.2. Benchmark Bond Interest Rate

Block 4: Foreign Exchange Market Block
- 4.1. Foreign Exchange Basket (0.5$ + 0.5€)
- 4.2. Real Exchange Rate

Using these listed components, the indicator of financial stability is established through the below equation.

$$FSI_t = \omega_{FSC} FSC_t \tag{1}$$

In this equation, FSI represents financial stability, FSC represents financial system components and ω_{FSC} stands for the weight of each component. Numerous methods are used to calculate weights ranging from personal observations or judgments to empirical methods. The empirical method is preferred in this study. For this reason, the following equation will be estimated.

$$y_t = \beta_0 + \beta_1 y_{t-1} + \beta_{FSC} FSC_{t-j} + \xi_t \tag{2}$$

In this equation y_t expresses real economic activity volume. β_{FSC} represents the vector of coefficients to be used to calculate weights.

The following equation will be used to calculate the weights.

$$\omega_{FSC} = \frac{1}{1'\beta_{FSC}} \beta_{FSC} \tag{3}$$

In this equation, a K × 1 dimension vector consisting of 1's is represented by $1'$.

In the study, FSI will be established by using quarterly data from the period of 2002–2017 and real economic activity volume will be measured by real GDP. The indicators for each block representing the financial system components and the volume of production can be followed from the Fig. 1.

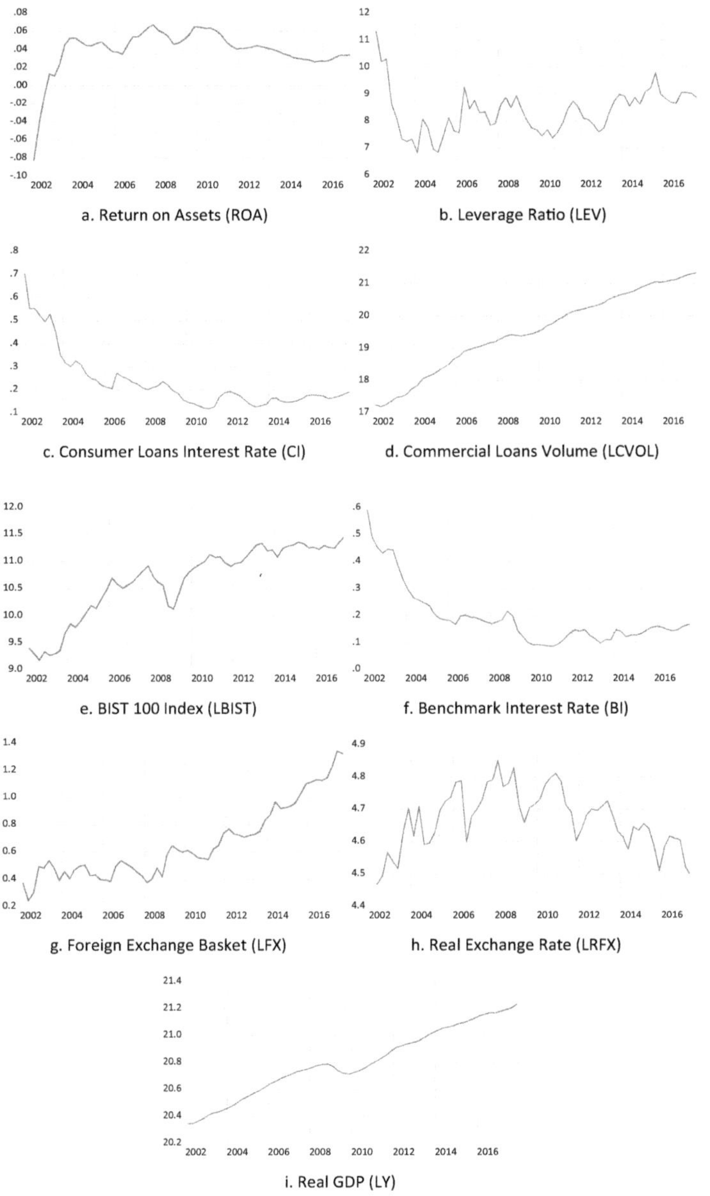

Fig. 1: *Financial system components*

In order to scale the above-given indicators, it is necessary to adjust the data. Since the increase in some indicators points out the tightening in financial conditions (such as interest rate, exchange rate, etc.), it is necessary to incorporate these types of variables into the model by taking reciprocal of them. In other words, if we express a variable by X, the model should have 1 / X value. On the other hand, variables that are non-ratio (Commercial Loans Volume, BIST 100 Index, Foreign Exchange Basket, Real Exchange Rate) are included in the model with their logarithmic levels.

The second stage in scaling is the normalization of the time series used. Since variables are expressed in different units, it is possible to put them together only if they are expressed on the same scale. Empirical normalization can be used to reduce the series to the same scale. The equation to be used for this purpose is given below:

$$X_i^n = \frac{X_i - X_{min}}{X_{max} - X_{min}} \tag{4}$$

In this equation, X^n represents normalized observation, X_{max} and X_{min} respectively represent the maximum and minimum observations in the relevant time series. The main advantage of this method is that it scales all the numerical values in the relevant time series in the [0, 1] range. When Fig. 1 is examined, it is seen that there are no outliers in the time series to be used. For this reason, the time series were normalized by the empirical normalization method.

In order to establish the financial stability indicator with the use of normalized data, it is necessary to weigh the determined variables. For this purpose, the previously given equation (2) was estimated and the results summarized in Tab. 1 were obtained.

Tab. 1: *Economic activity igita estimation results*

Variable	*Lag*[*]	*Coefficient*	*t-statistic*	*Marginal Significance*
Constant	-	0.138	3.514	0.001
y	1	0.733	7.467	0.000
roa	3	0.055	2.695	0.009
lev	3	0.094	2.938	0.005
ci	1	0.081	2.261	0.021
cvol	2	0.122	3.603	0.000
bist	3	0.069	2.312	0.025
bi	1	0.091	2.114	0.039
fx	2	0.068	2.096	0.041
rfx	1	0.030	1.831	0.073
AdjR^2	0.988	*Breusch-Godfrey*	1.521 (0.193)	
F	5.944 (0.000)	*White*	60.020 (0.267)	
Box-Pierce	10.386 (0.320)	*Chow*	1.199 (0.631)	

(*) The length of the lag is determined by the Akaike Information Criteria. In diagnostic tests, the values in parentheses represent marginal significance levels.

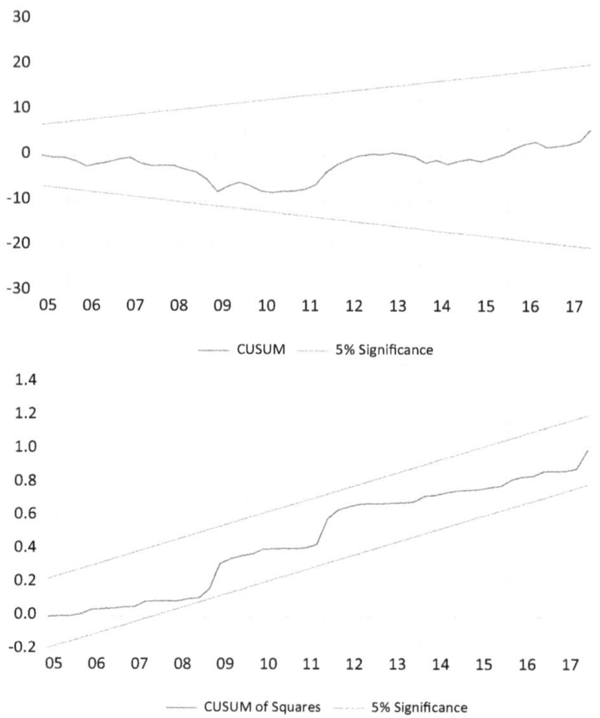

Fig. 2: *Structural break tests*

All coefficients estimated, according to the table, are statistically significant at the 5 % level of significance except the real exchange rate and coefficients also have the expected signs (The level of significance for the real exchange rate is 8 %). On the other hand, the traditional diagnostic tests in the lower part of the table and the stability tests given in Fig. 2 show that the estimated equation has no problem in the sense of empirical validity. The weights obtained by using the coefficient estimates of the variables represented by 4 blocks can be seen in Tab. 2.

Tab. 2: *Empirical weights of financial stability components*

Block	*Component*	*Variable*	*Coefficient*	*Weight*
Banking Sector	Return on Assets	*roa*	0.055	0.0902
Banking Sector	Leverage Ratio	*lev*	0.094	0.1541
Sum of Block				*0.2443*
Credit Market	Consumer Loans Interest Rate	*ci*	0.081	0.1328
Credit Market	Commercial Loans Volume	*cvol*	0.122	0.2000
Sum of Block				*0.3328*
Capital Market	BİST 100 Index	*bist*	0.069	0.1131
Capital Market	Government Bond Interest Rate	*bi*	0.091	0.1492
Sum of Block				*0.2623*
Foreign Exchange	Currency Basket Rate	*fx*	0.068	0.1115
Foreign Exchange	Real Effective Exchange Rate	*rfx*	0.030	0.0491
Sum of Block				*0.1606*

The weights in the last column of Tab. 2 are calculated according to equation (3) given above and are used to form the weight vector in equation (1). The course of the financial stability indicator obtained by using equation (1) can be observed in Fig. 3. Considering the process of building the FSI, naturally, the indicator value should be within the [0, 1] range. On the other hand, the approach of the indicator towards 0 indicates that the financial conditions have deteriorated and the approach of it towards 1 indicates that the financial conditions are improving. In other words, the downward trend of the indicator represents that the financial adversities increase, while the upward trend improvement in financial conditions.

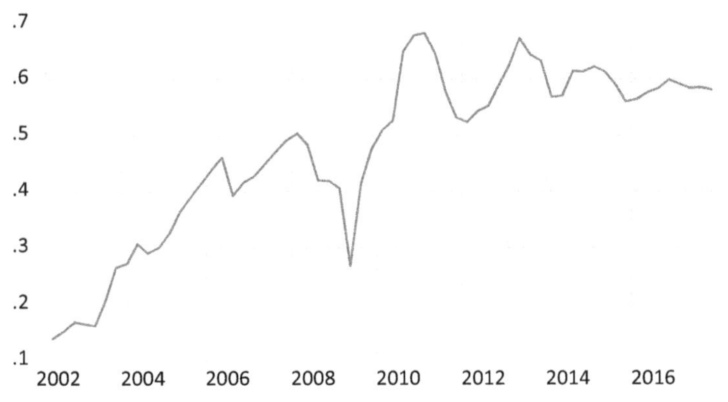

Fig. 3: *Financial stability indicator (2002 – 2017)*

4. Model and Estimation

In order to determine the effect of financial stability on economic growth, a standard neo-classical growth model will be used. The neoclassical growth model evaluates the per capita output as a Cobb-Douglas function of the capital per labor:

$$Y = A_0 e^g K^\alpha \tag{5}$$

In this equation A_0 is the initial level of technology and knowledge, Y is the output per capita and K is the capital for labor. Because total factor productivity is autonomous in the standard Solow model, the economic growth rate will be equal to parameter *g* in the steady state according to (5). Alternative specifications can be developed regarding total factor productivity determination (for instance assuming that the openness of the economy or financial development of the country determines it). In this study, it is assumed that financial stability is one of the factors that affect this variable in the linear form like:

$$g_t = g_0 + g_1 \left(FSI_{t-j}\right) \tag{6}$$

where FSI represents a scale variable related to financial stability. Including this definition in the traditional AK model generates the following:

$$Y_t = \left[A_0 e^{g_0 + g_1 \left(FSI_{t-j}\right)}\right] K^\alpha \tag{7}$$

Taking the log of both sides in the above equation we get

$$y_t = \gamma + g_0 + g_1 \left(FSI_{t-j}\right) + \alpha k_t \tag{8}$$

where lowercase letters represent the log of their level counterparts and $\gamma = ln\left(A_0\right)$. Considering the last equation, it is theoretically expected that output per capita positively responds to an increase in financial stability indicator (a favorable change in financial conditions) and an increase in the capital-labor ratio. If equation (4) is respecified in the first difference form defining $\theta_0 = \Delta\left(\gamma + g_0\right)$,

$$\Delta y_t = \theta_0 + \theta_1 \left(\Delta FSI_{t-j}\right) + \theta_2 \Delta k_t \tag{9}$$

is obtained where Δ is the first difference operator. Since the change in the capital stock equals the gross fixed capital formation (investments – I_t), the term Δk in equation (9) can be replaced by the following alternative definition:

$$z_t = \frac{log(I_t)}{\Delta log(L_t)} \tag{10}$$

Substituting this expression into equation (10) generates the final form of the economic growth function that will be used in this study:

$$\Delta y_t = \varphi_0 + \varphi_1 \left(\Delta FSI_{t-j}\right) + \varphi_0 z_t \tag{11}$$

One advantage of this specification is that the variable z provides the opportunity to determine not only the effects of a change in physical capital but also to see the effects of changes in human capital on economic growth.

The quarterly data related to national income accounts, employment, and population are obtained from the Turkish Statistical Institute for the 2002–2017 period, and the data related to financial stability indicators every quarter has been derived in the former part of this study for the same period. After the manipulation and transformation of the related time series indicated above, it is necessary to investigate the time series properties and whether they include unit root to decide the methodology to be used in the estimation process. The results of Augmented Dickey-Fuller (*ADF*) and Phillips-Peron (*PP*) tests to investigate the stationary in the data are given in Tab. 3.

Tab. 3: *Stationary test results*

Variable	Lag*	ADF Statistics	Probability	Band	PP Statistics	Probability	Integration
y	1	2,533**	0,303	5	0,922	0,750	I(1)
Δy	0	4,263	0,001	4	4,404	0,001	
FSI	0	2,202	0,208	0	0,202	0,208	I(1)
ΔFSI	0	6,899	0,000	0	6,899	0,000	
z	4	2,888**	0,173	2	1,653	0,450	I(1)
Δz	3	3,573	0,001	3	12,761	0,000	

Notes: (*) Lag lengths are determined by using Schwartz Information Criteria. (**) Indicates the inclusion of a linear time trend in the data

As Tab. 3 indicates, all of the time series used include a unit root in their levels but they are stationary in their first differences. In other words, both ADF and PP tests show that all of the time series used in this study present an I(1) characteristic. A cointegrating vector that would be found among non-stationary time series reveals that those variables present an equilibrium relationship in the long run. In order to investigate the existence of a cointegrating relationship among the variables we employed Johansen-Juselius multivariate cointegration tests and obtained the results presented in Tab. 4 below:

Tab. 4: *Johansen – Juselius cointegration test results*

Number of Cointegrating Vectors	Eigen Value	Trace Test	Probability	Maximum Eigen Value Test	Probability
0	0,409	47,788	0,015	31,572	0,008
1	0,161	16,216	0,475	10,534	0,562
2	0,090	5,682	0,502	5,682	0,502

Both trace and maximum eigenvalue tests indicate the existence of at least one cointegrating vector among variables at the 1 percentage level of significance. This shows us that there is a long-run equilibrium relationship between the mentioned variables and this relationship can be written as follows:

$$y_t = 0{,}478(FSI_t) + 3{,}338(z_t)$$

$$(0{,}078)\ (0{,}269)$$

The numbers in parentheses beneath the coefficient estimates are the standard errors. Both coefficients have the expected sign and are statistically significant. The existence of the cointegrating relationship among the variables states that the proper methodology to investigate the long-run relationship is the vector error correction model (VECM) which produces impulse–response functions for each of the variables in the model. By using the 4 lags and 1 cointegrating vector to estimate $VECM = (\Delta y_t, \Delta FSI_t, \Delta z_t)$, the following impulse–response functions depicted in Fig. 4 obtained:

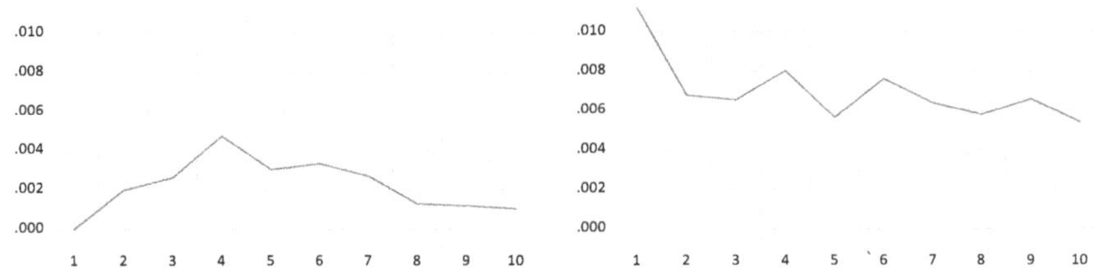

a. Response to innovations in FSI

b. Response to innovations in Z

Fig. 4: *Impulse – Response functions for per capita output – I*

Our theoretical expectations related to long-run relationships among the variables are revealed considering the impulse–response functions in both figures. First of all, a positive shock in the capital–labor ratio almost instantaneously increases the per capita output and this increase gradually diminishes up to the fifth quarter. After the fifth quarter, however, this increase turns out to be a stable and permanent effect on per capita output. To see the persistence of this effect the projection period extended from 10 quarters to 20 quarters as seen in Fig. 5. The related b parts of both figures state that the behavior of the relationship between per capita output and capital–labor ratio is consistent with the predictions of the Solow model. When we consider the financial stability indicator, especially, the short-run response to per capita output is remarkable. Since a positive shock in financial stability means that favorable conditions are present in the financial situation of the economy, we expect a positive response for the economic growth variable. According to "a" panel of Figs. 4 and 5, a positive shock measured by the one standard deviation innovation in the financial stability indicator causes an increase in the per capita output beginning from the first quarter and this effect lasts up to the fifth quarter. Although it diminishes gradually, from the beginning of the tenth quarter this effect turns out to be a persistent one. The persistence that both explanatory variables display in the estimated VECM proves their importance of them in the economic growth process. Depending on the definition of the capital-labor ratio in this study, increasing the quantity of investments per labor which positively affects economic growth shows that Turkey is far away from the capital shallowing process in the estimation period. On the other hand, the persistent effect of financial stability on economic growth, in the long run, indicates that financial instability and financial crisis periods in the Turkish economy impose a high economic cost on the society in terms of economic and social welfare.

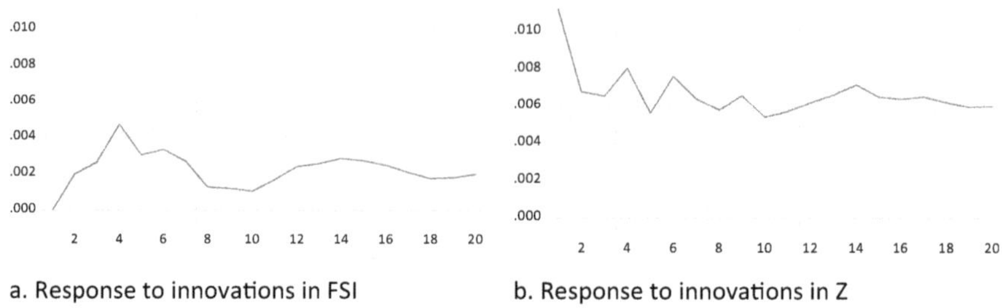

Fig. 5: *Impulse – Response functions for per capita output – II*

While the vector autoregressive methodology gives the opportunity to analyze the dynamic effects of variables on each other, it does not give any information about the direction of interactions among the variables in the model. Therefore, the direction of the causality needs to be tested to prove the theoretical expectations. One of the test methods frequently used for this purpose is the Granger causality test. Table 5 summarizes the test results.

Tab. 5: *Granger causality test results*

Null Hypothesis	**F-Test**	**Probability**	**Direction of Causality**
FSI does not cause y	3,468	0,033	FSI → y
y does not cause FSI	1,452	0,238	
z does not cause y	2,873	0,044	z ↔ y
Y does not cause z	4,004	0,012	

According to test results, the causality relationship between financial stability and economic growth is unidirectional and works from financial stability to economic growth at the 5% level of significance. This result confirms the already obtained results through Figs. 4 and 5. The causality between the capital-labor ratio and economic growth is bidirectional. While the capital-labor ratio affects economic growth the reverse is also true at the 5% level of significance. As we discussed in the construction of the alternative variable for capital accumulation, the inclusion of human capital in the total capital stock proves the predictions of the Solow growth model for the special case of Turkey.

5. Conclusion

The resilience of the economy against the possibilities that may destabilize the financial system as a result of unexpected situations can be defined as financial stability. Financial stability, in cases where it cannot be achieved, creates great negativities in the country's economy and social welfare. The existence of an effective and stable financial system is of great importance for economic growth. In addition, it became a generally accepted conclusion at the end of the 80s, when financial stability was a prerequisite for economic stability and sustainable economic growth.

In this study, a financial stability criterion has been developed for Turkey, which has experienced many financial crises due to both international markets and internal dynamics after 1980, and the relationship between financial stability and economic growth has been examined.

While creating the financial stability indicator for Turkey, the financial system components are formed from 4 blocks (Banking Sector, Credit Market, Capital Market, and Foreign Exchange Market) and their weighted average is used. The empirical is used to calculate the weight of each component. Thus, the FSI is created using quarterly data for the 2002–2017 period. When the empirical weights are examined, it is seen that the banking sector weighs approximately 25 %, the credit market 33 %, the capital market 26 %, and the foreign exchange market 16 %.

While examining the effect of financial stability on economic growth, the standard Neo-Classical Growth model is used. National income accounts, population, and employment data were obtained from Turkish Statistical Institute as quarterly data. It has been determined that these data and the financial stability indicator time series are stationary at the first difference. It has been observed that there is a long-term relationship between the variables; VECM is used to analyze this relationship. According to the test results, it has been determined that the causality relationship between financial stability and economic growth is unidirectional and from financial stability to economic growth at the 5% level of significance. It has been observed that the causality relationship between the capital-labor ratio and economic growth is bidirectional. As a result, in terms of the examined period, it is seen that financial stability is important in terms of making economic growth sustainable.

References

Ajello, A., Laubach, T., López, S. D., & Nakata, T. (2015). Financial Stability and Optimal Interest Rate Policy. Federal Reserve Board Working Paper, Washington.

Angeloni, I., Faia. E., & Lo Duca, M. (2015). Monetary Policy and Risk Taking. *Journal of Economic Dynamics and Control* (52), pp. 285–307.

Bagehot, W. (1873). *Lombard Street: A description of the Money Market*. Irwin, Illinois.

Beck, T. (2012). The Role of Finance in Economic Development – Benefits, Risks, and Politics. Denis, M. (Ed.), *Oxford Handbook of Capitalism*, Oxford University Press, New York.

Bencivenga, V., Smith, B. D., & Starr, R. M. (1995). "Transaction costs, technological choice and endogenous growth". *Journal of Economic Theory* (67), 153–177.

Bernanke, B. S., & Gertler, M. (1990). "Financial Fragility and Economic Performance." *Quarterly Journal of Economics* (105), 87–114.

Bernanke, B. S., & Gertler, M. (1989). "Banking in General Equilibrium". In W. Barnett & K. Singleton (Eds.), *"New Approaches to Monetary Economics"*. Cambridge University Press, Boston.

Bernanke, B. S., & Gertler, M. (1999). "Monetary Policy and Asset Price Volatility", *Federal Reserve Bank of Kansas City Economic Review* (4), 17–51.

Bernanke, B. S., & Gertler, M. (2001). "Should Central Banks Respond to Movements in Asset Prices?" *American Economic Review* (91), 253–257.

Demirgüç-Kunt, A., & Levine, R. (2008a). Finance and Economic Opportunity, World Bank Policy Research Working Paper No: 4468, Washington.

Demirgüç-Kunt, A., & Levine, R. (2008b). Finance, Financial Sector Policies, and Long-run Growth. World Bank Working Paper Series No: 4469, Washington.

Gilchrist, S., & Leahy, J. (2002). "Monetary Policy and Asset Prices", *Journal of Monetary Economics* (49), 75–97.

Goldsmith, R. W. (1969). *Financial Structure and Development*. Yale University Press, New Haven.

Greenwood, J., & Smith, B. (1997). Financial Markets in Development and Development of Financial Markets. *Journal of Economic Dynamics and Control* (21), 145–181.

King, R., & Levine, R. (1993). "Finance and Growth: Schumpeter Might be Right". *Quarterly Journal of Economics* (108), 717–737.

Levine, R. (1997). "Financial Development and Economic Growth Views and Agenda". *Journal of Economic Literature* (35), 688–726.

Loisel, O. (2014). "Monetary and Macroprudential Policy in an Estimated DSGE model for the Euro Area". *International Journal of Central Banking* (10), 237–247.

McKinnon, R. (1973). *Money and Capital in Economic Development*. Brookings, Washington.

Mishkin, F. S. (1999). "Global Financial Instability: Framework, Events, Issues". *Journal of Economic Perspectives* (3), 3–20.

Obstfeld, M. (1994). "Risk Taking, Global Diversification and Growth". *American Economic Review* (84), 10–29.

Schinasi, G. J. (2004). Defining Financial Stability. International Monetary Fund Working Paper No: 4, Washington.

Schumpeter, J. A. (1912). *The Theory of Economic Development*. Oxford University Press, London.

Shaw, E. (1973). *Financial Deepening in Economic Development*. Oxford University Press, New York.

Siklar, I., & Akca, A. (2018). "Macroprudential Policy and Financial Stability: The Turkish Case". *Research in Applied Economics* (10), 59–71.

Smets, F. (2014). "Financial Stability and Monetary Policy: How Closely Interlinked?" *International Journal of Central Banking* (10), 263–300.

Woodford, M. (2012). Inflation Targeting and Financial Stability. National Bureau of Economic Research Working Paper No: 17967. New York.

Zeynep Karal Önder[1]

Local Policies on Internal Migration: The Case of Andalusia[2]

1. Introduction

In this study, the effect of local government policies on internal migration is examined. The main question was to find the answer to the question of 'What is the effect of local government policy components on internal migration?' and to gain insight into internal migration and local government policies in developed country.

In this context, Turkey and Spain are similar two countries in terms of the ratio of local government expenditure in GDP. The purpose of the research demonstrates the effects of local government policy on residents in terms of the intention to migrate residents. Thereby, alternative internal migration policies without extra spending in Turkey is aimed at being determined.

In Spain, primary data through surveys to be conducted by resident were collected in the region that most migration and immigration. Impact of local government policies on migration potential was examined using discrete choice models (Probit and/or Logit) by using primary data.

Due to Spain's federal structure, the main services provided by the Andalusian Junta are education services, health services, and economic affairs. The items that local governments can influence migration in Andalusia are the areas where they directly serve the locals. These areas are also the areas where the most demands of the citizens arise.

2. The Relation Between Internal Migration and Local Government Policies

Every year, 3 % to 3.5 % of the population migrates in Turkey and this rate is well above the world average (Bell & Charles-Edwards, 2014, p. 8). The population migrating in Turkey is equal to the population of an average European country, and according to a study, the cost of a migrating individual

---

1 Anadolu University, Faculty of Economics, Department of Public Finance, zkaral@anadolu.edu.tr, ORCID: 0000-0002-7032-9448

2 This work is a part of 2219 Research Project (1059B191900855) supported by TUBITAK (The Scientific and Technological Research Council of Turkey).

to society is approximately 200 thousand TL (TÜRKONFED, 2018). For these reasons, managing internal migration is one of the problems that governments to create regulations. Experience and academic research demonstrate that local governments around the world create and carry out the majority of internal migration management policies, and that local governments' internal migration policies are more successful than central governments' internal migration policies (ECLAC, 2008, p. 231) (Yinanç, 2017, p. p. 29) (Afsar, 2003, p. 10) (Ecevit, 1997, p. 501).

In the framework of public choice theory, the preferences of individuals are more easily affected by local government policies (Maddox, 1960) (Buchanan, 1952) (Buchanan & Wagner, 1970) (Tiebout, 1956, p. 418).

Within the framework of Tiebout's statements, the research texts of the United Nations as well as local policies emphasize that individuals can lead to the idea of migration (ECLAC, 2008, p. 231). In the literature, internal migration is also seen as a cost-benefit problem between the policies offered by local governments and individuals (Sjaastad, 1962, p. 93). At the same time, each migration activity and migration geography should be evaluated in its own specific conditions (Ecevit, 1997, p. 501). As a result, all these, this study tries to reveal policy alternatives that local can implement by conducting field studies in the regions with the highest immigration in Spain.

3. Methodology

In this study, the effect of local government policies on internal migration was examined. The region that sends and receives the most immigrants in Spain is Andalucía (Andalusia) (INE, 2019). For this reason, the survey is carried out in Seville, the capital of Andalusia. Within the scope of this study, 1030 questionnaires were collected between November – February 2022. The questionnaires were collected online via the "Survey Monkey" platform. The distribution of the questionnaires collected in the Andalusia region is given in Tab. 1.

Tab. 1: *The regional distribution of participants*

Region	Collected Survey
Almería	163
Cádiz	109
Córdoba	183
Granada	135
Huelva	76
Jaén	51
Málaga	102
Sevilla	257
Total	1076

The effect of local government policies on internal migration has been examined using probability models and primary data obtained through a field study (survey) conducted with Andalusia residents who are the most immigrant and emigrants in Spain. According to the Regional Statistical Unit Classification, Andalusia is the region with the highest influx and reception in Turkey (INE, 2019). Primary data was analyzed with discrete selection models (Probit and/or Logit). The discrete selection model is one of the good solutions for cases where the dependent variable is qualitative (Greene, 1997). This model was preferred because migration intention can also be measured qualitatively.

In general, discrete selection models are modeled as follows, with y being the dependent variable and x being the vector of independent variables, which takes the value 1 if there is no discrete choice (Madalla, 1983).

$$Yi^* = \beta' x_i + \varepsilon_i \qquad (1)$$

y = 1 if intention/plan/will to migrate y = 0 if no intention/plan/will to migrate

By using the above model, we analyzed that the possibility that a person with an intention/plan/will to migrate will be affected by local government policies according to the functional classification. The model used in the analysis is as follows and Tab. 2 shows that the definitions of variables.

$$gn_i = \beta_0 + \beta_1 sex_i + \beta_2 education_i + \beta_3 employment_i + \beta_4 lincome_i + \beta_5 age_i + \begin{Bmatrix} \beta_6 P\_poss_i \\ \beta_7 P\_ecoaff_i \\ \beta_8 P\_envprot_i \\ \beta_9 P\_housing_i \\ \beta_{10} P\_healty_i \\ \beta_{11} P\_culture_i \\ \beta_{12} P\_edu_i \\ \beta_{13} P\_SSPS_i \\ \beta_{14} P\_GPS_i \\ \beta_{15} P\_defense_i \end{Bmatrix} \quad (2)$$

Tab. 2: *Definitions of variables*

Variables	**Definition**
gn_i	the intention to migrate: takes the value "1" if the participant has an intention to migrate and "0" if not
sex_i	the gender of the participants: it takes the value "1" if it is a woman and "0" if it is a man
$education_i$	the education level: "2" for primary school dropouts, "4" for primary school graduates, "8" for secondary school graduates, "12" for high school graduates, "14" for associate degree graduates, "14" for undergraduate students. for graduates, "16" takes the value "18" for a master's degree and "22" for a doctoral graduate.
$employment_i$	the employment status: takes the value "1" if the participant is employed in a place, and "0" if not
$lincome_i$	the logarithm of the income
age_i	declared age

Tab. 2: Continued

Variables	Definition	
P_poss_i	The Perception of Public Order and Security Services Quality	An index calculated by 1 for 'positive' responses, 0 for 'negative' responses and no value for 'I have no idea' and was calculated by taking the arithmetic mean
P_ecoaff_i	The Perception of Economic Affairs Services Quality	
$P\_envprot_i$	The Perception of Environmental Protection Services Quality	
$P\_housing_i$	The Perception of Settlement and Community Welfare Services Quality	
P_healty_i	The Perception of Health Services Quality	
$P\_culture_i$	The Perception of Resting, Culture and Religious Services Quality	
P_edu_i	The Perception of Educational Services Quality	
P_SSPS_i	The Perception of Social Security and Social Assistance Services Quality	
P_GPS_i	The Perception of General Public Services Quality	
$P\_defense_i$	The Perception of Defense Services Quality	

4. Results and Findings of the Discrete Selection Model Estimation

Summary statistics regarding the data obtained from 1076 questionnaires collected from field studies are given in Appendix-1. The estimation results of the probit model of the equation in Equation (2) are in Tab. 3, and the estimation results of the logit model are in Tab. 4. The results of the Probit/Logit models, in which we tested the effects of local government policies on the migration decision, have different aspects and are similar to each other. Variable-based interpretation was preferred to see the aspects and different aspects of both prediction results that support each other.

Tab. 3a: *Probit models results*

PROBIT MODELS	(1)	(2)	(3)	(4)	(5)	(6)
VARIABLES	**Basic M1.**	**Basic M2.**	**POSS**	**Eco. Aff.**	**Env. Prot.**	**Housing**
Sex	**0.264****	**0.361****	**0.361****	**0.368****	**0.354****	**0.364****
	(0.087)	(0.080)	(0.080)	(0.080)	(0.080)	(0.080)
Education	**-0.051****	**-0.051****	**-0.051****	**-0.050****	**-0.049****	**-0.050****
	(0.011)	(0.009)	(0.009)	(0.009)	(0.009)	(0.009)
Employment	**-0.177+**	-0.101	-0.103	-0.078	-0.082	-0.097
	(0.102)	(0.088)	(0.089)	(0.089)	(0.088)	(0.088)
Lage	**-0.279****	**-0.236***	**-0.236***	**-0.229***	**-0.235***	**-0.236***
	(0.107)	(0.101)	(0.101)	(0.101)	(0.101)	(0.101)
lincome	-0.033					
	(0.025)					
P_POSS			0.015			
			(0.078)			
P_Eco.Aff.				**-0.150***		
				(0.074)		
P_Env.Prot					**-0.148***	
					(0.067)	
P_Housing						-0.030
						(0.072)
Constant	2.307**	1.826**	1.826**	1.796**	1.809**	1.825**
	(0.446)	(0.391)	(0.391)	(0.391)	(0.391)	(0.391)
Observations	**840**	**1,007**	**1,007**	**1,007**	**1,007**	**1,007**
LR chi2(5)	57.60	66.23	66.26	70.38	71.10	66.40
Prob > chi2	**0**	**0**	**0**	**0**	**0**	**0**
Pseudo R2:	0.0505	0.0491	0.0492	0.0522	0.0527	0.0493

Standard errors are in parentheses.
** p<0.01, * p<0.05, + p<0.1

It is necessary to analyze the results in two stages. First, it should be examined whether the descriptive characteristics of the participants are compatible with other studies in the literature. According to the estimation results of the discrete selection models, men are more likely to migrate than women. The higher the education level, the lower the probability of migration. The older the participants, the less likely they are to migrate. These descriptive variables show results consistent with those in the literature.

Tab. 3b: *Probit models results (Continue)*

PROBIT MODELS	(7)	(8)	(9)	(10)	(11)	(12)
VARIABLES	Healthy	Culture	Education	SSPS	GPS	Defense
Sex	**0.359****	**0.362****	**0.360****	**0.363****	**0.360****	**0.367****
	(0.080)	(0.080)	(0.080)	(0.080)	(0.080)	(0.080)
Education	**-0.050****	**-0.051****	**-0.050****	**-0.051****	**-0.051****	**-0.049****
	(0.009)	(0.009)	(0.009)	(0.009)	(0.009)	(0.009)
Employment	-0.072	-0.098	-0.081	-0.093	-0.108	-0.057
	(0.089)	(0.089)	(0.089)	(0.089)	(0.089)	(0.089)
Lage	**-0.231***	**-0.236***	**-0.237***	**-0.237***	**-0.235***	**-0.229***
	(0.101)	(0.101)	(0.101)	(0.101)	(0.101)	(0.101)
P_Healty	**-0.159***					
	(0.066)					
P_Culture		-0.016				
		(0.067)				
P_Edu			-0.101			
			(0.068)			
P_SSPS				-0.040		
				(0.071)		
P_GPS					0.043	
					(0.072)	
P_Defense						**-0.181****
						(0.066)
Constant	1.807**	1.825**	1.827**	1.827**	1.826**	1.783**
	(0.391)	(0.391)	(0.391)	(0.391)	(0.391)	(0.390)
Observations	**1,007**	**1,007**	**1,007**	**1,007**	**1,007**	**1,007**
LR chi2(5)	72	66.29	68.47	66.54	66.58	73.75
Prob > chi2	**0**	**0**	**0**	**0**	**0**	**0**
Pseudo R2:	0.0534	0.0492	0.0508	0.0494	0.0494	0.0547

Standard errors are in parentheses.
** $p<0.01$, * $p<0.05$, + $p<0.1$

Although a significant effect of employment could not be reached in the predicted discrete selection models, migration tendencies decrease as the probability of employment increases as the education level increases. When we examine the descriptive statistics obtained from field studies, the main reason for migration in Andalusia is employment. For this reason, it is normal that the probability of emigration decreases as the level of education increases. Since the income variable could not be collected regularly, it was included in the estimates in the basic model, and no significant effect was found. The income variable was not included in the other estimates, as a significant effect could not be achieved and the number of observations was considerably reduced.

The second part of the estimation results shows the effect of direct local government expenditures on the migration decision. The opinions of the participants for each item of functional expenditure were included in the models separately. According to the estimation results of the Probit and Logit models, as the satisfaction of the residents of the district with the services provided by the local government increases, their intention to migrate decreases.

Tab. 4a: *Logit models results*

LOGIT MODELS	(1)	(2)	(3)	(4)	(5)	(6)
VARIABLES	**Basic M1.**	**Basic M2.**	**POSS**	**Eco. Aff.**	**Env. Prot.**	**Housing**
Sex	**0.427****	**0.427****	**0.585****	**0.599****	**0.574****	**0.591****
	(0.142)	(0.142)	(0.130)	(0.131)	(0.131)	(0.131)
Education	**-0.086****	**-0.086****	**-0.086****	**-0.085****	**-0.083****	**-0.086****
	(0.018)	(0.018)	(0.016)	(0.016)	(0.016)	(0.016)
Employment	**-0.278+**	**-0.278+**	-0.157	-0.115	-0.120	-0.148
	(0.168)	(0.168)	(0.147)	(0.146)	(0.146)	(0.146)
Lage	**-0.477****	**-0.477****	**-0.399***	**-0.386***	**-0.398***	**-0.401***
	(0.183)	(0.183)	(0.170)	(0.168)	(0.169)	(0.169)
lincome	-0.054					
	(0.041)					
P_POSS			0.007			
			(0.128)			
P_Eco.Aff.				**-0.255***		
				(0.120)		
P_Env.Prot					**-0.251***	
					(0.110)	
P_Housing						-0.056
						(0.117)
Constant	3.895**	3.895**	3.079**	3.039**	3.066**	3.081**
	(0.769)	(0.769)	(0.661)	(0.659)	(0.660)	(0.661)
Observations	840	840	1,007	1,007	1,007	1,007
LR chi2(5)	58.33	58.33	66.72	71.25	71.97	66.95
Prob > chi2	0	0	0	0	0	0
Pseudo R2:	0.0512	0.0512	0.0495	0.0529	0.0534	0.0497

Standard errors are in parentheses.
** p<0.01, * p<0.05, + p<0.1

When we analyze the effect of local government expenditures on migration intention at the functional classification level, there is a significant effect of Economic Affairs, Environmental Protection Services, Health and Defense services. Due to Spain's federal structure, the main services provided by the Andalusian Junta are education services, health services, and economic affairs. The items that local governments can influence migration in Andalusia are the areas where they directly serve the locals. These areas are also the areas where the most demands of the citizens arise. Consistent with these results, preliminary findings show that local governments should focus on the most basic human needs while forming their expenditure components within the scope of their objectives of having the optimum population size in their jurisdiction. As a result, the estimations made for the Andalusia region are compatible with the literature and provide the opportunity for local governments to choose between functional level expenditure alternatives and to make predictions about their effects.

The most critical output of the project is to determine which of the functional expenditure items is more effective. This output determines the policy preferences of local governments. When we examine the results of both descriptive and econometric analysis, it has been concluded that local governments should focus on the most basic human needs while forming their expenditure components within the scope of their objectives of having the optimum population size in their jurisdiction.

Tab. 4b: *Logit models results (Continuous)*

LOGIT MODELS	(7)	(8)	(9)	(10)	(11)	(12)
VARIABLES	**Healthy**	**Culture**	**Education**	**SSPS**	**GPS**	**Defense**
Sex	**0.583****	**0.586****	**0.584****	**0.589****	**0.583****	**0.595****
	(0.131)	(0.130)	(0.131)	(0.130)	(0.130)	(0.131)
Education	**-0.085****	**-0.086****	**-0.085****	**-0.086****	**-0.086****	**-0.083****
	(0.016)	(0.016)	(0.016)	(0.016)	(0.016)	(0.016)
Employment	-0.106	-0.150	-0.124	-0.140	-0.166	-0.086
	(0.147)	(0.146)	(0.146)	(0.147)	(0.146)	(0.147)
Lage	**-0.390***	**-0.399***	**-0.402***	**-0.401***	**-0.399***	**-0.389***
	(0.169)	(0.169)	(0.169)	(0.169)	(0.170)	(0.169)
P_Healty	**-0.264***					
	(0.108)					
P_Culture		-0.030				
		(0.109)				
P_Edu			-0.164			
			(0.110)			
P_SSPS				-0.076		
				(0.115)		
P_GPS					0.057	
					(0.116)	
P_Defense						**-0.294****
						(0.108)
Constant	3.058**	3.077**	3.081**	3.084**	3.076**	3.010**
	(0.661)	(0.661)	(0.660)	(0.661)	(0.662)	(0.660)
Observations	1,007	1,007	1,007	1,007	1,007	1,007
LR chi2(5)	72.80	66.79	68.95	67.15	66.96	74.19
Prob > chi2	0	0	0	0	0	0
Pseudo R2:	0.0540	0.0496	0.0512	0.0498	0.0497	0.0550

Standard errors are in parentheses.
** p<0.01, * p<0.05, + p<0.1

The second important result reached within the scope of this study is that the policies carried out by local governments in areas where they are authorized and do not have problems in resource allocation directly reach residents within the boundaries of local governments, and they can provide limited services to residents in areas where they have limited authority. The policies carried out by local governments are of great importance in the policies to be carried out with respect to the spatial distribution of the population. The most important reason for this is that the rural-urban distribution, urbanization stories, and the formation of urban agglomerations are geographical-specific processes in every geography. In these processes, it should be carried out by institutions established within the scope of the principle of decentralization, which know the strengths and weaknesses of the geography and have a command of its characteristics. (Pınar A., 2017, s. 131).

5. Conclusion

The construction of a balanced economic and social system depends on the population's spatial distribution within a country. Geographically balanced population distribution ensures economic efficiency and equitable social class creation. Changes in the population's spatial distribution could lead to a variety of economic and social issues, including fast urbanization and population concentration, a reduction in the population of rural areas, issues with urban management, squatting, and the appearance of displaced people.

The impact of local government policies on internal migration was examined in this study. It seeks to do this by conducting field research in Spain's Andalusia region and presenting policy ideas that local governments might implement. Fieldwork with residents who use local government services and intend to move was used to gather the information for these questions. The first topic that field studies attempted to address was whether or not the migration strategy is impacted by local government policy. The results show that the services that directly impact citizens are successful in reducing internal migration. The most critical output of the study is to determine which of these functional expenditure items is more effective. When we examine the results econometric analysis, it has been concluded that local governments should focus on the most basic human needs while forming their expenditure components within the scope of their objectives of having the optimum population size in their jurisdiction. Prioritizing the policies of Education and Health Services and Economic Affairs by local governments is the policy basket that has the most influence on immigration decision

References

Afsar, R. (2003). *Internal Migration and The Development Nexus: The Case of Bangladesh*. Dhaka: Regional Conference on Migration, Development and Pro-Poor Policy Choices in Asia. 2–3 Aralık 2003.

Bell, M., & Charles-Edwards, E. (2014). Measuring Internal Migration Around the Globe: A Comparative Analysis. KNOMAD Working Paper.

Buchanan, J. M. (1952). Federal Grants and Resource Allocation. *Journal of Political Economy*, *60*(3), 208–217.

Buchanan, J. M., & Wagner, R. (1970). An Efficiency Basis for Federal Fiscal Equalization. In J. Margolis, *The Analysis of Public Output* (s. 139–162). NBER.

Ecevit, M. C. (1997). İç Göçün Unutulan Kaynakları: Tarımsal Farklılaşma ve Dönüşüm Dinamikleri. In II. Ulusal Sosyoloji Kongresi Toplum ve Göç (s. 493–501). Mersin: T.C. Başbakanlık Devlet İstatistik Enstitüsü - Sosyoloji Derneği.

ECLAC. (2008). *Social Panorama of Latin America 2007*. Santiago: United Nations Publications.

Greene, W. (1997). *Econometric Analysis*. Third ed. New Jersey: Prentice Hall.

INE. 2019. Instituto Nacional de Estadistica. Erişim Tarihi: 20.07.2019. https://www.ine.es/dynt3/inebase/en/index.htm?padre=3700&capsel=3701

Madalla, G. (1983). *Limited Dependent and Quatitave Variables in Econometrics*. Cambridge: Cambridge University Press.

Maddox, J. G. (1960). Private and Social Costs of Movement of People Out of Agriculture. *The Amerikan Economic Review*, *50*(2), 393–402.

Pınar, A. (2017). Maliye Politikalarının Sektörel ve Bölgesel Etkileri. In A. Taraktaş, *Maliye Politikası II* (s. 124–141). Eskişehir.

Sjaastad, L. A. (1962). The Costs and Returns of Human Migration. *Journal of Political Economy*, *70*(5/2), 80–93.

Tiebout, C. M. (1956). A Pure Theory of Local Expenditures. *Journal of Political Economy*, *64*(5), 146–424.

TÜRKONFED. (2018). TÜRKONFED 39.Girişim ve İş Dünyası Konseyi Gümrük ve Ticaret Bakanı Tüfenkçi'nin Katılımıyla Diyarbakır'da Gerçekleşti. Erişim Tarihi: 04.10.2018 . TÜRKONFED: http://www.turkonfed.org/tr/detay/1357/turkonfed-baskani-kadooglu-dogu-ve-guneydogudan-ic-gocun-maliyeti-70-milyar-tl/

Yinanç, A. (2017). Değişen Süreçler Türkiye ve Dünyada Yerel Yönetimler ve Kentsel Altyapı Planlaması. T.C. Çevre ve Şehircilik Bakanlığı Altyapı ve Kentsel Dönüşüm Hizmetleri Genel Müdürlüğü. Ankara: T.C. Çevre ve Şehircilik Bakanlığı.

Appendix 1: *Summary statistics of variables*

Variable	Obs	Mean	Std. Dev.	Min	Max
no	1076	538.5	3.107.587	1	1076
Migration intention	1034	.6179884	.4861145	0	1
Sex	1076	.527881	.5123258	-1	1
Age	1049	4.338.894	1.210.654	18	1999
Maritual Status	1068	.4925094	.5345952	-1	1
Education	1076	1.612.454	490.821	0	22
Employmnet	1076	.66171	.4733478	0	1
Income	946	6940.73	14486.11	0	100000
POSS	1076	.2839219	.5315723	-1	1
Eco.Aff	1076	.1914498	.5577666	-1	1
Env. Prot.	1076	.2032218	.6098299	-1	1
Housing	1076	.1598513	.5690715	-1	1
Healty	1076	.2047708	.624143	-1	1
Culture	1076	.2143742	.615641	-1	1
Education	1076	.1824659	.6117356	-1	1
SSPS	1076	.1417286	.5806062	-1	1
GPS	1076	.1442379	.5710653	-1	1
Defense	1076	.1830855	.6293748	-1	1

Özlem Genç[1] & Ceran Arslan Olcay[2]

Evolution of The EU Budget via Digitalisation and Greening Priorities

1. Introduction

The European Union budget is based on own resources composed of revenues of import duties of the Union plus Gross National Product shares and Value Added Tax contributions of member states. The resources are pooled to implement policies and finance institutions of the Union. How the implementation of policies will be financed are determined focusing on the needs of the Union and priorities are decided. Since 1988, budgeting process is based on multiyear financial programmes called multiannual financial framework. The most recent multiannual financial framework has been set to prevail during the period 2021–2027. The 2021-2027 Multiannual Financial Framework has come into force with the Next Generation EU that has been established to contain the damaging effects of COVID 19 on member state economies.

The 2021–2027 Multiannual Financial Framework has culminated in essential amendments. A new item of own resources called plastics own resource has been put forward. Additionally, Next Generation EU has made possible the loan mechanism to finance Resilience and Recovery Fund, and thus has raised concerns over need to generate resources and questions on the repayment of the common debt.

This study aims at analysing 2021–2027 Multiannual Financial Framework and Next Generation EU established under the circumstances of COVID 19 crisis. In this context, changes on the revenue and expenditure items of the budget will be evaluated focusing on the significance and the common grounds of digitalisation and greening priorities in line with the future perspective of the European Union.

1 Ph.D., Research Assistant, Ankara University, Faculty of Political Sciences, ogenc@law.ankara.edu.tr, Department of Public Finance, ORCID: 0000-0001-6253-1120.

2 Ph.D., Assistant Professor, Ankara University, Faculty of Political Sciences, Department of Economics, colcay@ankara.edu.tr, ORCID: 0000-0002-2114-4076

2. The European Union Budget

The European Union (EU) budget can be considered as a financial act compromised among the institutions of the Union- the Commission, the Council, and the Parliament. The budget is a pool of resources contributed by member states to implement policies established to achieve goals of the EU and finance the institutions founded to this end (European Union, 2022b). While revenues are accrued mainly through contributions of member states and import duties, spending is determined in the light of the priorities of the Union and distributed by means of the funds founded to realise the Union's objectives. The main budgeting principle is laid out in the Treaty on the Functioning of the EU article 312 stating that the expenditure must be matched by revenue. That is to say, spending should stay in the limit of the revenue (European Union, 2022a).

The EU budget is designed as multiannual financial frameworks since 1988 and composed of the contributions of the member states to carry out and finance policies of the Union. The main sources of revenue called the own resources consist of customs duties, Gross National Income (GNI) based and Value Added Tax (VAT) based contributions coming from the member states. Budgeting system based on own resources has gone through transformations due to enlargement and deepening processes of the Union (European Union, 2022a). The most recent transformation in terms of revenue has occurred in the budgeting process of the 2021–2027 Multiannual Financial Framework which has coincided with the period of COVID 19. In this respect, while conventional own resources have been maintained, new own resource based on the non recycled plastic packaging waste, in short, plastics own resource, has been established coherent with "green objectives" (European Commission, 2022a). Furthermore, the Commission has made proposals to establish new resources based on emissions trading system, carbon border adjustment mechanism and reallocated profits of multinationals (European Commission, 2021). As a recent development, in December 2022, the Council adopted a directive on taxing large groups and multinationals with a combined turnover of at least 750 million Euros at a minimum rate of 15 % via Pillar 2 of the OECD's reform of international taxation. (European Council, 2022).

Spending side of the budget is a common accord of the Union to finance priority areas which are determined in compliance with the needs of the Union cyclically. Priority areas stated as headings are decided considering the needs of the Union for that period. Headings of spending for the 2021–2027 Multiannual Financial Framework have been determined as follows: single market, innovation and digital; cohesion, resilience and values; natural resources and environment;

migration and border management; security and defence; neighbourhood and the world; European public administration. (European Union, 2022b)

3. 2021–2027 Multiannual Financial Framework and Next Generation EU

The most recent multiannual financial framework planned to prevail for a 7 year period covers the 2021–2027 cycle. Since the drafting and coming into effect of the plan have coincided with COVID 19 crisis, a complementary element to combat the crisis-Next Generation EU-has come into force in tandem. In terms of the size of the budget, Multiannual financial framework(MFF) and Next Generation EU(NGEU) together form a vast amount (worth 2018 billion Euros in 2022 prices) and offer a huge amount of financial facility to recover from the damage caused by COVID 19 crisis and achieve the transformation of the economy the EU has been anticipating such as the twin objectives of green and digital (European Union, 2022b).

2021–2027 MFF has been drafted in the atmosphere of COVID 19 and the priority areas have been determined taking into consideration combating crises of COVID 19, climate, illegal migration and even Brexit. Confluence of those factors have led the EU to establish a more comprehensive one off solution by establishing the NGEU. The process of establishing the NGEU has set the stage for challenging debates that reflect divergences in the Union (Fabbrini, 2022: 189). How the resources will be created, at what rate the resources will be allocated as loans and grants, how the repayments will be made have been the hot topics of the discussions (Kaygusuz, 2020: 8). The notorious divide between northern and southern member states have appeared as Frugal Four versus Irresponsible South during this crisis. Austria, Denmark, Sweden, and Netherlands forming the frugal four have confronted establishing a bail out fund or issuing common debt by blaming southern member states for profligacy, while southern member states have emphasized solidarity (Bialasiewicz, 2020). Consequently, Recovery and Resilience Fund as a part of NGEU has been founded with the capacity to grant 338 billion Euros and to lend 385.8 billion Euros (in 2022 prices) with the accord of Germany, France and the Commission (Tesche, 2022: 489). Recovery and Resilience Fund (RRF) is based on a loan mechanism that the Commission raises funds by borrowing in capital markets. Debt issuance in this context has started as of June 2021 and is anticipated to take place between the period of 2021–2026. Yet, repayment will be done between 2028–2058. (European Commission, 2022c). This loan mechanism brought about by the NGEU had been on the agenda during the global crisis of 2008 and sovereign debt crisis thereafter, however could not be realised ever since .

A number of debates have emerged with the establishment of the NGEU. To begin with, loan mechanism has brought about approaches such as setting of this mechanism may lead to accomplishing financial union. Common borrowing and responsibility have paved the way for such arguments. Concerning how member states will apply for the fund, member states' programmes prepared to benefit from the RRF, have been conditioned to be consistent with green and digital transition roadmaps. Last but not least, maintaining rule of law has been emphasized in this respect. Future perspective and European values can be said to reflect to the running of the RRF (Fabbrini, 2022: 192).

However there are some issues that pose great challenges on NGEU. Those issues are as follows: concerns on running the loan mechanism, the need of the Union to create new sources of revenue for the repayment of borrowing, Russia-Ukraine war's exacerbating effect on concerns over energy and increasing pressure on finding new sources of energy, prospective problems in the repayments of loans, the fear of pressure of rising inflation on investments (The Economist, 2022).

4. Revenue and Headings of Spending in the Context of the 2021–2027 MFF and NGEU

The current long term budget (MFF) and NGEU together form an amount of 2017.8 billion Euros. 2021–2027 MFF is worth 1210.9 billion Euros, while NGEU makes up a total of 806.9 billion Euros. As is known, main resources of revenue are formed through customs duties (the traditional own resource), GNI and VAT contributions of member states. According to the Own Resources Decision, member states transfer %75 of customs duties after deducting %25 (up from %20 in the previous MFF) as collection costs. (Council Decision 2020/2053; European Parliament, 2022). In terms of GNI contributions, revenue ceiling is determined considering the estimated EU GNI. For the period 2021–2027, revenue ceiling to cover annual commitments has been determined as 1.46 % (up from 1.29 % in the previous MFF) of EU GNI, while the ceiling of annual payments 1.40 % (up from 1.23 % in the previous MFF). Those figures are the maximum amounts of resources which can be requested. As a joint guarantee to issue bonds to finance NGEU, revenue ceilings have been temporarily raised to 2.06 % of EU GNI for commitments and 2 % for payments respectively. (European Commission, 2022 f; Bisciari et al., 2021: 11). In terms of VAT contributions, the application of a uniform call rate of 0.30 % has been specified, while a uniform call rate of 0.80 Euro per kilogram for the new plastics own resource has been determined. (Council Decision 2020/2053)

Tab. 1: Displays the allocation of resources per heading

Headings of Spending	**Multiannual Financial Framework**	**Next Generation EU**	**Total**
Single market, innovation and digital	149,5	11.5	161
cohesion, resilience and values	426.7	776.5	1203.2
natural resources and environment	401	18.9	419.9
migration and border management	25.7	-	25.7
security and defence	14.9	-	14.9
neighbourhood and the world	110.6	-	110.6
European public administration	82.5	-	82.5
Total	1210.9	806.9	2017.8

Source: European Commission, https://ec.europa.eu/info/strategy/eu-budget/long-term-eu-budget/2021-2027/spending/headings_en, (17.10.2022)

Table 1 displays the allocation of resources per heading. Investments under the headings of single market, innovation and digital, cohesion, resilience and values, natural resources and environment have the largest shares of the budget in total. Those headings are also contributed via NGEU (European Union, 2022b). With the contribution of NGEU, almost 60 % of the budget is devoted to cohesion, resilience and values. Under this heading, mitigating damaging effects of COVID 19 on economies has been targeted by strengthening cohesion among member states and raising resilience of the economies by reducing disparities among regions. RRF, ReactEU and RescEU serve under this heading. The European Social Fund whose aim is focusing on youth employment, re-skilling workers and reducing poverty is also under the scope of this heading. (European Commission, 2022 g) 161 billion Euros are allocated for single market, innovation, and digital heading while 419.9 billion Euros are planned to be spent for the purposes of natural resources and environment heading. NGEU reinforces single market heading through contributing to the programmes of InvestEU and Horizon Europe. Under the heading of natural resources and environment, NGEU supports by contributing to Rural Development and Just Transition Funds. Components of NGEU and its allocations on other programmes are seen in Tab. 2.

Tab. 2: Components of and allocation of NGEU on other programmes (billion Euros in 2022 prices)

Recovery and Resilience Facility (RRF)	€723.8 billion	Contribution of NGEU under the heading of Cohesion Resilience and Values Heading
of which, loans	*€385.8 billion*	
of which, grants	*€338.0 billion*	
ReactEU	€50.6 billion	
RescEU	€2 billion	
InvestEU	€6.1 billion	Contribution of NGEU under the heading of Single Market, Innovation and Digital Heading
Horizon Europe	€5.4 billion	
Rural Development	€8.1 billion	Contribution of NGEU under the heading of Natural Resources and Environment
Just Transition Funds (JTF)	€10.9 billion	
Total	€806.9 billion	

Source: European Commission, https://ec.europa.eu/info/strategy/recovery-plan-europe_en, (17.10.2022)

RRF, the largest component of the NGEU is composed of 723.8 billion Euros in 2022 prices. 338 billion Euros as grants and 385.8 billion Euros as loans have made up this amount. 83.1 billon Euros have been allocated to other programmes as contribution of NGEU while 50. 6 billion Euros have been channelled to ReactEU which aims to combat youth unemployment and deterioration of welfare. In addition, 2 billion Euros have been transferred to RescEU which aims to combat disasters and crises. For the purposes of research, 5.4 billion Euros have been channelled to Horizon Europe while InvestEU has been reinforced with the contribution of NGEU by 6.1 billion Euros. In terms of green transition, 8.1 billion Euros have been channelled to Rural Development Fund and 10.9 billion Euros have been allocated for Just Transition Fund whose aim is to provide transition to climate neutrality.

To be able to benefit from RRF, member states are obliged to prepare national RRF programmes consistent with green and digital transition roadmaps. Member states have completed their national RRF programmes as of July 2022 (most member states have completed their programmes in 2021 with the exception of Netherlands submitting in 2022). National RRF programmes are expected to contain green and digital reforms and public investments planned to be carried out until 2026 with the support of RRF. In addition, the weight of green investments are anticipated to reach 37 % and digital 20 % respectively.

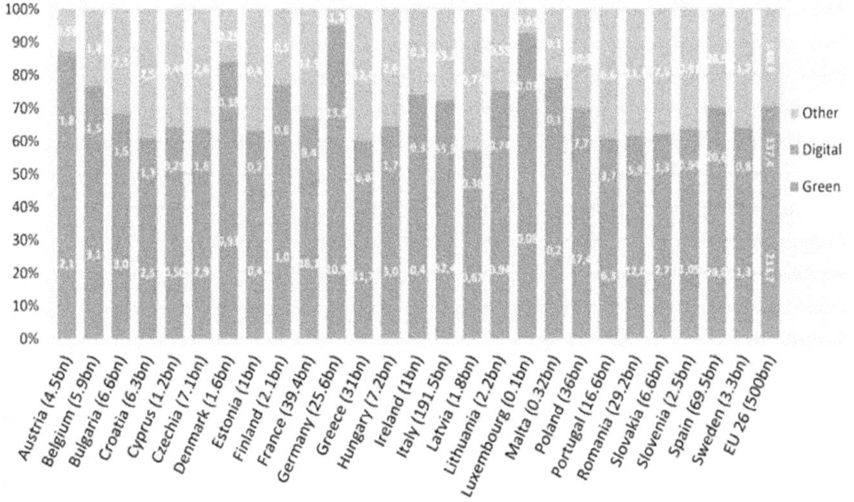

Fig. 1: Overall resource allocation in national recovery and resilience plans (% of total and billion Euros)

Source: Bruegel, https://www.bruegel.org/dataset/european-union-countries-recovery-and-resilie nce-plans (14.12.2022). Note: Calculations have been made by Bruegel based on submitted recovery plans. Numbers on the horizontal axis show the amount of the plan to be financed by RRF while the numbers over the bars denote digital, green and other types of investments in billion Euros. While the numbers show only grants for other countries, the numbers for Italy show both grants and loans.

Fig. 1 shows the weight of planned green, digital, and other investments of 26 EU countries in their national RRP programmes based on the calculations of Bruegel. According to the findings of this study, the required ratios of digital and green transition objectives can be said to have been attained by member states.

Tab. 3 shows updated maximum grant allocations of RRF and amounts of grants and loans requested by member states as of 2022.

Tab. 3. Maximum grant allocations, requested grants and loans of RRF

Country	Maximum Grant Allocations (billion Euros) (updated on 30 June 2022)	Requested Grants (billion Euros)	Requested Loans (billion Euros)
Belgium	4.5	5.9	-
Bulgaria	5.7	6.6	-
Czechia	7.7	7.1	-
Denmark	1.4	1.6	-
Germany	28	27.9	-
Estonia	0.9	1	-
Ireland	0.9	1	-
Greece	17.4	17.8	12.7
Spain	77.2	69.5	-
France	37.4	40.9	-
Croatia	5.5	6.4	-
Italy	69	68.9	122.6
Cyprus	0.9	10	0.2
Latvia	1.8	1.8	-
Lithuania	2.1	2.2	-
Luxembourg	0.1	0.1	-
Hungary	5.8	7.2	-
Malta	0.3	0.3	-
Netherlands	4.7	4.7	-
Austria	3.8	4.5	-
Poland	22.5	23.9	12.1
Portugal	15.5	13.9	2.7
Romania	12.1	14.3	15
Slovenia	1.5	1.8	0.7
Slovakia	6	6.6	-
Finland	1.8	2.1	-
Sweden	3.2	3.3	-
EU 27	338	342.3	166

Source: Maximum Grant Allocations; European Commission, https://commission.europa.eu/system/files/2022-06/2022_06_30_update_maximum_financial_contribution_rrf_grants.pdf, (14.01.2023).
Requested Grants and Loans; Bruegel, https://www.bruegel.org/dataset/european-union-countries-recovery-and-resilience-plans (14.01.2023).

Grant allocations of RRF have been decided to be disbursed in the period of 2021–2023. 70 % of the grants have been decided to be disbursed between 2021 and 2022. The remaining 30 % has been decided to be made available in 2023. The disbursement for 2021–2022 would be subject to an allocation key reflecting the 2019 population, the inverse of GDP per capita and 2015–2019 average unemployment. As for the allocation key for 2023, the latter criterion would be replaced, in equal proportion, by the loss in real GDP observed over 2020 and by the cumulative loss in real GDP observed over the period 2020–2021. Final allocations would be calculated by 30 June 2022 considering those developments (Darvas, 2020; Bisciari et al., 2021: 6).

Finally, the largest shares of grants have been allocated to Spain, Italy, and France. Loans, on the other hand, have been requested by Greece, Italy, Cyprus, Poland, Portugal, Romania, and Slovenia which reach the amount of 166 billion Euros in 2022 prices. (See Tab.3.)

5. Future Perspectives and the EU Budget

The objectives of the European Union as promoting sustainable development based on balanced economic growth, price stability, full employment, a highly competitive social market economy, a high level of protection of the environment in the framework of peace, freedom, justice, and security put forward since 1950s are being complemented by the objectives of green and digital single market recently. The essence of MFF and NGEU realising green and digital transition. Specifically, NGEU encourages member states to make green and digital investments.

In the draft of Shaping Europe's Digital Future, artificial intelligence, meta data analysis, 5G network and digital skills have been determined as priority areas. Digital investments are attached great importance in terms of competition with global rivals such as United States of America and Asian economies and considered to be a solution in the field of employment (European Commission, 2022d).

Tab. 4. Financing of digitalisation in the context of 2021–2027 MFF (billion Euros in 2022 prices)

Programmes	**Contribution of the Programmes to Digitalisation (billion Euros)**
Digital Europe	7.6
Connecting Europe	2.07
Horizon Europe (total capacity 95.5) (%35)	33.25 (share of digitalisation)
Invest EU (total capacity 26.2) (%10)	2.62 (share of digitalisation)
Creative Europe MEDIA	1.4
EU For Health (total capacity 5.3)(%10)	0.53
Recovery and Resilience Facility (total capacity 672.5) (%20)	134.5 (share of digitalisation)
Total	181.97

Source: European Commission, https://digital-strategy.ec.europa.eu/en/activities/funding-digital, (17.10.2022).

Financing of digitalization in the context of 2021–2027 MFF is provided through the programmes of Digital Europe, Connecting Europe, Creative Europe MEDIA and EU for Health. Horizon Europe, the largest research programme of the EU, Invest EU and RRF contribute to digitalisation either. In total, resources invested into digitalisation are estimated to sum up to 181.97 billion Euros in 2022 prices (European Commission, 2022e). In the economies especially considered as advanced economies, digitalization and greening are very much linked to each other. These two concepts can be regarded as complementary as both add value to sustainable development. Greener economy requires radical reforms in very key sectors such as industrial production, transport, energy which needs big capital investment for making the economy more environmentally friendly and regarding climate change emergencies. This proves the digitalization in economic processes and greening the economies have strong ties. Therefore, the Union has allocated one third of MFF to green transition. With the NGEU contribution, spending under the heading of natural resources and environment is estimated to sum up to 419 billion Euros. Investment in the field of climate action, environment, sustainable development and energy fall into the scope of green transition. Green Deal is a roadmap to the green transition in this respect (European Commission, 2022j).

Confluence of factors such as Russia–Ukraine war's intensifying effect on finding new sources of energy and the necessity for green transition has paved the way for the Union to adopt the RePowerEU Plan in December 2022 in this field.

Through RePowerEU, Russian fossil fuels are planned to be phased out which are computed to cost European taxpayers 100 million Euros per year. Additional source of 210 billion Euros will be needed until 2027. To finance RePowerEU, member states are allowed to use the remaining RRF loans worth 225 billion Euros (166 billion Euros of RRF loans have been requested by member states by the time of writing. See Tab. 3.). A new RRF grant through Emission Trading System worth 20 billion Euros is another planned source of finance. The decision of RePowerEU imposes member states the requirement to introduce RePowerEU chapters in their RRF plans and make necessary reforms accordingly.

6. Conclusion

The budget of the EU is formed based on the own resources gathered to implement the policies of the Union to achieve common objectives stated as promoting sustainable development, balanced economic growth, price stability, full employment, establishing a highly competitive social market economy, a high level of protection of the environment in the framework of peace, freedom, justice and security. Own resources consist of revenues obtained from import duties, and GNI and VAT shares of member states. Designed as multiyear financial programmes, the budget is decided with the common accord of the Commission, Council and the Parliament. In terms of spending, priority areas are designed taking into account the needs of the Union. The current MFF has brought a new own resource and proposals of the Commission are prepared to pave the way for the new ones. Complementary element of the 2021–2027 MFF, NGEU has also brought an essential practice in which the Commission generates funds by borrowing in capital markets. This loan mechanism is subject to common borrowing and responsibility. Therefore, it has raised questions on how new sources will be generated and how repayment will be made.

In terms of the spending side of the current MFF and NGEU, priority areas have been determined as single market, innovation and digital; cohesion, resilience and values; natural resources and environment; migration and border management; security and defence; neighbourhood and the world; European public administration. Spending side of the budget reflects circumstances under which the budget has been drafted. Those areas have been focused to combat damaging effects of COVID 19, and green and digital transitions. The budget is projected to bear green and digital elements. Thus, half of the budget is allocated to green and digital investments. In this context, digitalisation is anticipated to be financed through programmes founded for digitalisation purposes and the contribution of wide ranging programmes such as Horizon Europe, Invest EU and RRF. Contribution of programmes to digitalisation amounts to 181.97 billion Euros in 2022 prices.

Apparently, the future of EU is being re-designed in the interlinked level between digitalisation and greening by prioritising research & development, protecting the environment and values supporting green economy and MFF is being re-designed through those priorities. Specialisation, commercial activities and new business models become more effective with new technologies, and a paradigmatic transformation is created in which corporate functioning becomes easier. Moreover, with the broad interpretation of the Commission's definition of structural reform, this process can be explained as structural reform towards a more digital, stronger, competitive and greener EU. From this point of view, by means of the priorities within the scope of the MFF, the EU has also acknowledged reinforcing and deepening the innovative approaches of the digitalisation contributing to greener EU and being the key to the future.

Bibliography

Bialasiewicz, L. (2020). "National stereotypes in times of COVID-19: the 'frugal four' and the 'irresponsible South' ", https://www.opendemocracy.net/en/can-europe-make-it/national-stereotypes-in-times-of-covid-19-the-frugal-four-and-the-irresponsible-south/, 26.02.2021.

Bisciari, P., Butzen, P., Gelade, W., Melyn, W., & Van Parys, S. (2021). "The European Union budget and the Next Generation EU Recovery Plan: a game changer?", NBB Economic Review September 2021, https://www.nbb.be/en/articles/european-union-budget-and-next-generation-eu-recovery-plan-game-changer, 10.12.2022.

Council Decision (EU,Euratom) 2020/2053 of 14 December 2020 on the System of Own Resources of the European Union and repealing Decision 2014/335/EU, Euratom.

Darvas, Z. (2020). "Having the cake, but slicing it differently: how is the grand EU recovery fund allocated?", https://www.bruegel.org/blog-post/having-cake-slicing-it-differently-how-grand-eu-recovery-fund-allocated, 14.01.2023.

Darvas, Z. et al, (2022). "European Union countries' recovery and resilience plans" https://www.bruegel.org/dataset/european-union-countries-recovery-and-resilience-plans 14.12.2022

European Commission. (2021). Future-proof Taxation-Commission Proposes New, Ambitious Business Tax Agenda, https://ec.europa.eu/commission/presscorner/detail/en/ip_21_2430, 17.10.2022.

European Commission. (2022a). Plastics Own Resource, https://ec.europa.eu/info/strategy/eu-budget/long-term-eu-budget/2021-2027/revenue/own-resources/plastics-own-resource_en, 17.10.2022.

European Commission. (2022b). Headings: Spending Categories, https://ec.europa.eu/info/strategy/eu-budget/long-term-eu-budget/2021-2027/spending/headings_en, 17.10.2022.

European Commission. (2022c). Next Generation EU, https://ec.europa.eu/info/strategy/eu-budget/eu-borrower-investor-relations/nextgenerationeu_en, 17.10.2022.

European Commission. (2022d). Shaping Europe's Digital Future, https://ec.europa.eu/info/strategy/priorities-2019-2024/europe-fit-digital-age/shaping-europe-digital-future_en, 17.10.2022.

European Commission. (2022e). Funding for Digital in the 2021–2027 Multiannual Financial Framework, https://digital-strategy.ec.europa.eu/en/activities/funding-digital, 17.10.2022.

European Commission. (2022f). Revenue Ceilings, https://commission.europa.eu/strategy-and-policy/eu-budget/long-term-eu-budget/2021-2027/revenue/revenue-ceilings_en, 14.01.2023.

European Commission. (2022g). Headings: Spending Categories, https://commission.europa.eu/strategy-and-policy/eu-budget/long-term-eu-budget/2021-2027/spending/headings_en, 14.01.2023.

European Commission. (2022h). RRF: Update of the maximum financial contribution, https://commission.europa.eu/system/files/2022-06/2022_06_30_update_maximum_financial_contribution_rrf_grants.pdf, 14.01.2023.

European Commission. (2022i). REPowerEU: affordable, secure and sustainable energy for Europe, https://commission.europa.eu/strategy-and-policy/priorities-2019-2024/european-green-deal/repowereu-affordable-secure-and-sustainable-energy-europe_en#financing-repowereu, (14.12.2022).

European Commission. (2022j). Green Transition, https://reform-support.ec.europa.eu/what-we-do/green-transition_en#just-transition, 14.01.2023.

European Council. (2022). Digital Taxation, https://www.consilium.europa.eu/en/policies/digital-taxation/, 14.01.2023

European Parliament. (2022). EU customs control mechanisms and their possible improvement, https://www.europarl.europa.eu/RegData/etudes/BRIE/2022/733135/IPOL_BRI(2022)733135_EN.pdf, 14.01.2023.

European Union. (2022a). Revenue, https://european-union.europa.eu/institutions-law-budget/budget/revenue_en, 17.10.2022.

European Union. (2022b). Spending, https://european-union.europa.eu/institutions-law-budget/budget/spending_en, 17.10.2022.

Fabbrini, F. (2022). "The Legal Architecture of the Economic Responses to COVID-19: EMU beyond the Pandemic", Journal of Common Market Studies, 49(2), pp. 193–217.

Kaygusuz, Ö. (2020). "COVID-19 Krizi ve AB'nin Yeni Dönüşüm Dinamikleri Gelecek Nesil AB Mümkün mü?", Boğaziçi Üniversitesi-TÜSİAD Dış Politika Forumu Araştırma Raporu, DPF2020-AR02.

Tesche,T. (2022). "Pandemic Politics: The EU in Times of the Coronavirus Emergency", Journal of Common Market Studies, 60(2), pp. 480–496.

The Economist. (2022, May, 26). The EU's covid-19 recovery fund has changed how Europe spends money, https://www.economist.com/europe/2022/05/26/the-eus-covid-19-recovery-fund-has-changed-how-europe-spends-money, 07.06.2022.

Bora Azamet Korkmaz[1] & Şebnem Tosunoğlu[2]

The Effect of Government R&D Expenditures on Emissions[3]

1. Introduction

Due to its significant economic and social effects, such as transportation, security, health, agriculture, politics, and international relations, energy is a vital source. Governments structure the most essential policies, including the economy and defense, on the axis of energy, which has become the most powerful weapon of diplomacy. National energy policies are determined by considering and being influenced by many factors, such as energy security, energy prices, international relations, globalization, and international organizations (Prontera, 2009). Energy policies are presently governed by a variety of international organizations due to their importance, and a consistent strategy is being attempted to build in order to assure global energy security. These organizations emphasize international cooperation on energy access and air pollution issues. Thus, modern energy policies are designed to achieve energy security, effective and efficient use of energy, diversification of energy resources, and environmental protection.

For many years, the world energy system has been based mainly on fossil fuels and partially on nuclear energy. However, the sustainability of energy policies was called into question due to problems such as the oil crisis in the 1970s, large-scale nuclear accidents, and high air pollution in the atmosphere, and most countries are seeking alternative energy sources to ensure economic stability and sustainable growth due to the adverse impact of oil price fluctuations on many economies as well as increasing environmental concerns arising from the consumption of

---

1 Research Assistant, Anadolu University, Faculty of Economics and Administrative Sciences, Department of Public Finance, bakrkmz@gmail.com, ORCID: 0000-0001-5273-2893

2 Ph.D., Professor, Anadolu University, Faculty of Economics and Administrative Sciences, Department of Public Finance, ssel@anadolu.edu.tr, ORCID: 0000-0002-5591-4403

3 This paper is derived from the master's thesis titled "The Relationship Between Public R&D Expenditures in the Field of Energy and CO2 Emissions: The Case of OECD Countries", which was carried out under the supervision of Prof. Dr. Şebnem Tosunoğlu and defended by Bora Azamet Korkmaz at the Institute of Social Sciences, Anadolu University on 18.07.2022.

fossil fuels. In order to tackle the energy issues caused by dependence on fossil fuels, most governments are attempting to shift from an oil-based economy to a bio-based economy by increasing their focus on technological advancement and innovations in the field of energy. One of the most important indicators showing innovations in the field of energy is R&D activities (Bointner, 2014). Governments spend on R&D for several reasons. In the past, fossil and nuclear sources were the most popular ones for energy innovation; however, with the transformation in energy policies over the past 20 years, governments have focused mainly on energy efficiency and renewable energy technologies. The main purpose of this study is to mention the importance of R&D expenditures made by governments in the field of energy and to reveal the effect of these expenditures on emissions, considering energy policy change. The studies that focused on this topic can be categorized into two groups. The first group of studies consists of those that use time series analysis to provide country-specific findings. Among these group, (Lantz & Feng, 2006) in Canada between 1970 and 2000; (Cantos et. al., 2013) in Spain between 1992 and 2008; (Lee & Min, 2015) in Japan between 2001 and 2010; (Wenwen et al., 2017) in China from 1997 to 2014; (Shahbaz et al., 2018) in France between 1955–2016; (Shao et al., 2021) in the USA from 1990 to 2019, find a significantly negative relationship between technological advancements or R&D expenditures and emissions. The second group of studies consists of those that use panel data analysis for certain country groups. While (Garrone & Grilli, 2010) and (Koçak et al., 2021) do not find a significant relationship of R&D expenditures on the carbon emissions; (Balsalobre et al., 2014) in some OECD nations between 1994 and 2010; (Alvarez-Herranz et al., 2016) in OECD countries between 1990 and 2014; (Fernández et al., 2017) in 15 EU countries the USA and China between 1990 and 2013; (Alvarez-Herranz et al., 2017) in 17 OECD countries between 1990 and 2012; (Mensah et al., 2018) in OECD nations between 1990 and 2014; (Paramati et al., 2021) in 25 EU nations, detected R&D expenditures had a significantly reducing effect on greenhouse gas emissions.

2. Importance of Government R&D Policies in the Field of Energy

In the context of modern energy policy, states intervene in the energy field using a wide range of tools due to the failure of the competitive market to meet its needs. Externalities and natural monopolies necessitate governmental action and regulations. In addition to these factors, the importance of energy in the modern world, social and economic challenges, and concerns regarding equality and security mean that the energy industry cannot be left to the market entirely.

Despite the recent liberalization trend, the presence of the state in the energy sector remains in both developed and developing countries. States utilize a variety of instruments to regulate the energy sector (Bhattacharyya, 2011). In general, these tools discourage the use of fossil resources while promoting the use of renewable ones (Ellis & Peake, 1996). Feed-in tariffs, feed-in premiums, the renewable portfolio standard, tender procedures, net metering, emission trading systems, and other regulations are some of the most often implemented regulatory measures. In addition to these measures, governments adopt fiscal incentives for energy intervention. The main objective of fiscal incentives is to make renewable resources more accessible to investors by alleviating the burden of generally high initial investment costs and reducing output costs. Fiscal incentives such as investment and production, research and development, waste management, and energy tax are all contained within renewable energy investment incentives.

Increasing energy efficiency is known to be the most cost-effective and fastest way to reduce CO2 emissions, which has become one of the main policy goals of modern energy policy. However, the devices and machinery that are necessary for more efficient energy production and consumption are commonly more expensive on the market compare with traditional ones. Correspondingly, their market shares remain limited. Therefore, financial incentives are necessary to stimulate manufacturing and sales of these energy-efficient products (Markandya et al., 2009). R&D is crucial to achieving the desired efficiency and innovation capacity in the energy sector. Hence, governments develop specific financial incentive programs that help to extend R&D activities. In this context, governments can use mechanisms such as providing incentives to firms operating in the field of energy through loans and grants and indirect financing through tax incentives, as well as directly engaging in R&D activities. R&D deductions, which exist in many countries' tax systems, allow firms to deduct their R&D-related expenses within a certain time frame. According to this technique, R&D expenditures are considered the same as investment expenditures. Companies that hire R&D professionals receive a variety of tax benefits. R&D gets tax breaks from income, corporate, and value-added taxes, as well as insurance premiums. Tax incentives such as tax deductions, additional exceptions and exemptions, tax holidays, tax deferral, patent box regime, and accelerated depreciation are provided to companies engaged in R&D activities. Additionally, corporations may be eligible for tax credits for R&D expenses. Based on energy policy, states might also undertake R&D activities directly through public institutions and organizations.

From a theoretical point of view, there are many reasons for the public sector to promote policies that boost R&D expenditures in the field of energy, such as market failure, environmental externalities, and energy security.

The prime objective of government intervention in the innovation market is to promote the spread of new technologies. Additionally, it is intended to give a competitive edge in both national and international markets, expand employment, and provide environmentally friendly and safe manufacturing alternatives. In this regard, governmental support is crucial, particularly in sectors where new technologies are not yet utilized adequately, such as energy. Tosunoglu (2016) identifies the publicity of knowledge, externalities, uncertainties, and risks as the primary causes of market failure in innovation.

Due to its non-excludability and non-competitiveness, knowledge is recognized as a public good. Due to the spread of knowledge, R&D investments yield rising returns to scale in the generation of new information. Owing to the spread of knowledge, R&D expenditures provide increasing returns on scale in the production of new knowledge. The spread of knowledge accelerates the generation of new knowledge, but in the absence of government funding, the private sector considers the spread as a risk and does not make the necessary expenditures for R&D activities. Insufficient investments in R&D activities retard innovation and lead to market failure. Since knowledge production produces societal benefits, it should be promoted by the government. The fact that the social benefit of R&D activities exceeds the private benefit is the primary cause of innovation market failure. Universities and other public research institutions have been established for this reason in order to improve social benefits through knowledge creation. The knowledge created by the public sector is spread, and many private corporations benefit from it (Tosunoğlu, 2016). As a public good, knowledge generates positive externalities for society. However, since new knowledge can be used by anyone as soon as it becomes publicly available, intellectual property rights such as patents have emerged to protect the right to use the knowledge. Moreover, the creation of new knowledge increases the number of prospective adopters and the probability of market failure. Therefore, R&D activities, particularly the fundamental research processes, should be funded by the state. This is since firms tend to invest in R&D for initiatives that are lower risk and shorter term. Studies have indicated that it is more effective to concentrate government R&D spending in the field of energy on long-term and risky research activities. Furthermore, it is believed that spending on emerging technology produces more effective results (Bointner, 2014).

As knowledge is fundamentally a public good, R&D spillovers may result in inadequate investment in energy-efficient technologies. Firms do not fully realize the rewards of their innovation efforts and must share some of the benefits with other enterprises and customers (Gillingham et al., 2009). Positive externalities limit the willingness of private firms to undertake R&D activities aimed at improving energy efficiency (which helps reduce carbon intensity) of existing products, technologies, and equipment. For this reason, governments provide direct funding to universities and research centers or stimulate private sector R&D investments through subsidies and grants. Public R&D expenditures in the field of energy are also a technology-driven climate policy type. If public R&D funding is focused on early-stage technologies and high-risk initiatives, it has the potential to reduce obstacles to innovation in the energy sector. Thus, government R&D expenditures in the energy sector represent a pushing factor for technological advancement (Garrone & Grilli, 2010).

Furthermore, the private sector is generally reluctant to invest in this field due to the high costs, uncertainties, and risks associated with scientific research. R&D activities are high-risk, long-lead, challenging to predict results, prone to failure, and difficult to estimate costs. Because of the high initial investment costs and unpredictability, small and medium-sized businesses, in particular, are hesitant to invest in R&D. Moreover, finding external finance for innovation initiatives is more challenging than for investments in fixed capital because the product, new knowledge, and technology to be obtained as a result of the R&D activity cannot be mortgaged.

Besides, energy prices do not represent the entire social cost of energy use. The production and consumption of many energy resources raise greenhouse gas emissions, resulting in environmental externalities, or, in other words, costs borne by others. In the absence of regulatory interventions, high energy use and insufficient investment in energy efficiency occur. Although the presence of environmental externalities, mostly in the form of air emissions, is indisputable, their magnitude and the amount of internalized by individuals are ambiguous and difficult to quantify. Unless energy prices internalize these externalities, the market will provide a very slight amount of socially acceptable energy efficiency (Gillingham et al., 2009). Among the public measures undertaken to mitigate the risks and social costs of the climate crisis, the energy R&D policy stands out. Energy innovation plays a major role in achieving the goal of reducing carbon emissions. Because technological change is necessary to reduce emissions from energy consumption in the long run. When energy technologies are not developed to the desired level, excessive energy use and emissions arise. Policy makers mostly take energy innovation into account when determining climate policies (Garrone & Grilli, 2010).

Combating environmental externalities, a global threat resulting from energy consumption, is one of the most essential goals of modern energy policies. Increasing the usage of renewable energy sources is one of the most fundamental changes that must be undertaken in order to achieve the established environmental objectives. However, renewable energy projects generally require high technology, so at this point, the importance of R&D in the field of energy emerges. Reducing the high cost of renewable energy projects is possible through R&D. Through subsidies for energy-related R&D, governments play a crucial role in this transition. Utilizing more efficient materials, processes, and technologies, R&D seeks to decrease energy demand. The way to protect the environment without adversely affecting economic growth is through the development and widespread use of R&D technologies. Although the state cannot supply all of these services on its own, it should prepare the way for the private sector through the regulations it establishes. It is clear that, without government regulations, the private sector will not protect the environment.

Another reason for states to make R&D expenditures in the field of energy is to ensure energy security. The purpose is to minimize import dependency by expanding the use of modern energy technologies. The dependency of countries on specific energy supplies, particularly oil and natural gas from insecure regions of the world, entails an external cost, such as a national security threat (Gillingham et al., 2009). When the price of oil and natural gas rises, it has a negative impact on many economies all over the world. In this context, there is a transition from oil-based economies to bio-based economies as nations seek alternative resources to secure their economic stability and sustainable growth. In order to deal with the energy crises caused by dependence on fossil fuels, focus is placed on technological innovations and advancements in the energy sector (Wonglimpiyarat, 2010). Energy efficiency needs to be increased in order to reduce environmental externalities and ensure energy security. Increasing R&D expenditures in this area is the most sustainable solution to accomplish the objective of improving energy efficiency.

3. Methodology

Using panel data analysis, this study aims to demonstrate the environmental effect of government R&D expenditures in the energy sector in OECD countries between 2000 and 2020. The Augmented Mean Group (AMG) Estimator was preferred in order to reveal the long-term relationship. Before estimation, cross-section dependency, homogeneity, unit root, and cointegration tests are performed, respectively.

Standard dynamic panel estimators may not always be suitable for the estimation of macroeconomic data since most estimators assume panel cross-sections are homogenous, i.e. most do not account for heterogeneity. In addition, many estimators do not consider cross-sectional dependence, which may lead to erroneous and inconsistent results. To solve this issue, the AMG estimator was developed by (Eberhardt & Bond, 2009; Eberhardt & Teal, 2011; Bond & Eberhardt, 2013). The AMG estimator is a robust long-run cointegration estimator that allows for heterogeneity among slope coefficients, cross-sectional dependency, and able to estimate coefficients for non-stationary variables.

$$\Delta y_{it} = \alpha_i + \beta_i \Delta x_{it} + \gamma_i f_t + \Sigma_{t=2}^{T} \delta_i \Delta D_i + \varepsilon_{it}$$
$$\widehat{\beta}_{AMG} = N^{-1} \Sigma_{i=1}^{N} \widehat{\beta}_i$$

In the preceding equations, Δ is the first difference operator; α_i is constant term y_{it} and x_{it} are observable variables; β_i is country-specific estimators of the coefficients; f_t is unobserved common factors that take into account the heterogeneous effect on the dependent variable, the so-called common dynamic process δ_i represents the coefficient of the time dummies; ε_{it} is error term; $\widehat{\beta}_{AMG}$ indicates the average group estimator.

Prior to using the AMG estimator, it is necessary to evaluate the cross-sectional dependency among the units. The existence of cross-sectional dependency indicates that a positive or negative economic shock affecting one of the horizontal sections of panel data may also affect the others. As in this study, cross-sectional dependency is expected to exist, especially among countries in certain groups such as the OECD, G7, EU, etc. To determine whether there is cross-sectional dependence between units, (Pesaran, 2004) CD and (Pesaran, 2015) CD_{NT} tests were prefered.

The second prerequisite for using the AMG estimator is to test the homogeneity of the slope coefficients. Testing the homogeneity of the slope coefficients is to test whether the effect of a change in the independent variables on the dependent variable differs across units. In order to test the homogeneity of the slope coefficients, (Pesaran & Yagamata, 2008) and (Blomquist & Westerlund, 2013) tests were preferred.

Unit root test is performed to determine whether the variables are stationary or not. The preferred unit root test changes depending on whether the units are cross-sectionally dependent. If cross-section dependency exists, one of the first- or second-generation unit root tests must be run. In this study, one of the second-generation unit root tests (Pesaran, 2007) is preferred.

In panel data analysis, cointegration tests are performed to test whether there is a long-run relationship between the variables in the model. The second generation cointegration test (Westerlund, 2008), which can be used in cases of unit root detection in variables and takes into account cross-sectional dependence and heterogeneity, is used in this study.

4. Model Specification and Data

In this study, using a panel data set, the following model is created in order to examine the impacts of government R&D expenditures on carbon emissions:

$$lnCO2_{it} = \alpha_0 + \beta_1 lnEC_{it} + \beta_2 lnGDP_{it} + \beta_3 lnPERD_{it} + \beta_4 ENTAX_{it} + \varepsilon_{it}$$
$$i = 1,2,3,\ldots,N \; ve \; t = 1,2,3,\ldots,T$$

CO2: Carbon dioxide emissions,
EC: Energy consumption,
GDP: Gross domestic product,
PRDE: Public research and development expenditures,
ENTAX: Environmental tax

Considering the availability of data, the scope of the study was determined to cover the years 2000–2020. The time dimension (T) of the study consists of 21 years, and the cross-sectional dimension (N) consists of 23 countries. As the dependent variable, carbon dioxide (CO2) emission is chosen, and the independent variables are energy consumption, national income, environmental taxes, and government R&D expenditures in the field of energy. Logarithmic forms of all variables except taxes were used. Table 1 provides details about the variables:

Tab. 1: *Data set and variables*

Name of Variable	Code of Variable	Description of Variable	Unit of Variable	Data Source
CO2 Emissions	lnCO2	CO2 emissions per capita	Million tons	OECD
Energy Consumption	lnEC	Energy consumption	Mtoe	BP Statistical Review of World Energy 2019
Gross Domestic Product	lnGDP	per capita income	US$ at 2015 fixed prices	World Development Indicators
Public Energy R&D Expenditures	lnPRDE	Energy Public R&D Expenditures	Million dollars (US$ at 2020 fixed prices and PPP)	IEA
Environmental Taxes	ENTAX	Environmental Taxes	Share of GDP (%)	OECD

5. Empirical Results

Tab. 2: *(Pesaran,2004) and (Pesaran, 2015) cross-section dependency test (CSD) results*

Variable	CSD (2004)	p-value	CSD (2015)	p-value
lnCO2	34.74***	0.000	38.933***	0.000
lnEC	10.78***	0.000	10.915***	0.000
lnGDP	47.25***	0.000	56.583***	0.000
lnPRDE	14.86***	0.000	14.077***	0.000
ENTAX	20.76***	0.000	29.411***	0.000

*** Indicates that it is significant at the 1 % level.

According to Tab. 2, the null hypothesis Ho is rejected at a 1 % significance level because $p<0.01$ for all variables in both tests, and cross-sectional dependency between the units is inferred. In other words, an economic shock occurring in one of the countries in the model also affects the others.

Tab. 3: *(Pesaran and Yamagata, 2008) and (Blomquist & Westerlund, 2013) slope coefficient homogeneity test results*

	Pesaran, Yagamata (2008)		Blomquist, Westerlund (2013)	
	Delta	P-value	Delta	P-value
$\widehat{\Delta}$	14.583***	0.000	12.777***	0.000
$\widehat{\Delta}_{adj}$	17.787***	0.000	15.584***	0.000

*** Indicates that it is significant at the 1 % level.

Table 3 displays the results of the homogeneity test. Since p<0.01 in both (Pesaran & Yagamata, 2008) and (Blomquist & Westerlund, 2013) tests, the Ho hypothesis is rejected at the 1 % level of significance, and it is concluded that the slope coefficients are heterogeneous. In other saying, the independent variables of the model have varying impacts on CO2 emissions among countries.

Tab. 4: *(Pesaran, 2007) unit root test results*

	CIPS			
Variables	Level		First Difference (Δ)	
	Constant	Trend	Constant	Trend
lnCO2	1.210	-0.455	-10.052***	-7.631***
lnEC	-1.669*	-2.004*	-13.080***	-10.506***
lnGDP	0.047	3.056	-6.027***	-4.046***
lnPRDE	-8.588***	-8.290***	-17.156***	-15.075***
ENTAX	-0.745	0.822	-9.289***	-6.250***

***, ** and * indicate that the coefficients are significant at the 1 %, 5 % and 10 % levels.

According to the findings of the unit root test in Tab. 4 (Pesaran, 2007), lnEC and lnPRDE variables are stationary at level; however, the ln CO2 and ENTAX variables are not stationary at level. The null hypothesis is rejected at a 1 % significance level when the first difference of the variables is computed and all of them are found to be stationary.

According to the (Westerlund, 2008) cointegration test results in Tab. 5, both test statistics reject the Ho hypothesis, indicating the existence of a cointegration relationship between the variables.

Tab. 5: *(Westerlund, 2008) cointegration test results*

	Test Statistics	P-value
DH_g	1.881	0.030**
DH_p	2.345	0.010***

***, ** and * indicate that the coefficients are significant at the 1 %, 5 % and 10 % levels. Table critical values are 1 %=2.333 5 %=1.645 10 %=1.28.

Table 6 below, presents the findings obtained for 23 OECD countries for the period 2000–2020 using the AMG estimator.

Tab. 6: *AMG estimation results*

Dependent Variable: lnCO2	
Variables	**AMG**
lnEC	0.678***
	(5.44)
lnGDP	0.258**
	(2.41)
lnPRDE	-0.00334**
	(-2.33)
ENTAX	-0.0141**
	(-2.00)
_cons	-3.272***
	(-5.86)

***, ** and * indicate that the coefficients are significant at the 1 %, 5 % and 10 % levels.

According to the AMG estimate findings generated using the weighted average, a positive and statistically significant relationship was observed at the 1 % level between energy consumption and CO2 emissions. A 1 % increase in energy consumption increases CO2 emissions by 0.678 %. Similarly, a positive and statistically significant relationship at the 5 % level was found between national income per capita and CO2 emissions. A 1 % rise in per capita national income increases CO2 emissions by 0.258%. On the contrary, a negative and statistically significant relationship at the 5 % level was found between public

R&D expenditures in the field of energy and CO2 emissions. A 1 % increase in public R&D expenditures in the field of energy reduces CO2 emissions by 0.00334 %. Similarly, a negative and significant relationship at the 5 % level was found between environmental taxes and CO2 emissions. Increasing environmental taxes by 1 % decreases carbon dioxide emissions by 0.014 %.

Based on the estimation, energy consumption and GDP have a rising impact on emissions. Despite a growing interest in renewable resources, 79 percent of the OECD's overall energy supply still consists of fossil fuels. In all OECD countries except Iceland, Norway, and Sweden, fossil fuels account for the largest share of energy supply. Moreover, only in Austria, Denmark, Norway, and Sweden is the share of renewable energy in total energy supply above 30%, while in 14 countries the share of fossil fuels is above 70%. Consequently, emissions continue to rise as energy consumption increases. This effect is expected to persist unless the majority of energy supply shifts to environmentally friendly sources.

According to the results obtained, similar to energy consumption, economic growth also increases emissions. The primary reason for this is that economic policies are not always designed with environmental concerns in mind. Despite the fact that this is a relatively common circumstance, particularly in emerging nations where economic expansion is the major objective, it is evident that a large proportion of wealthy nations still do not accord the environment the necessary attention.

It was found that there was a statistically significant negative long-term relationship between the total expenditure on R&D and emissions. It is notable that the calculated coefficients for R&D spending are low. The main reason for this is that the share of countries' R&D expenditures in the field of energy in their GDP is quite low.

According to the findings, environmental taxes also have a mitigating effect on emissions. Increasing the share of environmental taxes in national tax systems, which is an alternative policy to reduce emissions, contributes significantly to this struggle.

6. Conclusion

After the 1990s, the costs of energy-induced ecological degradation started to emerge in the world and the issue of environmental security gained prominence in energy policies. Diversifying energy resources was a sufficient way to ensure supply security in the past, however, rising environmental concerns have necessitated new strategies. In order to ensure environmental security, policies to promote energy efficiency and use clean energy have also acquired prominence (Wonglimpiyarat, 2010). This research analyses the efficiency of government energy R&D expenditures of OECD member countries in resolving environmental issues, by panel data analysis method. According to the results obtained using the AMG estimator, a long-run negative relationship was found between public energy R&D expenditures and emissions. It is concluded that increasing energy consumption and national income, the other variables used in the study, increase emissions, whereas increasing environmental taxes decreases emissions.

The findings of the study indicate that the advancement of technology is a key factor that must be taken into consideration in order to make the transition to energy sources that are less harmful to the environment. So, government spending on R&D in the energy field is important if we want to have a secure energy supply and a safe environment in the future.

The trouble of a climate crisis and environmental destruction caused by the increase in greenhouse gas emissions from fossil fuels, which still provide the majority of the world's energy demands, has become a big threat to global sustainability. It is obvious that the world's energy demand will continue to rise inexorably. To ensure that carbon dioxide emissions do not continue to climb as energy consumption rises, it is necessary to considerably expand the share of renewable energy sources in energy consumption. Therefore, energy policy cannot be considered independent from the climate crisis. Energy security and the establishment of a sustainable energy policy cannot be achieved unless energy policies are considered alongside environmental policies.

In summary, as energy-related R&D expenditures grow, creative activities, processes, and products become more widespread, leading to greater energy efficiency and less resource consumption. Thereby, obtaining the same output while consuming fewer resources decreases emissions from energy usage. Furthermore, government R&D spending is critical to the development and spread of alternative energy sources like renewable energy. Consequently, the budget allocated by the public sector for R&D in the field of energy is an indicator for the level of greenhouse gas emissions. R&D expenditures are an indicator of how far innovation has spread. Accelerating the development of energy technology is widely regarded as one of the most essential steps that must be performed in order to reach the globally agreed target of minimizing carbon emissions to a certain level. Given that the findings of this study demonstrate that progress in energy technology helps reduce carbon emissions. States that wish to tackle the issues of energy and environmental security should invest more than they do now in energy R&D activities. For the development of energy technologies, public energy policies should be designed accordingly. It is clearly evident in every way that the amount of budget that governments spend on R&D needs to have a more significant role in determining energy policy.

References

Alvarez-Herranz, A., Balsalobre-Lorente, D., Shahbaz, M., & Cantos, J. M. (2016). Energy innovations-GHG emissions Nexus: Fresh empirical evidence from OECD countries. *Energy Policy*, 90–100.

Alvarez-Herranz, A., Balsalobre-Lorente, D., Shahbaz, M., & Cantos, J. (2017). Energy innovation and renewable energy consumption in the correction of air pollution levels. *Energy Policy*, (105), 386–397.

Balsalobre, D., Álvarez, A., & Cantos, J. M. (2014). Public budgets for energy RD&D and the effects on energy intensity and pollution levels. *Environmental Science and Pollution Research*, (22), 4881–4892.

Bhattacharyya, S. C. (2011). *Energy Economics, Concepts, Issues, Markets and Governance*. London: Springer-Verlag. doi:10.1007/978-0-85729-268-1

Blomquist, J., & Westerlund, J. (2013). Testing slope homogeneity in large panels with serial correlation. *Economics Letters*, 374–378. https://doi.org/10.1016/j.econlet.2013.09.012

Bointner, R. (2014). Innovation in the energy sector: Lessons learnt from R&D expenditures and patents in selected IEA countries. *Energy Policy* (73), 733–747.

Bond, S., & Eberhardt, M. (2013). Accounting for unobserved heterogeneity in panel time series models. *University of Oxford*, 1–11. https://lezme.github.io/markuseberhardt/BEMC.pdf

Cantos, J. M., & Balsalobre Lorente, D. (2013). Incidencia del gasto público en I+D+i energético sobre la corrección medioambiental en España / Impact of Public R&D in Energy on Environmental Correction in Spain. *Estudios de Economia Aplicada* (31–1), 93–126.

Eberhardt, M., & Bond, S. (2009). Cross-section dependence in nonstationary panel models: a novel estimator. *Munich Personal RePEc Archive*.

Eberhardt, M., & Teal, F. (2011, February). Econometrics for Grumblers: A new look at the literature on cross-country growth empirics. *Journal of Economic Surveys, 25*(1), 109–155.

Ellis, J., & Peake, S. (1996). Renewable energy promotion in IEA countries. *Renewable Energy, 1–4*(9), 1175–1178.

Fernández, Y. F., López, M., & Blanco, B. (2017). Innovation for sustainability: The impact of R&D spending on CO2 emissions. *Journal of Cleaner Production* (172), 3459–3467. https://doi.org/10.1016/j.jclepro.2017.11.001

Garrone, P., & Grilli, L. (2010). Is there a relationship between public expenditures in energy R&D and carbon emissions per GDP? An empirical investigation. *Energy Policy, 38*(10), 5600–5613. https://doi.org/10.1016/j.enpol.2010.04.057

Gillingham, K. & Newell, R.G. & Palmer, K. (2009). Energy efficiency economics and policy. *Annual Review of Resource Economics, Annual Reviews*, 1(1), 597–5620.

IEA. (2020b). *Energy Technology RD&D Budgets.* Paris: IEA.

Koçak, E., Kınacı, H., & Shehzad, K. (2021). Environmental efficiency of disaggregated energy R&D expenditures in OECD: a bootstrap DEA approach. *Environmental Science and Pollution Research*, 19381–19390. doi:https://doi.org/10.1007/s11356-020-12132-w

Lantz, V., & Feng, Q. (2006). Assessing income, population, and technology impacts on CO2 emissions in Canada: Where's the EKC? *Ecological Economics, 57*(2), 229–238.

Lee, K.-H., & Min, B. (2015). Green R&D for eco-innovation and its impact on carbon emissions and firm performance. *Journal of Cleaner Production, 108*(Part A) 534–542.

Markandya, A., Ortiz, R. A., Mudgal, S., & Tinetti, B. (2009). Analysis of tax ıncentives for energy-efficient durables in the EU. *Energy Policy, 12*(37), 5662–5674. doi:10.1016/j.enpol.2009.08.031

Mensah, C., Long, X., Boamah, K., Bediako, I. A., Dauda, L., & Salman, M. (2018). The effect of innovation on CO2 emissions of OCED countries from 1990 to 2014. *Environmental Science and Pollution Research* (25), 29678–29698.

OECD. (2020b, Şubat 1). *R&D Expenditures.* OECD Data: https://stats.oecd.org/BrandedView.aspx?oecd_bv_id=enetech-data-en&doi=be26ccf4-en#

Paramati, S. R., Alam, M. S., Hammoudeh, S., & Hafeez, K. (2021, October). Long-run relationship between R&D investment and environmental sustainability: Evidence from the European Union member countries. *International Journal of Finance & Economics, 26*(4), 5775–5792. https://doi.org/10.1002/ijfe.2093

Pesaran, M. H. (2004). General Diagnostic Tests for Cross Section Dependence in Panels. *Cambridge Working Papers in Economics*, No. 0435.

Pesaran, M. H. (2007). A simple panel unit root test in the presence of cross-section dependence. *Journal of Applied Econometrics, 22*, 265–312. https://doi.org/10.1002/jae.951

Pesaran, M. H. (2015). Testing weak cross-sectional dependence in large panels. *Econometric Reviews, 34*(6–10), 1089–1117. https://doi.org/10.1080/07474938.2014.956623

Pesaran, M. H., & Yagamata, T. (2008). Testing slope homogeneity in large panels. *Journal of Econometrics*, 50–93. https://doi.org/10.1016/j.jeconom.2007.05.010

Prontera, A. (2009). Energy Policy: Concepts, Actors, Instruments and Recent Developments. *World Political Science Review, 1*(5), 1–30.

Shahbaz, M., Nasir, M. A., & Roubaud, D. (2018). Environmental degradation in France the effects of FDI, Financial Development, and Energy Innovations. *Energy Economics* (74), 843–857.

Shao, X., Zhong, Y., Li, Y., & Altuntaş, M. (2021). Does environmental and renewable energy R&D help to achieve carbon neutrality target? A case of the US economy. *Journal of Environmental Management*, 1–10.

Tosunoğlu, Ş. (2016). *Kamu İnovasyon Destekleri: Türkiye'de İnovasyon Odaklı Kamu Politikaları.* Eskişehir: Nisan Kitabevi.

Wenwen, L., Wang, W., Wang, Y., & Qin, Y. (2017). Industrial structure, technological progress and CO2 emissions in China: Analysis based on the STIRPAT framework. *Natural Hazards: Journal of the International Society for the Prevention and Mitigation of Natural Hazards*, 1545–1564.

Westerlund, J. (2008). Panel cointegration tests of the Fisher effect. *Journal of Applied Econometrics,* (23), 193–233. doi:https://doi.org/10.1002/jae.967

Wonglimpiyarat, J. (2010). Technological change of the energy innovation system: From oil-based to bio-based energy. *Applied Energy,* (87), 749–755.

Celali Yilmaz[1]

How Many Companies Had Been Founded in Ottoman?

1. Introduction

Our knowledge of Ottoman financial history consists of limited repetitions. One of these repetitions is the number of companies established in the Ottoman Empire.

There are sources that cite different figures on the number of joint stock companies established until the collapse of the Ottoman Empire. However, the common point in almost all of them is that "there was very little corporatization during the Ottoman period and most of the existing commercial enterprises were under the control of foreigners". While pontificating with the comfort of knowing the ending of the movie, one should pay attention to the conditions of the period. There is a de-facto failure. But is this failure in *establishing* companies or in keeping them alive? Analyzing what the real situation is and what are the references of today's information seems to be a candidate for interesting results.

This study will try to reach a realistic number by comparing the information in different sources that give figures about the number of joint stock companies established in the Ottoman Empire.

2. How Many Joint Stock Companies Were Established in the Ottoman Empire?

The question in the title was inspired by the statements of an important Ottoman historian that appeared in a newspaper in 2010.

In an interview with Prof. Kemal KARPAT, one of the most important Ottoman historians, the following information was given (Karpat: 2010):

> "As Prof. Carter FINDLEY has noted in a preliminary study, by 1918 Turkish and Muslim merchants and producers had assumed an important position in the economy. For example, whereas in 1908 there were only 9 Ottoman-owned companies, in

1 Ph.D., Professor, Istanbul Medeniyet University, Faculty of Political Sciences, Department of Public Finance, celali.yilmaz@medeniyet.du.tr, ORCID: 0000-0003-2767-1149

> 1918 this number had risen to 129, and Turks showed a great interest in economic entrepreneurship."

The emphasis in the above paragraph is on the rapid pace of development, as the number of joint stock companies increased from "only 9" in 1908 to "129" in a short period of ten years. It is also admirable that this development was achieved in an environment of successive wars. However, the numbers "only 9 companies before 1908" and "129 companies in total in 1918" lose their meaning when we try to calculate "which companies were these?". Because when we count the joint stock companies known to have actually existed at that time, these numbers are easily exceeded.

It is also possible to see the "magic number 129" in some other sources that provide information on the number of Ottoman joint stock companies.

For example, many prominent contemporary researchers such as Doğan Avcioğlu (1968: 130), Tevfik Çavdar (1971: 100–101), Sina Akşin (1980: 281–282), Zafer Toprak (1982: 63) and Erik Jan Zürcher (2004: 126) repeat similar numbers when providing information on the situation of joint stock companies in the last years of the Ottoman Empire.

When the references of these contemporary studies are examined, it is noteworthy that the common source in all of them is a book by Ahmet EMİN [YALMAN] published in English in 1930.

An analyzing of Ahmet Emin (1930) reveals that the section on Ottoman joint stock companies consists of the following paragraph (Ahmet Emin 1930: 143):

> According to some general statistics published in the Constantinople papers on September 9, 1918, the companies created during the War included 42 that were commercial and industrial; 15, building and transport; 9, insurance; 6, agricultural; and 16, financial. The commercial companies had a nominal capital of £T2,298,800, the industrial £T2,863,000, the agricultural, £T495,000, the financial, £T542,000, the building and transport, £T2,019,000, the insurance, £T1,403,950. In all, the total was £T16,623,150, of which £T6,194,689 was actually paid up. Of joint-stock companies organized in Turkey before and during the War, 3 were organized in 1909, 13 in 1910, 22 in 1911, 8 in 1912, 5 in 1913, 10 in 1914, 15 in 1915, 15 in 1916, 29 in 1917, and 19 during the first months of 1918. Of the total of 139, 95 had their head offices in Constantinople.

As can be seen, the figures on Ottoman joint stock companies in Ahmet EMİN (1930) are based on "some general statistics published in the Istanbul newspapers[2] on September 9, 1918".

When the "Istanbul newspapers dated September 9, 1918" were examined to reach Ahmet Emin (1930)'s reference, no information that could be called "general statistics" on Ottoman joint stock companies was found in any newspaper.

However, we have noticed from Toprak (1982: 63) that a few days after that date, in the *Vakit* Newspaper (of that period) dated September 14, 1918, there is an article published under the signature of "Mehmet ASIM [US]". In the article titled "*İktisâdî İnzibat*" ("Economic Order"), the information and figures in Ahmet Emin (1930) on Ottoman joint stock companies are given.

Mehmet ASIM's article in the September 14, 1918 issue of *Vakit* Newspaper is an overview of a book titled "Memalik-i Osmaniye'de Osmanlı Anonim Şirketleri" (Ottoman[3] Joint Stock Companies in Ottoman Empire, in short "*Ottoman Catalog*"), which was published "recently" by the Ministry of Trade and Agriculture. As a matter of fact, the figures given in Mehmet ASIM's newspaper article are compiled from this book.

It is very comforting to reach this observation, as it reveals the sequence that the information on Ottoman joint stock companies repeated in many academic studies today follows towards its ultimate source. To recapitulate the information given above chronologically in order of time;

2 Although Ahmet Emin (1930) does not explicitly mention the newspaper in which the article in question was published and refers to it as "Istanbul newspapers", the newspaper *Vakit* was founded in October 1917 by Ahmet EMİN [YALMAN] himself, together with Mehmet ASIM [US]. In other words, Ahmet Emin (1930) is the founder of the "Istanbul newspaper", the primary source whose name is not explicitly mentioned. In March 1923, Ahmet EMİN left this newspaper, which he co-founded, and started publishing *Vatan* newspaper on his own. (See Tezcan, 2007)

3 The emphasis on "Ottoman" in the title of the companies is important. This is because at the time, there were also companies that did not have the status of "Ottoman joint stock company" (OAS). For example, the Ottoman Bank was not an OAS. An OAS is a company incorporated under Ottoman law in Ottoman territory, and in many cases its owners and managers were Ottoman citizens.

1. The Ministry of Trade and Agriculture published a book on Ottoman Joint Stock Companies in 1918 (Ministry of Trade and Agriculture 1918, *primary source*).
2. During the days when this book published, *Vakit* Newspaper published a review article about this publication of the Ministry of Trade and Agriculture (Mehmet ASIM 1918, *secondary source*).
3. In a book published in English in 1930, some information on the number of Ottoman joint stock companies was given by indirectly referring to the information in the book review in *Vakit* newspaper (Ahmet Emin 1930, *citer from secondary source*).
4. The information in the book published in English in 1930 by one of the most important journalists of the last years of the Ottoman Empire and the first years of the Republic has been the main reference for many contemporary and major studies [e.g. Avcioğlu (1968), Çavdar (1971), Akşin (1980), Toprak (1982), Zürcher (2004) *citers from the citer of secondary source*].
5. As a result, we now have a sufficiently reliable reference that "the number of Ottoman joint stock companies existing in 1918 was 129". Moreover according to Karpat (2010), these figures remain keeps a reference for the new work of other important historians such as FINDLEY. [see (Findley 2011) in English and (Findley 2012), in Turkish]

But was this information accurate and was it always presented correctly?

For example, although the *Vakit* newspaper review of the book published by the Ministry of Trade and Agriculture mentioned some basic deficiencies regarding the scope of the book, Ahmet Emin (1930), who referenced the newspaper article, did not mention these deficiencies, so naturally, no subsequent work referencing this book included information about these deficiencies.

However, as Mehmet ASIM pointed out in the aforementioned newspaper article, the data in the book published by the Ministry of Trade and Agriculture is incomplete. Aside from the fact that companies that were not considered "Ottoman" were completely ignored[4], many companies were also overlooked as it was not possible to collect regular information on companies during the Wars.[5] In fact, the *Ottoman Catalog* was published as a "nazire" on Edgar PECH's

---

4 For example, one of the best known ottoman company the Ottoman Bank is not included in the *Ottoman Catalog* because it was not an "Ottoman joint stock company" (its place of incorporation was Paris and its founders were foreigners), despite the "Ottoman" in its title and its function as the central bank issuing Ottoman banknotes.

5 It is known from some surviving company documents and official documents in the Ottoman Archives that there were economic institutions that existed at the time but

French Catalog, which had been published only a few years earlier (See Pech, 1911). Because Pech (1911) is a catalog of mostly the utility companies owned by Europeans and operating in Ottoman territory. The *Ottoman Catalog* (1918), on the other hand, seems to have been published in order to say "There are these companies in the Ottoman territories, not only those in *French Catalog* (Pech 1911)".

On the other hand, the single paragraph of information in Ahmet Emin (1930) contains numerous errors. Toprak (1982: 64) draws attention to several errors in that quote.

First, the date of publication of the statistics on Ottoman joint stock companies in "Istanbul newspapers" is September 14, 1918, not September 9, 1918.

Secondly, Ahmet Emin (1930), for example, has increased the number of joint stock companies established in 1918–1919, probably taking into account that the *Ottoman Catalog* only covers joint stock companies established in the first months of 1918 (exactly until February 14, 1918). However, it is assumed that all of the "12"[6] companies added to the list, assuming that they were established after February 14, 1918, were established in Anatolia. This is because the number of companies stated to have been established in Istanbul was left at 95, the number in Mehmet ASIM (1918).

Thirdly, the number of *joint stock* companies is given as the number of all companies established in those years. However, these are the companies that were "alive" as of the date the *Ottoman Catalog* was printed (1918). In other words, companies that had been established in previous years, but had not survived the wars and the political strife in the Ottoman Empire in the economic and political environment of that period, which could not be considered stable,

---

were not included in the *Ottoman Catalog*. For example, although Ziraat Bank, founded in 1888, was a significant bank at the time, it was not included in the *Ottoman Catalog*. One reason for this may be that Ziraat Bank was perceived as a public institution rather than a company at the time. In fact, the transformation of Ziraat Bank into a joint stock company took place immediately after the Republic, with the Budget Law of 1924. However, Ziraat Bank is mentioned in (Pech, 1911: 125–129). On the other hand, considering that unauthorized public offerings can be observed even at the beginning of the 21st century, it does not seem realistic to assume that such attempts would not have occurred a hundred years ago, and in a politically and economically chaotic environment.

6 In fact, this number is also 11. In the *Ottoman Catalog*, the year of foundation of a company, which should have been 1918, was mistakenly written as 1917; this error was not noticed in Mehmet Emin (1918) because only the years were counted, and this error was repeated in Toprak (1982).

and did not reach the last year of the First World War, were considered not to have been established at all.

However, the errors in Ahmet Emin (1930: 143) are not limited to those mentioned above. The figures given in the paragraph quoted above regarding the total capitalization of Ottoman joint stock companies by sector are identical to the figures in Mehmet ASIM (1918). In other words, the number of companies founded in 1918, which was "7"[7] in Mehmet ASIM (1918), was increased to 19 in Ahmet Emin (1930), but the total capital size of the companies was not changed! Therefore, according to this information in Ahmet Emin (1930: 143), all of the new companies were established with "zero capital"! This is of course not possible according to the minimum capital requirement. However, this is the situation created by the fact that the total capital figure was not changed while the number of companies was increased.

Another error in the information given in Ahmet Emin (1930) is in the figure for the total capitalization of financial companies. The figure of 7,542,000 Ottoman liras[8] in Mehmet ASIM (1918) (quoted from the table in the appendix of the *Ottoman Catalog*) appears as "542,000" in Ahmet Emin (1930: 143). The omission of the digit "7", in only one digit destroyed more than 90 % of the capitalization of the financial companies established in the Ottoman period.[9] On the basis of this information, it is now easy to claim that "financial companies in the Ottoman period were very tiny in terms of paid in capital" However, despite this numerical error in the sector information, the overall total figure has not been changed.

On the other hand, Ahmet Emin (1930) increased the number of joint stock companies established in 1918, taking into account that "joint stock companies

7 This number should essentially be 8.

8 If we pay attention to Ahmet Emin (1930: 143), the sign of the Ottoman lira is £T (in fact, it should be £O). The "£" sign used today for the British currency, the pound sterling, is also used for the Ottoman lira. This is due to the fact that at that time "lira" was used to mean "gold coin". As a matter of fact, the symbol (£) of the British pound, which is still used today, is in the form of the letter L. Likewise, just as the phrase "British Lira" is frequently used for the British pound (See *Ottoman Catalog* 1918), there are also books that use the phrase "Turkish Pounds" for the Ottoman lira (See *German Catalog* 1983).

9 Considering that Ahmet EMİN [YALMAN]'s book is used as the main source for Ottoman economic history studies, could one of the sources of the judgment that "there was no capital accumulation in the Ottoman Empire and domestic companies were very small" be this numerical error in a book published in 1930 and still considered a "fundamental" reference?

established only in the first months of 1918" were included in the Ministry of Trade and Agriculture (1918). However, despite the increased number 19, the phrase "... in the first months of 1918..." was retained in the text. According to this statement, the total number of companies established in 1918 should be even higher than the 19 mentioned in Ahmet Emin (1930).

Another error in Ahmet EMİN's book concerns the total number of commercial and industrial companies. Ahmet Emin (1930: 143) states the total number of companies in these two sectors as 42. However, Mehmet ASIM (1918) mentions "42 commercial and 42 industrial" Ottoman joint stock companies. Following this error in the sectoral breakdown of the number of companies, the total number of companies given in Ahmet Emin (1930: 143) is only 88. Since the total number of companies is stated as "129", the question of "which sectors the companies not mentioned in the sectoral distribution list belong to?" remains unclear, apart from the 88 companies whose sectoral distribution is given.

On the other hand, although the number of companies is given as 42 for "commercial and industrial" companies together, commercial and industrial companies are mentioned separately when sectoral capital sizes are given. Therefore, whichever way one looks at it, numerical inconsistencies are noteworthy.

What has been mentioned so far can be considered as insignificant errors. However, the most fundamental error is in the total number of companies. Although the number "129" is repeated in all the sources mentioned above, the original source is the *Ottoman Catalog* (1918). Although there are 130 companies in that book, due to a numbering error, the last company's sequence number is listed as "129" in the book. The number, which is repeated in all sources starting from Mehmet ASIM (1918) and which is understood to be used in new sources in 2010s, continues to be 129 and in this sense seems to deserve the characterization of "magic number".

The information on Ottoman joint stock companies in all of the above sources is based on the *Ottoman Catalog* (1918), as mentioned earlier. However, the information in that book is not complete. Moreover, when the information in that book was taken from secondary sources, the part of the primary source containing explanations on the scope and nature of these figures and the calculation errors of the secondary source were not taken into account, and some parts were transferred incorrectly. The continuation of this situation in tertiary sources rendered the erroneous information almost "indisputably correct".

However, even if it is assumed that only Ottoman joint stock companies are included in the "magic 129" number, it is not possible to rely on the "magic 129" number, considering that some of the famous "national companies" founded by

Kara Kemal during these years (e.g. the National Ekmekçi Joint Stock Company, Milli Ekmekçi Anonim Şirketi, founded in 1917) and even some companies[10] classified as joint stock companies in the "1913–1915 Industry Statistics (1917)" book published by the Ministry of Trade and Agriculture only one year before the *Ottoman Catalog* were not included.[11]

Finally, while the approach in the newspaper article by Mehmet ASIM (1918) is something to be taken into consideration when using it as an academic reference, as it carries a "reflex of defense of the [new] Second Constitutional Monarchy against the [old] Abdul Hamid era" in terms of economic practices, the statements in Ahmet Emin (1930) are similar in terms of a "reflex of defense of the [new] Republican era against the [old] Ottoman era".[12]

Çakır & Akkuş (2015) do not fall into the "magic 129" error, but although they give the correct number of companies in the Ottoman Catalog, they assume that all companies were only those in that *Ottoman Catalog*.

However, aside from the errors and omissions in computing the "magic 129" figure, there are sources that show that the total number of companies in 1908 was much higher.

---

10 For example, companies such as "*Borkard İstikrazat-ı Uzviye Fabrikası*", İstanbul, Yedikule (1917: 180), "*İstinye Tamir Havuzları Şirketi*", İstanbul, İstinye (1917: 183), "*Pedoti Tuğla Anonim Şirketi*", İstanbul, Tuzla (1917: 84) are examples of joint stock companies that are included in the Trade and Agriculture Ministry's Industrial Statistics (1917) but not in the *Ottoman Catalog* (1918). Likewise, the two founders of the merged company that would merge in 1919 and take the title "*Arslan ve Eskihisar Müttehid Çimento Fabrikaları Anonim Şirketi*" (Oyak Aslan Çimento A.Ş., which is now listed on the Istanbul Stock Exchange), "*Eskihisar Müttehid Çimento Fabrikaları Anonim Şirketi*". Although both companies, "*Eskihisar Sun'i Portland Cement and Water Lime Ottoman Joint Stock Company*", Eskihisar, Istanbul, and "*Arslan Ottoman Joint Stock Company*", Darıca, Istanbul, were listed in the 1913–1915 Industrial Statistics (1917: 87), only Eskihisar (Yılmaz, 2011: 104; OAŞ 10) was included in the *Ottoman Catalog*. Therefore, the "magic 129" does not include the Arslan Cement factory, which existed in 1918 and met all the conditions for inclusion in the *Ottoman Catalog*.

11 Ministry Trade and Industry (1917), *1329–1331 Seneleri Sanayi İstatistiki*, İstanbul, Matbaa-i Amire, [H]1333. For the transcription see Ökçün (1984).

12 In fact, the development of joint stock companies can be considered as the first examples of the "we inherited wreckage, we created wonders" culture that has now become a political tradition. Naturally, companies whose economic continuity is disrupted due to the fact that they belong to the "old and lost era" in terms of their ownership structure are not the subject of scrutiny in every change of "transfer". An example of this is the joint stock companies founded by the "Unionists" during the period of the National Economic Policy, in the case of the *Ottoman Itibar-ı Milli Bank*.

For example, in an article titled "*Memleketimizde Ticaret ve Sanayi Şirketlerin Vaziyeti*" (The Current Situation of Trade and Industry Companies in Our Country), published in 1925 in the Journal of Istanbul Chamber of Commerce and Industry under the signature of Mehmet Vehbi [SARIDAL], it is stated that there were 53 joint stock companies in 1908 and 34 new companies were established in 1918 alone[13] (Toprak 1982: 65). Likewise, in the *German Catalog* (1983: 1), despite some errors in numbers and dates, the number of companies established in the Ottoman borders until 1906 is stated as 60 and the distribution of these 60 companies according to sectors is also given.

According to another source (Toprak, 1995: 117–118); "A total of 236 companies were established between 1908 and 1918 thanks to the incentives and patronage. The number of joint stock companies that started operations in the first five years of the Constitutional Monarchy was 113. In 1918, 120 of the 129 companies that continued to operate were companies established under the Union and Progress government. During the war years, the number of foreign companies decreased and Turkish companies increased. Of the 129 companies, 42 were active in trade, 41 in industry, 16 in finance, 15 in construction and transportation, 9 in insurance, and 6 in agriculture."

The number of companies established in the Ottoman period has also been the subject of statements in the Grand National Assembly of Turkey (TBMM). For example, the figures given by Mustafa Rahmi Bey, Deputy Minister of Trade, in the TBMM in 1927 on the number of companies in the Ottoman period support the figures in Toprak (1995): "The number of joint stock companies until the war was 68. During the war 70 companies were established. In 1919, 12, in 1920, 8, in 1921, 4 and in 1922, 5 companies were established. After the conclusion of the Treaty of Lausanne, the peace and stability established in the country and the continuation of the peace led to an increase in such economic organizations, eleven companies were established in 1923, 42 companies in 1924, 50 companies in 1925, 26 companies in 1926. The total of these companies is more than all the companies that were established in 40–50 years. The number of existing companies, national companies, is 310. The number of foreign companies is 175. The number of existing banks is 66. Of these, 30 are foreign banks and 36 are local banks. The authorized capital of local banks is 40 million liras. After the publication of the Chambers of Commerce Law, 228 chambers were established.

---

13 Mehmet Vehbi [Saridal] (1925), According to the article in question, the number of joint stock companies established between 1909 and 1917 are as follows, respectively: 10, 21, 33, 13, 11, 9, 10, 14 and 30.

The services of these institutions are very beneficial for the country." [TBMM Minutes, 16.4.1927, Quoted by Sirma (2011)]

However, it is also possible to accept that the sources that give the number of joint stock companies existing in 1908 as 9 are "fair". Indeed, Kivilcimli (1974: 111), without any reference, claims that "5 companies were established from 1863 to the 1908 revolution, 37 companies from 1909 to 1914 and 55 companies in the period 1914–1918".

Although Kivilcimli (1974) does not provide any reference for the information on the number of Ottoman joint stock companies, an examination of the Bibliography at the end of the book reveals that the source of this information should be Tahsin and Saka (1930). However, such an interpretation of the information in Tahsin and Saka (1930) requires a repetition of the assessment made for Ahmet Emin (1930). This is because, based on the available "balance sheet"[14] of joint stock companies as of 1930, it is not possible to assume that no joint stock company, other than the ones existing at that time, could have been established in the past and closed before that date. The erroneous figures in Kivilcimli (1974) are basically based on this erroneous assumption.

3. Conclusion

Although the period covering approximately the first quarter of the 20th century is not quite long in terms of calendar years, starting with the removal of Abdul Hamid II from power, a number of political and economic changes, some of which have been described as "revolutions" and others as "traumas", have taken place one after the other. The deposition of Abdul Hamid II and the proclamation of the Second Constitutional Monarchy, the coming to power of the Committee of Union and Progress, the Tripoli, Balkan and World War I wars, the loss of power by the Committee of Union and Progress, the armistice and occupation years, The political end of the Ottoman Empire, the establishment of the Ankara Government, the proclamation of the Republic and finally the Economic Depression of 1929 cannot be considered as a healthy operating ground for the survival of economic enterprises. Although there were many attempts to

14 To draw an analogy from accounting, just as the balance sheet is a "stock" and the income statement is a "current" value, the *Turkish Catalog* is a balance sheet as of 1930. It shows the companies that were still "alive" as of that year. However, it is not sufficient to reach a *conclusion about which companies were established and closed in the Ottoman period until that year.

establish joint stock companies within the framework of the "National Economy" policy despite the war conditions in that period, especially in the environment that emerged after the Second Constitutional Monarchy, the life span of these companies was very short.

Even if some of these major changes (e.g. the Constitutional Monarchy and the proclamation of the Republic) are perceived as positive changes, even this cannot be accepted as a positive situation for all economic enterprises. For example, some joint-stock companies* founded by "Ittihad ve Terakki notables" suffered after the proclamation of the Republic due to their ownership structure and were largely liquidated. For example, many joint stock companies mentioned in the *Ottoman Catalog* (1918) were either closed or "in liquidation" by the time the *Turkish Catalog* (1930) was published. The common characteristic of most of these companies is that their founders were "Unionists". Considering that even routine changes of power in the democratic period affected the "success" of some companies and businessmen, it is impossible to think that a much more radical political transformation such as the transition from the Ottoman Empire to the Republic had no impact on the continuity of economic enterprises. Although the effects of this factor in the Republican period have been the subject of academic study (Buğra 1995), this "transformation effect" on Ottoman joint stock companies has not yet been taken into account. Therefore, it does not seem easy to reach a clear conclusion about a period by only looking at the "most recent balance sheet".

On the other hand, as partially explained above, almost all of today's popular information on the number of Ottoman joint stock companies is a hand-to-hand, erroneous and incomplete transfer of information from a source that provides partial information on that period.

To return to Mehmet ASIM's newspaper article, it should be remembered that the total number of Ottoman joint stock companies and their activities were not even known by the relevant public institution at the time. Therefore, it is inevitable that those who have read the article so far with the hope of learning the total number of Ottoman joint stock companies will be disappointed. Because in 1918, the Ministry of Commerce of the time did not know this number either!

However, even though the total number of Ottoman joint stock companies is not yet known, there is no doubt that this number is at least several times higher than the figures given in Kivilcimli (1974), and considering the companies included in *French Catalog* (Pech 1911) and the omissions in the *Ottoman Catalog* (1918), this number is several times higher than the "magic 129" number.

References

Ahmet Emin [Yalman] (1930). *Turkey in the World War*, New Haven, Yale University Press.

Akşin, S. (1980). *Jön Türkler ve İttihat ve Terakki*, İstanbul, Gerçek.

Avcıoğlu, D. (1968). *Türkiye'nin Düzeni*, Ankara, Bilgi.

Buğra, A. (1995). *Devlet ve İşadamları*, İstanbul, İletişim.

Çakır, C., & Akkuş, Y. (2015). "İstanbul'da Kurulan Anonim Şirketler", *Antik Çağdan XXI. Yüzyıla Büyük İstanbul Tarihi*, Volume 6, pp. 191–197.

Çavdar, T. (1971). *Milli Mücadele Başlarken Sayılarla "Vaziyet ve Manzara-i Umumiye"*, İstanbul, Milliyet.

Findley, Carter V. (2011). *Turkey, Islam, Nationalism and Modernity*, USA, Yale University Press.

Findley, Carter V. (2012). *Modern Türkiye Tarihi: İslam Milliyetçilik ve Modernlik 1789–2007*, İstanbul, Timaş.

Historische Wertpapiere: Ottomanisches Kaiserreich und Turkei – Aktien und Anleihen: 1854-1938, Frankfurt Freunde Historicher Wertpapiere, 1983, "*German Catalog*".

Karpat, K. (2010). "İttihat ve Terakki Dönemi", *Zaman*, "*Yorumlar*", 17.03.2010.

Kivilcimli, H. (1974). *Türkiye'de Kapitalizmin Gelişimi*, İstanbul, Tarih ve Devrim.

Mehmet Vehbi [Saridal]. (1925). "Memleketimizde Ticaret ve Sanayi Şirketlerinin Vaziyeti", *İstanbul Ticaret ve Sanayi Odası Mecmuası*, Kânunısani 1341 [Ocak 1925], No: 1, s. 656.

Ökçün, G. (1984). (Edt.) *Osmanlı Sanayi 1913–1915 İstatistikleri*, İstanbul, Hil Yayın.

Pech, E. (1911). *Manuels des Societes Anonymes Fonctionnant en Turquie*, 5e.Edition, Constantinople, "*French Catalog*".

Sirma, İ. (2011). "Osmanlı Anonim Şirketlerinde Kâr Dağıtımı", *Akdeniz University, International Journal of Alanya Faculty of Business*, *3*(2), pp. 117–136.

Tahsin, H., & Saka R. (1930). *Sermaye Hareketi*, İstanbul, Amedî Matbaası, "*Türkçe Katalog*".

TBMM (1927). (Grand National Assembly of Turkey) *Minutes*, 16.4.1927.

Tezcan, A. (2007). "Ahmet Emin Yalman: Dönemi ve Gazeteciliği (1918–1938)" (PhD Thesis), Ankara University, Ankara.

Ticaret ve Sanayi Nezareti. (1917), *1329–1331 Seneleri Sanayi İstatistiki*, İstanbul, Matbaa-i Amire.

Toprak, Z. (1982). *Türkiye'de Milli İktisat (1908–1918)*, Ankara, Yurt.

Toprak, Z. (1995). *Milli İktisat-Milli Burjuvazi*, İstanbul, Tarih Vakfı Yurt.

Yilmaz, C. (2011). *Osmanlı Anonim Şirketleri*, İstanbul, Scala, "Ottoman Catalog"

Zürcher, Erik Jan. (2004). *Turkey: A Modern History*, New Edition, New York, I.B.Tauris

Burçin Bozdoğanoğlu[1]

Nft As a New Generation Investment Instrument and Its Taxability

1. Introduction

NFT (Non-Fungible Tokens) is a concept that has become popular recently, especially as a product of Blockchain technology. Considering this concept, which is often referred to with works of art, in this period when digital investment instruments were increasingly diversified and widespread. Its English abbreviation is "Non-Fungible Token", and it is possible to express the meaning of the word in Turkish as "it cannot be substituted, changed, cannot be multiplied".

Although NFT is particularly associated with works of art, NFT's creation is not limited to works of art. Apart from this, materials such as interviews, photographs, videos, prominent signs, etc., the creation of digital goods and brand-qualified NFTs are also possible. In addition, with the metaverse alternative universe, it is possible to create NFTs for the sale of properties in the digital environment of the places and places of the virtual world and for these transactions, and NFTs for game characters and items that are traded with game money.

In the study, the NFT creation process, the differences between NFT Marketplaces from crypto asset trading platforms and the need for the legal regulation of the NFT trading process will be discussed. The taxability of NFTs, which reached a high transaction volume in a short time in the last period of the digitalization process, is the main subject of the study. In general, it is known that there are difficulties in the applicability of classical taxation rules to new digital products and business models. In particular, the rapid progress of the digitalization process, the changes in taxation and the slow pace of adaptation to the process cause the value created to be excluded from taxation. In this context, in this study, different countries and regions, such as the UK, USA and Norway will be included in the study regarding the taxability of NFTs. Also, suggestions

1 Prof. PhD., Bandırma Onyedi Eylül University, Faculty of Economics and Administrative Sciences, Public Finance Department, bbozdoganoglu@bandirma.edu.tr

will be made regarding the arrangements that can be made by taking into account the existing tax laws in Turkey.

2. NFT Concept and Features

NFT is the abbreviation of the English term "Non-Fungible Tokens" and appears as one of the innovations blockchain technology has included in our lives. The Turkish equivalent of NFT, which is expressed as the meaning of the word cannot be substituted, changed, or duplicated, has been determined as a "Qualified Intellectual Deed" by the joint work of the Presidency Digital Transformation Office and the Turkish Language Institution.

These tokens also referred to as unique tokens, usually provide rights such as access to certain content or granting royalties. NFTs, like other tokens, work on the blockchain. The main features of these tokens are that they are cryptographic and non-mutual; In other words, they are unique. NFTs are also not divisible. In addition, one NFT cannot replace another NFT (Blockchain Türkiye, 2021: 12).

It is also possible to define NFT as the recording or tokenization of a digital or real-world asset through Blockchain technology and smart contracts in a way that cannot be substituted, changed, deleted or divided (İçten, 2022: 139). Within the framework of all these explanations, it can be said that NFTs are characterized by the following elements (Di Bernardino et al., 2021):

Uniqueness: An NFT represents a unique digital or otherwise object that can be clearly associated with a user or a virtual wallet.
Indivisibility: Indivisible
Immutability: NFTs are not replaceable and not repeatable

3. Technological Components of NFTs

It is possible to develop different versions of NFTs on Ethereum and other next-generation blockchains. Typically, NFTs are created using Ethereum's ERC 721 Token Standard to create an inherited crypto-asset. Ethereum is an open-source, decentralized computing platform built on blockchain technology developed by Vitalik Buterin. Similar to Bitcoin, Ethereum is a decentralized public blockchain network; but there are some technical differences between them (Buterin, 2014).

Considering the technology used, it is seen that NFTs were created as digital assets with a discordant quality with Ethereum's ERC-721 token standard. In this respect, the technological components behind the existence, formation and transaction of NFTs in the market can be listed as blockchain technology, smart contract, ERC-721 standard, data encoding, address and transactions.

Blockchain Technology: Blockchain technology is a set of digital methods to store the same data in multiple places. A blockchain is thought of as a database that stores the number of accounting units held by each user (Hays & Valek, 2018: 8). With an encrypted password, usually called a public-private key pair, users can access account units called cryptocurrencies and make transactions within the duration of this password. A blockchain is a collection of information known as a node that is not held by the physical entity but is spread across all computers in the network. The massive processing power of this blockchain is secured by cryptographic proofs, known as "mining", which uses distributed servers to verify and process transactions that involve a contest to receive payment and complete the transaction. Because the person who wants to override the blockchain control rules must have at least 51 % of the computing power in the code chain (Hays & Valek, 2018: 9).

Smart Contracts: The concept of smart contracts was first used by Nick Szabo, a software expert and cryptographer, in the early 90s. Szabo defines smart contracts as "a computerized transaction protocol that fulfills the terms of a contract" (Szabo, 1994). A smart contract is a computer science term that refers to computer code that runs on certain blockchain systems and ensures that the same predefined results occur when predetermined conditions are met (German, 2022). Smart contracts enable unknowing parties and decentralized participants to trade fairly without a trusted third party. Applications running on smart contracts rely on state transition mechanisms. The participants share situations with instructions and parameters. As one of the most important applications of blockchain technology, smart contracts form the basis of decentralized autonomous organizations (DAO) and financing methods such as NFT, ICO and STO.

Address and Transactions: Blockchain addresses and transactions are the most fundamental concepts in cryptocurrencies. The address in the blockchain is a unique identifier given to each user for the purchase and sending of assets, and with this feature, it resembles a bank account. This address consists of a fixed number of alphanumeric characters from public keys and private passwords. For NFT transfer, the owner must prove that he has the relevant private key and send the assets to another address(es) with a correct digital signature. This is usually done using a cryptocurrency wallet (Valeonti et al., 2021).

Standards and Protocols: This includes token standards related to NFTs, including ERC-20, ERC-721 and ERC-1155. The most well-known token standard is ERC-20. Exchangeable tokens that can be issued on Ethereum after meeting the requirements are created based on this standard. With the ERC-20 standard, tokens become identical in both type and value. Many public chains and various blockchain-based DApps get adequate initial funding this way.

Data Encoding: Encoding is the process of transforming data from one form to another. Many files are usually encoded in efficient, compressed formats to save disk space or in an uncompressed format for high quality/resolution. Major blockchain systems such as Bitcoin and Ethereum use hexadecimal values to encode transaction elements such as function names, parameters, and return values. This means that raw NFT data must follow these rules. If someone claims to own NFT-based intellectual property, they essentially have the original hexadecimal values signed by the creator. Others can freely copy the raw data but cannot claim property ownership. Based on this, it is possible to state that similar to the basic processing procedure of smart contracts, NFT-related activities (e.g. buy/sell/trade/auction) should be processed in these four stages (Wang et al., 2021)

In the Ethereum blockchain, where most NFTs find applications, the NFT creation process is called "mint". The name comes from the English figurative term minting money (Araalan, 2022). NFTs are produced or transferred to digital media; It is formed by making images, gifs, video, or audio files a part of the blockchain, that is, by "minting" them. Today, anyone with a digital wallet can turn their work into NFT for a certain price and sell it on the platforms in the market.

Generating, storing and trading NFTs costs the user a fee called a gas fee. The Gas Fee is the fee for using an Ethereum blockchain function. These fees, measured in the "gwei" unit, are directly proportional to the effort spent performing a function. The higher the effort spent on performing a function on the Ethereum blockchain, the higher the gas fee. For this reason, smart contract manufacturers prefer that the code they write is free from complexity. To complete a simple NFT trade, a transaction fee of between $60–100 is required for each transaction (EC, 2021: 28).

4. Evaluation of Intellectual Property

It is important to understand that ownership of the NFT does not always mean the intellectual property of the asset represented in the NFT. NFTs can represent photos, videos, music, artwork, online gaming content, tweets, and other digital files. At issue here is the electronic representation of this property. It will not cover essential intellectual property, such as the copyright of NFT and the work NFT represents unless specifically included (Beyer, 2021).

Making an NFT sale will not automatically transfer the intellectual property rights to the related NFTized work to the buyer. However, all or some of the intellectual property rights can be transferred by adding provisions in this direction to the smart contract that forms the basis of the sales transaction. When the practical applications are examined, in general, only the ownership of the relevant NFT is transferred in the sale of the NFT, and the intellectual property rights of the brought work are not transferred. In accordance with Article 52 of the Law on Intellectual and Artistic Works No. 5846 in Turkish Law, financial rights such as the right to distribute, reproduce, and process work must be transferred in writing and in a way that these rights are shown separately. In this context, although these rights can be specified separately in the smart contract, whether the smart contract will meet the written requirement of the transfer of rights within the scope of the law in question is a separate issue. Although NFT works of art clearly show by which crypto wallet account the work was registered to the blockchain, when it was exported, and by which crypto wallet account the work was purchased, such as a registry record, it does not offer direct information about who made these transactions and whose intellectual product the work was (Cumhuriyet & Narin, 2022).

NFTs are digital intangibles that typically represent a property or other right. However, an NFT is not the underlying asset but an electronic record proving its ownership. Thus, owning an NFT does not result in ownership of the underlying asset of the NFT unless that NFT specifically involves the transfer of rights such as copyright (PwC, 2022: 13). So what then is it that millions of US dollars are given and taken? For example, what the person who "buys" Dorsey's first tweet actually receives is not the rights on that work, but an alphanumeric value that gives other people the right to say that they "got their first tweet from Jack Dorsey." Regarding the nature of what is taken here, we encounter a familiar ambiguity constantly in discussions about the legal nature of crypto assets and the "right" to data in general. In order to meet this and create a general framework, ready-made framework license projects such as the "NFT License" are created (Güçlütürk, 2022).

5. NFT Trading and NFT Marketplaces

NFT marketplaces; Platforms where NFTs can be stored, traded, viewed and created, often different from crypto asset trading platforms. Accordingly, NFT is not just a brokerage service in marketplaces; services such as project design, different marketing techniques, creating strategies, tracking and keeping on the agenda, and creating customers are also offered. NFT marketplaces, which have experienced strong growth, especially after 2017, are a relatively new phenomenon. In this short period, the NFT market has experienced huge heights, especially with the success of CryptoKitties (Ante, 2021: 17). In terms of NFT Marketplaces, and storage is especially a problem. As a matter of fact, it is still being determined where the real image of a digital asset produced as NFT is stored (Ante, 2021: 18).

Separate regulation and supervision of NFT marketplaces are essential, as NFTs can be sold cheaply and repurchased at a high price to evade taxes or launder money. The issuance and sale of NFTs take place on what is called the NFT platform or NFT Marketplace. In this respect, they operate differently than the platforms where crypto assets are traded. The most known NFT marketplaces; OpenSea, Nifty Gateway, SuperRare, Rarible, Mintable, Binance, Marketplace, and Decentraland.

Crypto asset wallet use is required for NFT generation and trading. MetaMask and Coinbase are generally preferred as wallets. The NFT purchase process starts with purchasing "ETH", or crypto money that can be used in the transaction, from crypto asset trading platforms and loading them into the crypto asset wallet. Afterwards, this wallet is connected to the NFT marketplace. The process is completed by loading the NFT token, which is paid with the cryptocurrencies in the wallet, into the crypto asset wallet. NFT tokens are generally traded over the cryptocurrencies of the platforms they are issued. For example, ETH, MANA, SANDbox etc. These coins do not represent any NFT, even though they are traded on multiple crypto-asset platforms. Although NFTs are essentially tokens, trading transactions are made in exchange for tokens of double quality. However, recently, well-established marketplaces such as Nifty Gateway and platforms such as Shopify and Coinbase have added traditional methods such as credit cards and fintech to their payment options for purchasing processes.

NFTs, mostly identified with works of art, can be created in many different areas. As a matter of fact, the NFT market can be examined at two levels: "project level" and "ownership level". At the project level, the NFT market is divided into six main segments: art, collectables, sports, utility, metaverse, and games. In these matters, NFT can cooperate with brands and foundations, and the amount earned can be converted into scholarship support by selling the digital work used in a movie or TV series decor. The NFT market is segmented at the ownership level into Primary and Secondary Markets. Platforms such as Opensea.io, Rarible.com, Binance, and Mintable.app enable players to print, trade, buy and auction NFTs through a metamask wallet account that connects the platform and cryptocurrency exchanges with fiat banking assets (Mukhopadhyay & Ghosh, 2021).

6. Taxability of NFTs and Country Practices

6.1. Foreign Country Examples

United Kingdom: The UK currently has no legislation specifically regarding NFTs, and although HMRC acknowledges that NFTs are classified as a separate entity from cryptocurrency, guidance on HMRC's tax treatment generally only covers crypto assets. Since NFT is an asset, tax liability will arise if it is sold for more than the amount purchased. In the absence of official legislation or guidance regarding NFTs, it seems more reasonable to subject them to capital gains tax by treating them as physical works of art or collectables, recognizing that the profits and losses associated with NFTs arise when these assets are sold or given to someone else. Therefore, NFTs will also be considered assets for other taxes, such as Inheritance tax (Lowe, 2022).

USA: The IRS has fine-tuned annual tax filing regulations to account for non-fungible tokens (NFTs), replacing the term "virtual currency" with "digital assets," which includes NFTs. Due to the rapid rise of the NFT market in 2021, taxation has been discussed by many public authorities. The IRS has also stated that NFTs carry some risks as they can be used for money laundering purposes. The IRS has also announced the warning on its website, dated April 28, 2022, prepared by J5 (The Joint Chiefs of Global Tax Enforcement) (IRS, 2022).

Today, what the IRS lists as collectables have no other tangible properties. This raises questions about whether other items on the list, such as artwork, should also be physical. There are no clear guidelines. NFTs that do not fall into one of the above categories are unlikely to be considered collectables under tax regulations. If NFTs are considered a collection product, they will be taxed at a flat rate as part of capital gains. Long-term crypto capital gains are taxed at 20 %, compared to 28 % for NFTs. NFT investments defined as short-term (less than one year) are taxed at 37 % (Valburn, 2022).

Norway: Norway was the first country to publish guidance on NFT taxation. The Tax Administration recognizes NFT as an asset, and tax rules are regulated similarly to other virtual assets. In Norway, all income from the virtual currency is taxable under tax regulations regarding virtual assets. In terms of taxation, virtual currencies such as cryptocurrency, digital tokens and other digital assets are considered assets. Income from assets is considered capital income and is taxed at %22 (Norwegian Tax Administration, 2022).

Income from virtual currencies is included in the calculation of net wealth tax with market value as of January 1 in the following year. Virtual currencies are subject to general tax regulations for assets. They are not subject to the exemptions and special tax rules that apply to fiat currencies, stocks, bonds, financial instruments or other types of assets with special exemptions. This means, among other things, that the exemption method does not apply to virtual currencies and that the upward correction factor for the income earned does not apply (Norwegian Tax Administration, 2022).

The tax treatment of virtual currencies must be considered for each product/service. The name of the product or service does not affect this assessment. Creating an NFT, often referred to as minting, is not taxed.

6.2. Evaluation of the Current Situation in Turkey

Although there is no definition of crypto assets and NFTs in our tax legislation, crypto assets are defined as "intangible assets" in the regulation of the Central Bank of the Republic of Turkey.

This definition does not mean that crypto assets will no longer be taxable. According to Article 73 of our Constitution, there is a need to make a legal regulation regarding these assets to make taxation on crypto assets in accordance with the provision that taxes will be set, abolished and changed by law. However, it is possible to interpret the current legal provisions (income tax, corporate tax and VAT) in terms of the tax status of NFTs, parties to NFT transactions and NFT types. However, although NFTs are inseparable, immutable, and indelibly mapped to the source entity, there is no doubt that they are virtual entities. Therefore, it is clear that evaluations to be made through convergence regarding the virtual/digital equivalents of the regulations made for physical assets in the current tax laws will result in "taxation by comparison" and constitute a violation of Article 73 of the Constitution. For this reason, clear legal provisions regulating the subject are needed. In addition, clear definitions and assessments are needed for these virtual goods under the Tax Procedure Law, even if existing law provisions are used through convergence (İçten, 2022: 158).

NFTs are digital copies of physical assets or entirely digitally created artifacts, uniquely tokenized in a blockchain environment via smart contracts. From this point of view, in the case of benefiting from the existing tax laws in the taxation of NFTs, in accordance with the provision in the 73 articles of our Constitution that taxes will be imposed, abolished and amended by law, statements regarding NFTs should be added to the articles of the law on this subject (such as Article 18 of the Income Tax Law).

As a result, in terms of taxation of crypto assets, considering the current diversity of these assets, it is not a very appropriate method to adopt similar taxation approaches in terms of their proximity to the income elements in the Turkish tax system. Considering the developments in the digital field, especially using blockchain technology, the issue of how to tax crypto assets in a global sense is not clear. Recently, NFTs, DeFis (Decentralized Finance), and DaOs (Decentralized Autonomous Organizations), which are seen as crypto assets, have been added to these discussions. It is also possible to add different crypto assets to them in the future. The main starting point for the taxation of these assets, which attract attention from almost all segments of society and are open to using, is to determine the legal nature. When a global evaluation is made on this subject, it is seen that the financial administrations of the countries have similar positioning problems.

It is seen that the legal qualifications of these assets need to be regulated within the framework of other laws other than taxes. However, legal regulations cannot respond to the pace of development in digital assets. While there is no definition in the relevant law regarding the asset, it is not the right approach to make arrangements within the framework of tax laws.

It would be a more appropriate approach to define these digital assets, which are constantly evolving and changing, as "digital assets" in the Turkish tax legislation and the income from them as a new income element under the name of "digital asset earnings". In addition, the design of a separate tax regime for this newly defined income will be an important initiative that allows the Tax Administrations to act legally and quickly.

At this point, it may be possible to use the concept of "virtual digital asset" in the last regulation that came into force in India in order to determine the scope of the definition of "digital asset". Also in France, the category of digital assets was defined to include tokens and virtual currencies under European law. However, assets such as financial instruments were excluded from this category (SBL, 2021). In this context, digital assets are defined as intangible portable assets, including cryptocurrencies, within the framework of the French Council of State's decision (Marsac, 2021).

Such an arrangement will facilitate the understanding and taxation of new digital products and allow the countries' strategic approaches to be followed. It is suggested that the new taxation regime for "digital assets" in Turkey should include the following elements (İçten, 2022: 160):

- Flat and low taxation
- Taxation of all crypto asset trading gains
- Possibility of retroactive deduction
- Giving an exception to earnings below a certain amount
- Exemption or low taxation for holdings exceeding a certain period
- Taxation by declaration

- Applying the system not only to the earnings from crypto asset trading but also to the earnings from mining and lending transactions and allowing trading losses to be offset against these incomes.
- VAT exemption (approach with other countries)

The constant change in the structure of digital assets and technological infrastructure; shows a need for specialized staff to tax these assets. In addition, a separate Digital Asset department to be established within the Revenue Administration is important in terms of determining basic strategies for monitoring international developments and ensuring cooperation, informing public units about the needs in other laws, and increasing the basic knowledge level of citizens and taxpayers at the point of increasing the level of digital financial literacy.

7. Conclusion

NFTs, whose English abbreviation is "Non-Fungible Token" and Turkish equivalent is Qualified Intellectual Deed, is the mapping of a digital or physical asset exclusively with a token in a blockchain environment in a way that cannot be substituted, changed, deleted, indivisible, through smart contracts. NFTs, which mostly come to the fore with works of art, have recently spread to a wide area, from textile products of well-known brands, auction sales of jewellery brands, as well as virtual land, office sales, rentals, and from avatars in games to the game tools they acquire, especially in the metaverse universe.

On the other hand, the legal status of NFTs needs to be clarified worldwide. NFTs tend to be evaluated in the same category as cryptocurrencies in terms of different country applications. However, there is no consensus on this issue either. For example, while the United States considers cryptocurrencies a stock and taxes them accordingly, it has treated NFTs as a collection product and subjected them to different tax legislation. On the other hand, virtual currencies such as cryptocurrency, digital tokens and other digital assets are accepted as assets for taxation purposes in Norway.

When the domestic law provisions are evaluated in terms of our country, it is seen that the nature of the work of crypto assets is primarily handled in connection with financial rights, especially within the Law on Intellectual and Artistic Works framework. In this context, the legal "work" quality of NFTs, which can take many different forms, becomes controversial. On the other hand, considering NFTs that do not have a physical form within the scope of "goods" creates uncertainty regarding the Civil Code. Therefore, the taxation of NFTs, which needs to be clarified and how it will be defined legally brings debates at the point of departure.

As a matter of fact, similar hesitations are also in question in terms of the Tax Procedure Law. Since NFTs can take many forms, it is necessary to evaluate whether they are considered "commodities" or "intangible rights" within the current regulations, the exchange rate difference and interests incurred in their purchases, and whether they are subject to depreciation. In our country, there is no regulation at the law level regarding crypto assets. Only in the regulation issued by the Central Bank have crypto assets been described as "intangible assets". However, this qualification does not mean that NFTs can also be taxed as intangible assets, considering our country's constitutional provision of tax regulations. In the current situation, there are areas for improvement in the provisions of the current legislation in terms of taxation of NFTs, like other crypto assets. Suppose crypto assets are defined as "intangible assets" when the laws in the Turkish tax system are evaluated. In that case, there appears to be no regulation covering NFTs, a type of crypto-asset. Current regulations will not be expected to cover NFTs and other types of crypto assets or products of other digital technologies that will emerge in the blockchain environment or outside of blockchain technology.

At this point, it is very difficult to follow the pace of the development of crypto assets with legislative regulations. Therefore, it would be a correct approach for the regulation to be flexible to cover new technological infrastructure and assets that may arise in the future. Considering the point reached by digital technology, it is best to define a new "digital asset" to include this group of assets and to define the income and earnings from them as "digital asset gains" as a new income element, considering the necessity of showing a strategic and flexible approach to taxation.

In this regulation to be made for the taxation of NFTs in Turkey, first of all, a comprehensive definition of digital assets, similar to the definitions in India or France, will be determined in terms of determining the legal status of existing assets and then making the tax regulation specific to these assets in terms of the steps to be followed.

In line with the regulations made in this respect, by establishing a department within the Revenue Administration consisting of specialized staff on digital assets, it will be possible to take the necessary steps to inform the taxpayers, follow international developments, and make the necessary cooperation.

References

Ante, L. (2021). "Non fungible token (NFT) markets on Ethereum blockchain: Temporal development, cointegration and interrelations", Blockchain Research Lab, Working Paper Series No:22,13.08.2021, https://papers.ssrn.com/sol3/papers.cfm?abstract_id=3904683, (06.04.2022)

Araalan, C. (2022). "NFT'lerin Türk Hukuku Çerçevesinde Değerlendirilmesi", Legal Blog, 25.04.2022, https://legal.com.tr/blog/genel/nftlerin-turk-hukuku-cercevesinde-degerlendirilmesi/ (06.06.2022)

Beyer, G. W. (2021). Non-Fungible Tokens: What every estate planner needs to know, http://dx.doi.org/10.2139/ssrn.3965888, (23.10.2022)

Blockchain Türkiye (BCTR). (2021). Kriptovarlıkların Vergi-Muhasebe ve Denetim Yönünden İncelenmesi, https://bctr.org/dokumanlar/Kripto_Varliklarin_Vergi_Muhasebe_ve_Denetim_Yonunden_Incelenmesi.pdf, (27.07.2022)

Buterin, V. (2014). "Ethereum: A-Next Generation Smart Contract and Decentralized Application Platform", https://ethereum.org/669c9e2e2027310b6b3cdce6e1c52962/Ethereum_Whitepaper_-_Buterin_2014.pdf (21.12.2022)

Cumhuriyet, B. N., & Narin, C. E. (2022). "Non-Fungible Token (NFT) Nedir? Ve Telif Hakları", https://www.mgc.com.tr/non-fungible-token-nft-ve-telif-hakki/ (21.10.2022)

Di Bernardino, C., Chomczyk, P. A., Ellul J., Ferreira, A., Goldbeck, A., Herian, R., Siadat, A., & Siedler, N.-L., "NFT – Legal Token Classification" (22.07.2021). EU Blockchain Observatory and Forum NFT Reports, https://papers.ssrn.com/sol3/papers.cfm?abstract_id=3891872, (01.03.2022)

EC. (2021). Demystifying Non Fungible Tokens (NFTs), EU Blockchain Observatory and Forum, https://www.eublockchainforum.eu/sites/default/files/reports/DemystifyingNFTs_November%202021_2.pdf, (02.02.2022)

German, E. (2022). "The Recognition of Smart Contracts in Jersey", The Jersey and Guernsey Law Review, https://www.monocerosinnovation.com/wp-content/uploads/2022/02/E-German-The-Recognition-of-Smart-Contracts-in-Jersey-2021-Jersey-and-Guernsey-Law-Review-June-2021-p159.pdf (14.12.2022)

Güçlütürk, G. O. (2022). "NFT'lerin Oluşturulması ve Transferinin Eser Sahibinin Mali Haklarıyla İlişkisi", 25.03.2022, https://nasamer.ku.edu.tr/nftlerin-olusturulmasi-ve-transferinin-eser-sahibinin-mali-haklariyla-iliskisi/, (06.06.2022)

Hays, D. K., & Valek, M. J. (2018). Cryptoresearch Report, Vontobel Incrementum, June 2018, https://cryptoresearch.report/wp-content/uploads/2018/06/Crypto-Research-Report-June-2018-3.pdf, (20.12.2022)

IRS. (2022). "J5 Releases NFT Red Flags to Warn Public of Risks", 28.04.2022, https://www.irs.gov/pub/irs-utl/j5-media-release-4-28-2022.pdf, (20.12.2022)

Içten, T. (2022). "NFT Uygulamaları ve Vergilendirilmesi Mevcut Durum ve Öneriler", Vergi Dünyası, Ekim 2022, Yıl:42, Sayı:494

Lowe, H. (2022). "NFT's explained; what are the tax implications of buying and selling crypto assets?", 09.09.2022, Mercer&Hole, https://www.mercerhole.co.uk/insights/nfts-explained-what-are-the-tax-implications-of-buying-and-selling-crypto-assets/ (09.12.2022)

Marsac, S. T. (2021). "A French point of view: from crypto assets to digital assets", International Bar Association, https://www.ibanet.org/article/f59c675e-e95e-4c74-bdc3-ea5a42e8ef9c#:~:text=The%20following%20are%20considered%20to,public%20authority%2C%20is%20not%20necessarily (26.07.2022)

Mukhopadhyay, M., & Ghosh, K. (2021). Market Microstructure of Non Fungible Tokens, Five Shades of Emerging Business Cases, Eliva Press (Nov 2021), https://ssrn.com/abstract=3934676, (30.11.2022). (21.07.2022)

Norwegian Tax Administration. (2022). Tax regulations-virtual currency. https://www.skatteetaten.no/en/person/taxes/get-the-taxes-right/shares-and-securities/about-shares-and-securities/digital-currency/tax-regulations-virtual-currency/ (12.12.2022)

PWC. (2022). Annual Global Crypto Tax Report, https://www.pwc.com/gx/en/financial-services/pdf/global-crypto-tax-report-2022.pdf, (05.01.2022)

SBL. (2021) "French Tax Law, What Tax Treatment is applied to cryptocurrencies?" Schmidt Brunet Litzler, 06.10.2021, https://www.sbl.eu/our-news/french-tax-law-what-tax-treatment-is-applied-to-crypto-currencies/ (25.07.2022)

Szabo, N. (1994). "Smart Contracts", The George Washington University Law School, 1994, https://www.fon.hum.uva.nl/rob/Courses/InformationInSpeech/CDROM/Literature/LOTwinterschool2006/szabo.best.vwh.net/smart.contracts.html, (05.01.2023)

Valburn, M. (2022). "Understanding the Art of NFT Taxes", 07.06.2022, https://www.entrepreneur.com/money-finance/understanding-the-art-of-nft-taxes/401878, (09.08.2022)

Valeonti, F., Bikakis, A., Terras, M., Speed, C., HudsonSmith, A., & Chalkias, K. (2021). Crypto collectables, museum funding and OpenGLAM: challenges, opportunities and the potential of Non-Fungible Tokens (NFTs). *Applied Sciences*, *11*(21), 9931

Wang, Q., Li, R., Wang, Q., & Chen, S. (2021). Non-fungible token (NFT): Overview, evaluation, opportunities and challenges. https://arxiv.org/pdf/2105.07447.pdf, (03.08.2022)

Kadir Yasin Eryiğit[1] & Adnan Gerçek[2] & Esra Uygun[3]

An Econometric Study on Reasons of Tax Gap: The Case of Turkey[4]

1. Introduction

The tax gap is an integral part of economies. Almost every country has a tax gap. However, no tax administration has been able to develop a universal calculation method for measuring the tax gap that can be applied in other countries (Raczkowski & Mroz, 2018: 567).

The tax gap is that the taxpayers do not fully declare their tax obligations in their tax returns, pay their taxes incompletely despite fully declaring their tax obligations, or do not submit the necessary tax returns on time (Joint Committee on Taxation, 2019: 2). The tax gap indicates the general level of non-compliance of taxpayers for a given tax year. It includes deficiencies in income tax, corporate tax, expenditure taxes and other taxes. Country economies do not struggle with tax losses and evasion as long as the tax gap remains within reasonable limits. However, with the increase in the tax gap, it emerges as a major problem that prevents the collection of budget revenues and the fair distribution of income (Mróz, 2010: 96–118). Therefore, economies need to determine the tax gap to control the tax gap rate. Therefore, measurement of the tax gap serves as a system that can take the necessary measures to protect the financial interests of the countries in the public administration process (Raczkowski, 2015: 567).

1 Ph.D., Professor, Bursa Uludağ University, the Faculty of Economics and Administrative Sciences, Econometrics Department, kyeryigit@uludag.edu.tr, ORCID: 0000-0001-6857-7402

2 Ph.D., Professor, Bursa Uludağ University, the Faculty of Economics and Administrative Sciences, Public Finance Department, agercek@uludag.edu.tr, ORCID: 0000-0002-9495-2429

3 Ph.D., Lecturer, Tokat Gaziosmanpaşa University, Zile Vocational Scholl, Public Finance Department, esra.uygun@gop.edu.tr, ORCID: 0000-0001-5332-0831

4 This study is derived from the doctoral thesis titled "The concept, scope and measurement of the tax gap: Various country applications and implications for Turkey", completed in 2021 at Bursa Uludağ University under the supervision of Professor Doctor Adnan Gerçek.

Considering that the countries economic, social and financial structures are different, it is difficult to figure out the internationally acceptable tax gap limit precisely. However, statements to Schneider about the acceptable tax gap in his study. According to Schneider, the acceptable tax gap is approximately 5 % of GDP. Even if the tax gap exceeding this limit contributes to economic growth, it is incompatible with the requirements of possible sustainable development. It has a negative impact on the implementation of the factors of production. However, it should be noted that there are informal economic activities in both developed and developing countries (Schneider, 2002; Schneider et al., 2010: 405–430).

The United Kingdom is the country that conducts the most comprehensive study on the measurement of the tax gap. The UK has been measuring the tax gap by general and tax types every year since 2007 and has published a report. In a study published in 2018, Raczkowski and Mroz measured the tax gap of 35 countries, including 28 EU member states and Australia, Canada, Japan, New Zealand, Turkey and Switzerland (Raczkowski & Mroz, 2018: 567–583). Richard Murphy measured the tax gaps of EU member states in 2015 in his study published in 2019 (Murphy, 2019: 1–38).

Although the tax gap and its measurement have started to attract attention in recent years, a limited number of countries and institutions are working on this issue. The measurement of the tax gap requires a comprehensive study. It is difficult to measure the impact of tax avoidance activities on the tax gap. Therefore, these activities were not included in the study. In addition, considering the existence of the informal economy, it should be noted that its measurements are only estimations. There is currently no study on measuring the tax gap in Turkey. This study was planned to provide a source for the gap in the literature.

This study aims to examine the factors causing the tax gap and their effects on it, taking into account the tax gap rates of Turkey in the years 2006–2019. The problematic of the study What are the reasons for the tax gap in Turkey? What are the solutions for reducing the tax gap? In order to get answers to these questions, quarterly tax gap rate, informal economy rate, the share of public expenditures in GDP, tax burden, real GDP per capita, and informal employment rate data for the period 2006:1 – 2019:4 were used. The tax gap and informal economy rates are interpolated to obtain quarterly series using Baxter's (1998) method. The data were tested by Lee and Strazicich's (2003) Unit Root Test with Multiple Structural Breaks and the Johansen, Mosconi and Nielsen Co-integration Approach. Also, Johansen et al. (2000) approach take into account possible structural breaks in time series, and the unit root test method with multiple structural breaks, developed by Lee and Strazicich, was used as a unit root test.

For this purpose, first of all, a literature review is included in the article. Then, the factors causing tax deficit were analyzed by using "Multiple Structural Breakdown Lee and Strazicich Unit Root Test" and "Johansen, Mosconi and Nielsen Cointegration Approach". Finally, the obtained results are presented.

2. Literature Review

There are various concepts related to the tax gap in the literature. Some of the definitions are as follows: The tax gap is the difference between the tax revenues collected and the amount that should be collected in case of tax compliance (Brown & Mazur, 2003: 689–700; Mazur & Plumley, 2007: 569–576; Toder, 2005: 367–378). While defining the tax gap, it is divided into three components as declaration errors, under-reporting and underpayment (Plumley, 2005). He also expressed the tax gap as the hidden economy and hidden income. The value obtained by multiplying the income obtained illegally with the legal tax rate constitutes the tax gap (Giles, 1997(a); Giles (1997b): 63–67). The tax gap is the difference between the overdue taxes that taxpayers must pay and the amount of tax included in the state budget (Gemmell & Hasseldine, 2012: 1–31). According to another definition, the concept of a tax gap is related to the level of tax compliance. It represents the difference between the amount of income to be collected and the amount of income collected in full compliance with the tax (Gökbel, 2011: 22). The IRS defines the tax gap as the net tax gap and the gross tax gap. The gross tax gap is the difference between the tax liability imposed by law for a given tax year and the amount of tax that taxpayers voluntarily pay for that year (Bickley, 1). The gross tax gap is the total amount of the tax liability not paid voluntarily that year. The net tax gap is defined as the unpaid tax amount after all processes for the tax year are completed, and delayed payments are made (Thomas et. al., 1993: 2–20). Both gross and net tax gaps fall into three main groups. These are: undeclared gap, under-declared gap and under-payment gap (Plumley, 2005, 570; Raczkowski, 2015: 61)

In a study conducted to measure the tax gap of the European Union member countries in 2015, the total tax gap of the EU member countries was estimated as 750–900 billion Euros. The highest tax gap is in Italy, France and Germany (Murphy, 2019: 1–38). In another study covering the tax deficit measurement of EU member states for the years 2011–2014, the top five countries with the highest tax gaps for 2014 are Italy (295.9 USD billion), Germany (244.4 USD billion), France (186.5 USD billion), Spain (152 USD billion) and the United Kingdom (96.2 USD billion). The five countries with the lowest tax gaps are Croatia (3.1 USD billion), Latvia (2.9 USD billion), Southern Cyprus (1.4

USD billion), Luxembourg (1.0 USD billion) and Malta (1.0 USD billion) (Raczkowski, 2015: 69). In a study to measure the tax gap of 28 EU member states and 35 countries, including Australia, Canada, Japan, New Zealand, Turkey and Switzerland, the tax gap for 2015 was measured, it is lower in most of the countries (Raczkowski & Mroz, 2018: 568).

CASE has been conducting studies on VAT gap measurements in the European Union member states every year since 2013 and continues to publish its study reports. Last report includes VAT gap measurements for 2018, rapid VAT gap measurements for 2019 using a simplified methodology, and revised measures for 2014–2017. According to the report's results (CASE, 2020: 10–66). In 2018, most European Union (EU) member states saw a slight decrease in GDP growth rate, but economic conditions remained positive to improve tax compliance. The tax gap in the EU was calculated to be 11 % and 140 billion Euros. Among the EU-28, the smallest gaps are in Sweden (0.7 %), Croatia (3.5 %) and Finland (3.6 %), the largest in Romania (33.8 %), Greece (30.1 %) and Lithuania (25.9 %). Half of the EU-28 member states identified a gap of over 9.2 %. Nominally, the largest gap is in Italy (EUR 35.4 billion), the United Kingdom (EUR 23.5 billion) and Germany (EUR 22 billion) (CASE, 2020: 10–66). The UK Revenue Service Her Majesty Revenue and Customs (HMRC) has been working on measuring the tax gap for a long time. HMRC has been publishing the tax gap measurements prepared within its body every year since 2007. Unlike other countries, HMRC measures the tax gap as a general rate and classifies it according to a customer group, tax type and behavior. In the 2022 report, which includes 2020–2021 measurements, the amount of tax gap was measured as 32 billion dollars, and the rate was 5.1 % (HMRC, 2022). The United States, on the other hand, has announced tax gap measurements in specific years. In the 2019 report, the net tax gap for 2011–2013 was 381 billion dollars, and the gross tax gap was 441 billion dollars (IRS, 2019).

3. Econometric Methodology

The study estimated the factors leading to the tax gap and their effects on it by Johansen, Mosconi and Nielsen Co-integration Approach. The reason for adopting this method is that it allows the existence of structural breaks in the long-term relationship. Before performing the co-integration test and model estimation, it is necessary to determine the integration degrees of the series. The approach used for this is the multiple structural break unit root test methods developed by Lee and Strazicich (2003).

3.1. Lee and Strazicich Unit Root Test with Multiple Structural Breaks

Lee and Strazicich propose a two-break unit root test, implying orientation stability in the alternative hypothesis (Lee & Strazicich, 2003: 1082–1089). The Lee and Strazicich test takes into account Models A, B and C expressed in Perron (1989). The data creation process is described as:

$$Y_t = \delta' Z_t + \varepsilon_t \quad \varepsilon_t = \beta\varepsilon_{t-1} + \xi_t . \tag{1}$$

Where Z_t is a vector of exogenous variables, and $\zeta_t \sim i.i.d.N\left(0,\sigma^2\right)$. In Lee and Strazicich (2003), two structural breaks could be handled as follows; Model A $t \geq T_{Bj} + 1$, with $D_{jt} = 1$ and the others are zero $(j = 1,2)$, allows txo breaks at a level defined by $Z_t = [1, t, D_{1t}, D_{2t}]$, where T_{Bj} ise the time period in which the break emerged. Model C includes two breaks at orientation and level defined by $Z_t = [1, t, D_{1t}, D_{2t}, DT_{1t}, DT_{2t}]$, where $DT_{jt} = t$ for $t \geq T_{Bj} + 1$and zero$(j = 1,2)$ for the other cases. Note that data generation process contains breaks as zero $(\beta = 1)$ and stable in alternative $(\beta \langle 1)$ hypothesis. For instance, for A (similarly for Model C), depending on the value of β, zero and alternative hypotheses can be written as follows:

$$H_0 : Y_t = \mu_0 + d_1\beta_{1t} + d_2\beta_{2t} + \upsilon_{1t} \tag{2}$$

$$H_1 : Y_t = \mu_1 + \gamma_t + d_1 D_{1t} + d_2 D_{2t} + \upsilon_{2t} \tag{3}$$

where; υ_{1t} and υ_{2t} are stationary error terms and $\beta_{jt} = 1$ for $t = T_{Bj} + 1$ and $j = 1,2$ and the others are zero. Also $\left(d = d_{1,} d_2\right)'$. For Model C, D_{jt} terms should be added to Equation (3) and DT_{jt}terms should be added to Equation (2.41).

The two-break LM unit root test statistic could be obtained with the use of the following Equation:

$$\Delta Y_t = \delta' \Delta Z_t + \varphi \tilde{S}_{t-1} + \upsilon_t \tag{4}$$

where; with $t = 2,\ldots,T, \tilde{S}_t = Y_t - \psi_x - Z_t\tilde{S}, \tilde{S}$ are the first observations on ψ_x, Y_t and $Z_t$obtained with regression coefficients $Y_1 - Z_1\tilde{S}$ of $\Delta Y_t{}'$ on ΔZ_t. Accordingly, unit root test and LM statistic defined as $\phi = 0$ (Schmidt & Phillips) to test the following hypothesis:

$$\tilde{p} = T\tilde{\phi} \tag{5}$$

$$\tilde{\tau} = \phi = 0 \tag{6}$$

3.2. Johansen, Mosconi and Nielsen Co-integration Approach

Johansen et al. (2000: 216–249) created an alternative test of co-integration if the series for which a long-term equilibrium relationship was sought contained one or two structural breaks during the period they were examining. This co-integration approach is an alternative to the VECM-based co-integration analysis created by Johansen (Johansen, 1988; 231–254); Johansen and Juselius (1990: 169–210).

If Y_t is defined as a vector containing r-numbered p-dimensioned first-order integrated $I(1)$ vectors, then the model proposed by Johansen et al. (2000) could be expressed in VECM as follows:

$$\Delta Y_t = \alpha \begin{pmatrix} \beta \\ \gamma \end{pmatrix} \begin{pmatrix} Y_{t-1} \\ tE_t \end{pmatrix} + \mu E_t + \sum_{i=1}^{k-1} \Gamma_i \Delta Y_{t-i} + \sum_{i=1}^{k} \sum_{j=2}^{q} \psi_{i,i} D_{j,t-i} + \sum_{m=1}^{d} \Phi_m W_{m,t} + \varepsilon_t \tag{7}$$

where; with $t = \ldots, -1, 0, 1, \ldots$, Δ is the first difference operator, k is the number of lags,$E_t = \left[E_{1t} E_{2t} \ldots . E_{qt} \right]'$, for $T_{j-1} + k \le t \le T_j \left(j = 1, \ldots, q \right), E_{j,t} = 1$ and the others, accepted as zero, are q number of dummy variable vectors. Note that, the fist k observation of $E_{j,t} = 1$ effective sub-sample is set to zero. If $t = T_{j-1+i} \left(j = 1, \ldots q \right)$ for the ith observation of $D_{j,t-i,}$ j^{th} period, $D_{j,t-i} = 1$ are "impulse" dummy variables with a value of zero.

As recommended by Hendry and Mizon (1993), "intervention" dummy variable $W_{m,t} \left(m = 1, \ldots d \right)$ is incorporated into the model to normalize the residuals (Hendry & Mizon, 1993: 272–300). The β is cointegration level indicating (p x r)-dimensioned long-term balance relationship and α is a coefficient indicating proper adjustment rate to $\left(p \times r \right)$-dimensioned long-term balance. $\gamma = \left[\gamma_1 \gamma_2 \ldots \gamma_q \right]'$ is $\left(q \times r \right)$- dimensioned vector of long-term trend coefficients. With $i = 1, \ldots, k-1$, Γ_i is $\left(p \times p \right)$-dimensioned, with $j = 2, \ldots q$, $i = 1, \ldots k$ and$m = 1, \ldots d$, $\mu = \left[\mu_1 \mu_2 \ldots \mu_q \right]$ is $\left(p \times p \right)$- dimensioned, $\psi_{j,i}$ is $\left(q \times 1 \right)$-dimensioned and Φ_m, $\left(q \times 1 \right)$- dimensioned short-term parameter matrix and vectors.

For each sub-sample period, $\beta' Y_t + \gamma' t E_t$ indicates stationarity around level and trend breaks. Equation (7) is then called as linear trend model, $H_l \left(r \right)$, in which $\beta' Y_t$ trend and level of co-integration relationship varies from period to period. Note that with $\alpha \beta' = \Pi_{p \times p}$, if $rank \left(\Pi, \Pi_1, \Pi_2, \ldots, \Pi_q \right) \le r$, then the hypothesis for the existence of both deterministic non-stationarity and co-integration vector in each sub-sample is set as $H_l(r): rank(\Pi, \Pi_1, \Pi_2, ..., \Pi_q) \leq r$ rank. With the use of canonical correlation (CanCor)

$$\text{CanCor}\left\{\Delta Y_t, \begin{pmatrix} Y_{t-1} \\ tE_t \end{pmatrix} E_t, \Delta Y_{t-1}, \Delta Y_{t-2}, ..., \Delta Y_{t-(k-1)}, D_{j,t-i}, W_{m,t} \begin{matrix} i = 1, ..., k \\ j = 2, ..., q \\ m = 1, ..., d \end{matrix}\right\} \quad (8)$$

$1 \geq \lambda_1 \geq ... \geq \lambda_p \geq 0$ squared sample canonic correlation values are estimated and likelihood ratio for *r* co-integration relationship $H_l(r)$ against $H_l(p)$ alternative could be written as follows (Johansen et al., 2000).

$$LR\{H_1(r)|H_1(p)\} = -T \sum_{i=r+1}^{p} I_n(1 - \lambda_i) \quad (9)$$

If only the level of co-integration relationship varies from period to period, then the model given in Equation (3.21) is converted into the following form:

$$\Delta Y_t = \alpha \begin{pmatrix} \beta \\ \mu \end{pmatrix}' \begin{pmatrix} Y_{t-1} \\ E_t \end{pmatrix} + \sum_{i=1}^{k-1} \Gamma_i \Delta Y_{t-i} + \sum_{i=1}^{k} \sum_{j=2}^{q} \psi_{j,i} D_{j,t-i} + \sum_{m=1}^{d} \Phi_m W_{m,t} + \varepsilon_t \quad (10)$$

where; $\beta' Y_t + \mu' E_t$ indicates stationarity around level breaks and the level will differ for each period. Equation (3.24) is so called as $H_c(r)$ model. The $1 \geq \lambda_1 \geq ... \geq \lambda_p \geq 0$ squared sample canonic correlations will be obtained from the following estimation:

$$\text{CanCor}\left\{\Delta Y_t, \begin{pmatrix} Y_{t-1} \\ E_t \end{pmatrix}, \Delta Y_{t-1}, \Delta Y_{t-2}, ..., \Delta Y_{t-(k-1)}, D_{j,t-i}, W_{m,t} \begin{matrix} i = 1, ..., k \\ j = 2, ..., q \\ m = 1, ..., d \end{matrix}\right\} \quad (11)$$

In this case, likelihood ratio for *r* co-integration relationship hypothesis $H_c(r)$ against $H_c(p)$ alternative will be again as given in Equation (3.23). As recommended in Johansen et al. (2000), critical values for both $H_1(r)$ and $H_c(r)$ models are derived from Gamma distribution.

4. Model and Data

In this study, the endogenous variables vector to be considered to predict the long-term factors that cause the tax gap and their effects is as follows:

$$Y' = \left[se_t \quad tg_t \quad gdp_t \quad sem_t \quad pe_t \quad tb_t \right] \tag{12}$$

where; se_t represents informal economy, tg_t tax gap, gdp_t GDP per capita, sem_t informal employment, pe_t public expenditures and finally tb_t represent tax burden. With the expectation of two co-integrating vectors in the system and Johansen et al. (2000) multivariate cointegration approach after estimation, following abbreviation matrix is used to determine long-term relationships:

$$\begin{bmatrix} \beta \\ \gamma \end{bmatrix}' = \begin{bmatrix} -1 & 0 & \beta_{gdp} & \beta_{sem} & \beta_{pe} & 0 \\ \beta_{se} & -1 & 0 & 0 & 0 & \beta_{tb} \end{bmatrix} \tag{13}$$

In this matrix, β indicates long-term coefficients and γ represents trend coefficients of sub-periods for two structural breaks. Since Johansen et al. (2000) approach, the estimation method adopted for Equations (12) and (13) is takes into account also the possible structural breaks in the time series, the unit root test method with multiple structural breaks, developed by Lee and Strazicich (2003, 2004), was used as the unit root test in determining the integration degrees of the variables before the estimation.

The data used in the study are quarterly and cover the period 2006:1–2019:4. Informal economy rate, tax gap rate, real GDP per capita, the share of public expenditures in GDP, unregistered employment rate and tax burden are taken as data. The tax gap rate and the informal economy rate are interpolated using Baxter's (1998) method to obtain quarterly series from 2006:1 to 2019:4. Data were obtained from the Central Bank of the Republic of Turkey (TCMB), the Turkish Statistical Institute (TUIK), the World Bank database, and the Federal Reserve Economic Data (FRED). In addition, all series are used in terms of logarithms.

Before examining the long-run relationships between variables, non-stationary features were tested in the study. Using Lee and Strazicich (2003), the stationarity properties of the series in the presence of structural breaks were tested using the series' one and two break minimum LM unit root test. Unit root test results are in Table 1.

Tab. 1: Lee and Strazicich (2003, *2004) unit root test results*

Serial	*Model*	*Delay*	*Break Date*	*λ*	*T-Statistics*	*Critical Value*
se_t	C	2	2010:3 2015:2	0.4 0.6	- 5.21	- 5.67
tg_t	C	3	2008:3 2012:1	0.2 0.4	- 5.62	- 5.59
gdp_t	C	3	2008:2 2012:1	0.2 0.4	- 4.50	- 5.59
sem_t	C	3	2011:1 2014:4	0.4 0.6	- 5.12	- 5.67
pe_t	A	0	2008:4 2010:4	0.2 0.4	- 5.15	- 5.59
tb_t	C	0	2009:2 2018:3	0.2 0.8	- 4.02	- 5.71

Note: Critical values at the 5 % significance level are taken from Lee and Strazicich (2003, 2004).

Table 1 shows that the levels of all variables are not stationary, and there is nonstationarity in a significant structural break. It is observed that there is a structural break in the informal economy in the 2010:3 period and 2015:2 period. The 2010:3 period can be considered as the effects of the 2008 global crisis in Turkey, which began to be felt in the USA in September 2008, resulted in the sudden depreciation of the real estate market in the USA and the increase in personal bankruptcies, and affected the whole world in a short time. The impact of crisis periods covers the past and the next few years. Another structural break in the informal economy coincides with the 2015:2 period. This situation can be considered the initial effect of the foreign exchange and debt crisis, which started to be felt in Turkey in 2016. It started with fluctuations in foreign exchange prices. It began with the significant depreciation of the Turkish lira in waves. In the following periods, it showed its effect with the increased unpaid debts and the economic contraction. Inflation remained in double digits and led to stagflation. Income inequalities and the current account tax gap have increased. The foreign exchange and debt crisis, which started to become more evident as of 2016, was felt most socially and economically in the exchange rates and the foreign exchange reserves of the Central Bank of the Republic of Turkey (TCMB). The dollar rate, which was 2.95 TL in January 2016, became 3.76 TL in January 2018, 5.21 TL in January 2019, 5.97 TL in January 2020, and 7.36 TL in January 2021. Therefore, these developments in the economy also have a significant impact on the informal economy.

As seen in Tab. 1, a structural break is observed in the tax gap in the 2008:3 and 2012:1 periods. The year 2008 can be considered the reflection of the "2008 Global Economic Crisis" in the structural break.

The structural break in public expenditures is in the 2008:4 and 2010:4 periods. In the 2008:4 period, one of the periods when the 2008 crisis began to be felt, there was a decrease in tax revenues and GDP. It is normal to experience a decrease in tax revenues, which has the largest share of the state's income sources, and a decrease in public expenditures due to a decrease in GDP.

The structural breaks in the tax burden are in the 2009:2 and 2018:3 periods. In the Turkish Tax System, tax accrual-collection periods can be considered the reason for the fluctuations in the tax burden. Because the payment period of corporate tax, which has an important share in tax revenues, is April 30. Considering that it covers the first and second quarters, it is normal that tax revenues and tax burden rates are higher in these periods. We can relate the structural break in 2009:2 to this situation. Structural breaks in GDP are in the periods 2008:2 and 2012:1.

The fact that the breakdown in GDP coincided with the 2008 crisis period and the following years can be associated with the global crisis.

Finally, the structural breaks in informal employment are in the 2011:1 and 2014:4 periods. Employers, workers or self-employed try to hide their income by engaging in informal economic activities to avoid financial obligations such as taxes and insurance premiums and eliminate bureaucratic procedures. Many reasons, such as inflation, inequalities in income distribution, unemployment, and reduction costs to compete, the laws are not simple and clear, the penalties are not deterrent, and the low education level of the workforce is effective on informal employment. In recent years, great work has been carried out to reduce unregistered employment, and success has been achieved. The informal employment rate, which was 46.97 % in 2006, decreased to 39.02 % in 2012, 33.49 % in 2016, 33.42 % in 2018, and 30.59 % in 2020.

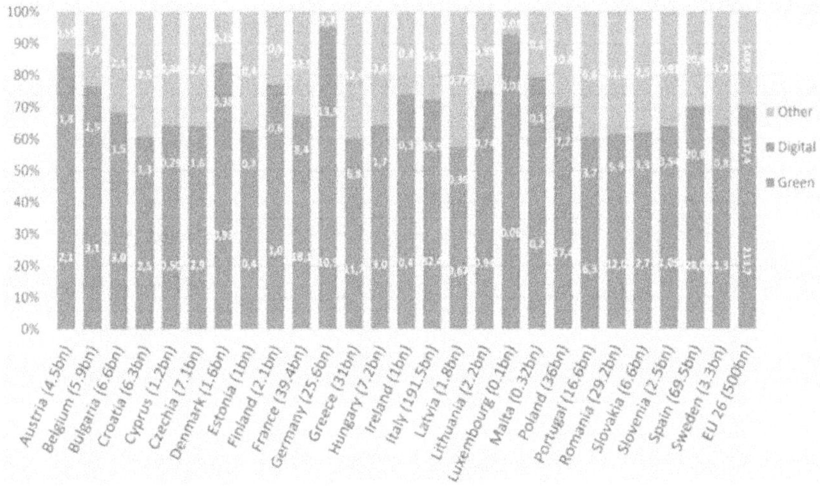

Chart 1: *Time Graphs in the Presence of Structural Breaks*

After examining the non-stationary properties of the series, the co-integration test in the presence of structural breaks was performed by Johansen et al. (2000) was used. The minimum value of the Akaike Information Criteria (AIC) was adopted to select the optimum lag length and the lag length was estimated as $k = 3$. Table 2 shows two co-integration vectors (r=2) for the $H_l\left(r\right)$ model, which shows the changes in level in the long run. LR statistics of VECM restriction tests are in Tab. 3.

Tab. 2: *2008:3–2012:1 for fracture pair* Johansen et al. (2000) *trace statistics*

$H_0\left(H_1\right)$	**Model** $H_l\left(r\right)$
$r = 0\left(r \geq 1\right)$	265.31 (173.08)
$r = 1\left(r \geq 2\right)$	163.24 (135.23)
$r = 2\left(r \geq 3\right)$	91.34 (101.44)
$r = 3\left(r \geq 4\right)$	53.45 (71.77)
$r = 4\left(r \geq 5\right)$	29.10 (46.02)
$r = 5\left(r \geq 6\right)$	13.19 (23.85)

Note: The parentheses give critical values derived according to the gamma distribution.

Tab. 3. *VECM test results for 2008:3–2012:1 fracture pair*

	Null Hypothesis (H_0)	**LR Statistics**
Individual Exclusion		
se_t	$\beta_{se} = 0$	15.408 (0.000)
tg_t	$\beta_{tg} = 0$	8.736 (0.012)
gdp_t	$\beta_{gdp} = 0$	24.998 (0.000)
sem_t	$\beta_{sem} = 0$	28.297 (0.000)
pe_t	$\beta_{pe} = 0$	40.212 (0.000)
tb_t	$\beta_{tb} = 0$	24.703 (0.000)
Weak Externality		
se_t	$\alpha_{se} = 0$	43.131 (0.000)
tg_t	$\alpha_{tg} = 0$	48.631 (0.000)
gdp_t	$\alpha_{gdp} = 0$	2.085 (0.35)
sem_t	$\alpha_{sem} = 0$	5.808 (0.05)
pe_t	$\alpha_{pe} = 0$	3.273 (0.19)
tb_t	$\alpha_{tb} = 0$	0.091 (0.95)
Presence of Structural Breaks		
For the first break (2008:3)	$\gamma_1 = \gamma_2$	26.604 (0.000)
For the second break (2012:1)	$\gamma_2 = \gamma_3$	36.023 (0.000)
Normality		
Asymmetry	$s = 0$	1.119 (0.358)
Kurtosis	$k = 3$	0.144 (0.704)
Asymmetry and kurtosis	$s = 0$ and $k = 3$	4.619 (0.464)

Note: Values in parentheses give marginal significance levels.

Table 3 shows that each variable is included in the co-integration space for the break test. In addition, the bottom panel of Tab. 3 shows that the informal economy and tax deficit are internal (endogenous), while GDP, public expenditures, informal employment and tax burden are external (exogenous). In addition, the null hypothesis that the two structural breaks do not affect their long-run relationship was rejected for both breaks. Apart from this, the residuals obtained from the predicted model could not be rejected for the null hypothesis of normality asymmetry, kurtosis and both asymmetry and kurtosis. Accordingly, the residues are normally distributed.

The existence of two co-integration vectors in the system and the endogenous nature of informal economy and tax gap at the same time necessitate the definition of long-term relationships. At least two constraints per co-integration vectors are required to fully describe the system (Pesaran & Shin, 2000: 49–87). The following equation of constraints in terms of economic prospects to determine long-run relationships was used in this study. Therefore, the long-run elasticities for r=2, q=3 and $H_I(r)$ model could be obtained by testing the following constraint matrix and defining the informal economy and tax gap equations.

$$\begin{bmatrix} \beta \\ \gamma \end{bmatrix}' = \begin{bmatrix} -1 & 0 & \beta_{gdp} & \beta_{sem} & \beta_{pe} & 0 & \gamma_{11} & \gamma_{12} & \gamma_{13} \\ \beta_{se} & -1 & 0 & 0 & 0 & \beta_{tb} & \gamma_{21} & \gamma_{22} & \gamma_{23} \end{bmatrix} \tag{1}$$

It can be obtained by testing the constraint matrix and defining the informal economy and tax gap equations.

The model is structured on two specified equations in one system. In the first equation of the system, the informal economy and its determinants, GDP, unregistered employment rates and the ratio of public expenditures to GDP are included. In the second equation, informal employment rates and tax burden rates are the tax gap and its components.

There is a positive effect between the informal economy rate and the tax gap rate. Table 4 gives the defined long-term equations and the identification test results. The fact that the constraints imposed as a result of the identification test cannot be rejected implies that the model is fully determined and that the parameters can be interpreted as long-term flexibility (Johansen, 2005: 93–104). Accordingly, when the informal economy equation is examined, it is seen that every 1 % increase in GDP decreases the informal economy by 0.015 %, and every 1 % increase in informal employment increases the informal economy by 0.587 %. Finally, every 1 % increase in public expenditures decreases the informal economy by 0.055 %. When the other determined equation, the tax gap equation, is examined, it is seen that every 1 % increase in the informal economy in economy increases the tax deficit by 0.726 %, and every 1 % increase in the tax burden increases the tax gap by 0.085 %. In addition, the adjustment coefficients are negative and significant. Accordingly, short-term deviations in the informal economy disappear by approximately 20 % each period, and short-term deviations in the tax gap by approximately 50 % each period.

Tab. 4: *Defined long-term coefficient matrix and identification test results*

Defined Equations	β_{se}	β_{tb}	β_{gdp}	β_{sem}	β_{pe}	β_{tb}	γ_1	γ_2	γ_3	α_{se}	α_{tb}	s
Shadow Economy	-1	0	-0.015	0.587	-0.055	0	-0.019	-0.032	-0.002	-0.19	0	6.008 (0.111)
Tax Gap	0.726	-1	0	0	0	0.085	-0.011	-0.019	0.003	0	-0.48	

5. Conclusion

The size of the tax gap gives information about the cyclical economic situation of the countries. It indicates that the countries' socio-economic policies are wrong and need to be corrected. In this respect, the tax gap measurement has gained importance, especially recently. There was no study on the measurement of the tax gap in Turkey. This study was carried out to provide a source for the gap in the literature.

For this reason, in this study, the factors causing the tax gap in Turkey and their effects on the tax gap were investigated. The study covering the period 2006:1, 2019:4, informal economy rate, tax gap rate, the share of public expenditures in GDP, tax burden, real GDP per capita, and unregistered employment rates were taken as data. Structural breaks identified in the study are as follows: 2010:3 and 2015:2 in the informal economy, 2008:3 and 2012:1 in tax deficit, 2008:4, 2010:4 in public expenditures, 2009:2 and 2018:3 in tax burden, 2008:2 and 2012:1 in GDP and unregistered employment in 2011:1 and 2014:4 periods. The results showed that there is a positive relationship between the informal economy rate and the tax gap rate. In other words, every 1 % increase in the informal economy increases the tax gap by 0726 %. In addition, the elasticity of the informal economy concerning GDP was found to be -1. Every 1 % increase in GDP reduces the informal economy by 0.015 %. Every 1 % increase in informal employment increases the informal economy by 0587 %. Every 1 % increase in public spending reduces the informal economy by 0.055 %. A positive relationship was also found between the tax burden and the tax gap. Every 1 % increase in the tax burden increases the tax gap by 0.085 %.

The excess tax burden is an important factor that increases the tax gap. High tax rates and inefficient tax collection lead taxpayers to informal activities. It is a situation accepted in the literature that as the level of taxation increases in an economy, the desire to participate in informal economic activities and the level of tax evasion increase. The increase in informal economic activities reduces the government's tax revenues. If the government, whose taxable income is decreasing, chooses to increase the tax rates more to increase its revenues, the informal economy will continue to grow. This situation puts governments in a vicious circle. The increase in the informal economy increases the tax deficit. Therefore, to reduce the tax gap, it is necessary to reduce the informal economy first. For this, the informal economy must be determined. Determining the size of the current informal economy in an economy is also very important in terms of economic policies. Because when the informal economy reaches significant dimensions, it causes deviations in economic policies by distorting the behavior of some variables such as GDP, unemployment rate, tax rates, tax revenues, and public expenditures.

Combating tax losses and evasion and ensuring efficiency in the financial system is one of the main tasks of governments. The tax gap is also a problem that occurs due to the existence of tax losses and evasion. In order to reduce the tax gap, it is necessary to fight against tax losses and evasion and to reduce the informal economy. For this purpose, there is a need for arrangements to prevent informality in the financial system. In addition, it is beneficial to increase the controls. The height of the informal economy indicates the ineffectiveness of the financial law system and tax audit. Therefore, deterrent and heavy tax penalties should be applied.

References

Baxter, M. (1998). *Interpolating Annual Data into Monthly or Quarterly Data. Methodological Series,* No. 6. The Government Statistical Service, UK.

Bickley J. M. (2012)"Tax Gap, Tax Compliance, and Proposed Legislation in the 112th Congress", Congressional Research Service.

Brown, R. E., & Mazur, M. J. (2003). "IRS's Comprehensive Approach to Compliance Measurement" *National Tax Journal, 56*(3), pp. 689–700.

CASE(Center for Social and Economic Research). (2020). Study and Report on the VAT Gap in the EU-28 Member States: Final Report, https://www.case-research.eu/en/study-and-reports-on-the-vat-gap-in-the-eu-28-member-states-2020-final-report-101489. (13.01.2021).

Gemmel, N., & Hasseldine J. (2012). "The Tax Gap-A Methodological Review", Working Paper 09/2012 in Public Finance, Victoria Business School, University of Wellington.

Giles, D. E. A. (1997a). "The Hidden Economy and the Tax Gap in New Zealand: A Latent Variable Analysis, New Zealand, " Working Paper 97-08. Department of Economics, University of Victoria. https://ideas.repec.org/p/vic/vicewp/9807.html. (15.09.2019).

Giles, D. E. A. (1997b). "Causality Between the Measured and Underground Economies in New Zealand," New Zealand, *Applied Economics Letters, 4*, pp. 63–67.

Gökbel, D. (2011). *Vergiden Kaçınmanın Önlenmesi*, Ankara, Seçkin Yayıncılık.

HMRC. (2022). Measuring Tax Gaps 2022 edition, London: HM Revenue & Customs, https://www.gov.uk/government/statistics/measuring-tax-gaps, (05.11.2022).

Hendry, D. F., & Mizon, G. E. (1993). Evaluating Dynamic Econometric Models by Encompassing the VAR, in Phillips, P.C.P. (Ed.), *Models, Methods and Applications of Econometrics*. Basil Blackwell, Oxford.

IRS. (2019). Understanding the Latest Tax Gap Estimates and Overall Taxpayer Compliance; https://www.irs.gov/newsroom/understanding-the-latest-tax-gap-estimates-and-overall-taxpayer-compliance, (09.11.2020).

Johansen, S. (1988). "Statistical Analysis of Cointegration Vectors", *Journal of Economic Dynamics and Control, 12*, pp. 231–254.

Johansen S, (2005). "Interpretation of Cointegrating Coefficients in the Cointegrated Vector Autoregressive Model", Oxford Bulletin of Economics and Statistics, *67*, pp. 1–134.

Johansen, S., & Juselius, K. (1990). "Maximum Likelihood Estimation and Inference of Cointegration with Application to the Demand for Money", *Oxford Bulletin of Economics and Statistics, 52*, pp. 169–210.

Johansen, S., Mosconi, R., & Nielsen, B. (2000). "Cointegration Analysis in the Presence of Structural Breaks in the Deterministic Trend", *Econometrics Journal, 3*, pp. 216–249.

Joint Committee on Taxation. (2019). Overview of the Tax Gap, (JCX-19-19), May 8, 2019. https://www.jct.gov/publications/2019/jcx-19-19/ (12.01.2020).

Lee, J., & Strazicich, M. C. (2003). "Minimum Lagrange Multiplier Unit Root Test With Two Structural Breaks", *Review of Economics and Statistics, 85*, pp. 1082–1089.

Mazur, M. J., & Plumley, A. H. (2007). "Understanding the Tax Gap." *National Tax Journal, 60*(3), pp. 569–576.

Mróz, B. (2010). "The Shadow Economy in Poland: Causes, Manifestations, Economic and Social Effects, Journal of Management and Financial Sciences", *Warsaw School of Economics, Collegium of Management and Finance, 3*(3), (April), pp. 96–118.

Murphy, R. (2019). The European Tax Gap, *Tax Research UK*, pp. 1–37.

Pesaran, M. H., & Shin Y. (2000). "Long-Run Structural Modeling", *Econometric Reviews, 21*, pp. 49–87.

Plumley, A. H. (2005). "Preliminary Update of the Tax Year 2001 Individual Income Tax Underreporting Gap Estimates", Paper Presented At the 2005 Internal Revenue Service Research Conference IRS, Washington, DC.

Raczkowski, K. (2015). "Measuring the Tax Gap in the European Economy," *Journal of Economics and Management, 21*(3) Poland Warsaw, pp. 58–72.

Raczkowski, K., & Mroz, B. (2018). "Tax Gap in the Global Economy," *Journal of Money Laundering Control, 21*(4), pp. 545–554.

Schneider, F. (2002). "The Size and Development of the Shadow Economies of 22 Transition and 21 OECD Countries," IZA Discussion Paper, No. 514, http://repec.iza.org/dp514.pdf. (14.01.2020).

Schneider, F., Buehn, A., & Claudio, E. M. (2010). "Shadow Economies All Over the World: New Estimates for 162 Countries from 1999 to 2007," Policy Research Working Paper, The World Bank Development Research Group Poverty and Inequality Team and Europe and Central Asia Region Human Development Economics Unit, No. 5356. http://documents1.worldbank.org/curated/en/311991468037132740/pdf/WPS5356.pdf. (15.09.2019).

Thomas, W., Convery, E. A., & Risler, M. H. (1993). "Federal Tax Compliance Research Gross and Net Employment Tax Gap Estimates for 1984–1997", Internal Revenue Services.

Toder, E. (2005). "What is the Tax Gap?" *Tax Notes, 117*(4), pp. 367–378.

Overwiew of The Tax Gap. (2019). Joint Committee on Taxation, 9 May 2019. https://www.jct.gov/publications/2019/jcx-19-19/ (12.01.2020).

Müslüm Gümüş[1] & Mustafa Erkan Üyümez[2]

The Concept of "Valuation" In Determining The Truth of Taxable Income[*]

1. Introduction

"Valuation", one of the end-of-period transactions that is critical in determining the fair value of taxable income, refers to recording the assets and liabilities of the enterprise with their fair values. Valuation, which involves the determination of the monetary value to be taken as a basis in the first recognition of assets and resources and their presentation in the financial statements in the following periods, is a process that directly affects the operating profit for the period (Duman & Yücenurşen, 2017: 1310). Valuation regulations are detailed in both the Tax Procedure Law, No. 213 (TPL)[3] and the Turkish Commercial Code, No. 6102 (TCC)[4].

While the Turkish Accounting Standards (TAS) and Turkish Financial Reporting Standards (TFRS) view valuation as the determination of the financial status of the enterprises, and accordingly the results of their activities (Duman & Yücenurşen, 2017: 1310), tax legislation considers it as the ascertainment of economic asset prices to determine the tax base (Küçük, 2018: 47). TAS/TFRS and TPL differ in their valuation criteria, as TAS/TFRS aims to present the economic assets in the financial statements over their current and fair values,

1 Hakkari University, FEAS, Department of Public Finance, muslumgumus@hakkari.edu.tr, ORCID:0000-0001-9790-7028

2 Anadolu University, FEAS, Department of Public Finance, meuyumez@anadolu.edu.tr, ORCID:0000-0001-7567-3486

* This paper is derived from the doctoral thesis titled "Ensuring Truth In Taxation Of Business Income: Problems And Solutions", which was carried out under the supervision of Prof. Dr. M. Erkan ÜYÜMEZ and defended by Müslüm GÜMÜŞ at Anadolu University Social Sciences Institute Department of Public Finance on the date of 28.06.2022. And also this paper was presented as a summary paper at the 36. International Public Finance Conference /Türkiye on 29.10.2022.

3 https://www.mevzuat.gov.tr/mevzuat?MevzuatNo=213&MevzuatTur=1&MevzuatTertip=4

4 https://www.mevzuat.gov.tr/mevzuat?MevzuatNo=6102&MevzuatTur=1&MevzuatTertip=5.

whereas the valuation provisions in the TPL aim to determine the tax claim (Ergin, 2016: 20). These differences also reveal two different profit-loss situations (Duman & Yücenurşen, 2017: 1323). Such use of different valuation measures in standards and tax legislation makes it difficult to determine the fair value of business profitability, affecting the truth in taxation.

2. Truth in Taxation

Conceptually, the concept of "*truth*" basically refers to "*what concretely and objectively exists independently of consciousness*" (Hançerlioğlu, 2016: 131). According to the Turkish Language Association (TDK), truth is defined as something that exists independent of consciousness, as opposed to things that are thought, designed, imagined, objective and resulting from the realization of possibility.[5] According to the Oxford Dictionary, truth is defined as "*the true facts about something, rather than the things that have been invented or guessed.*"[6] This is directly related to the concept of "actual nature" in the provision of "the taxable event and the actual nature of the transactions related to this event are essential" regulated in Article 3 of the TPL. This provision, regulated under the title of "Proof", is based on a rule regarding the economic approach in tax law rather than a proof rule (Öncel et al., 2018: 27). The economic approach, which is an application of the teleological interpretation, advises going beyond the legal form and taking into account the actual economic characteristics and contents in the determination of the taxable event and the interpretation of the provisions of the law. (Öncel et al., 2018: 27). Taxation, whose substance is based on economic activity, requires going beyond the form of the concrete material event and revealing the economic substance (Akkaya, 2002: 34).

Truth in tax law means that form and substance are the same. Truth in tax law necessitates dealing with real life events as they fulfill their tax obligations (Taylar, 2013: 202). Thus, truth in taxation means that taxation is performed on the basis of the taxable event and the transactions related to these events (economic substance), and that the events and transactions are regulated and determined on the basis of the criteria and principles that ensure justice in taxation. In other words, the truth in taxation means that tax legislation is regulated according to the principles that will ensure justice and that taxation is carried out on the basis

5 Glossary of Philosophy Terms – 1975. https://sozluk.gov.tr/.
6 https://www.oxfordlearnersdictionaries.com/definition/english/truth?q=truth.

of the actual nature and content of the taxable event and the transactions related to these events.

3. Taxation of Income

Income is the most important criterion in achieving the ability to pay taxes and ensuring equality in taxation. However, some problems are encountered in determining taxable income, which may have some adverse consequences for tax justice. Income, which essentially constitutes the subject, base and source of income tax, is structurally an economic concept (Turhan, 1993: 116). Therefore, definitions of income in economic and financial terms and income definitions in tax law may not match (Özer, 1975: 6). In general, income is defined as all kinds of earnings and revenues that a natural person earns in return for his/her work or wealth in a certain period (Özer, 1975: 6). Income can be described as surplus value resulting from capital and/or work. Income is described as the flow of values obtained in return for the inclusion of production factors in the production process (Aksoy, 1994: 357). In economic terms, income is defined as the sum of goods and services that a person can consume during a certain period (usually a year), provided that they remain at the same wealth at the beginning and end (Aksoy, 1994: 357).

In the "*Conceptual Framework for Financial Reporting*", income is defined as *"increases in assets or decreases in liabilities that lead to increases in equity, excluding contributions made by claimants on equity"*.[7] In financial terms, *income* means *profit* (Üyümez, 1998: 11).

Since accepting the definitions of *income* based on scientific criteria from different perspectives is not possible in the context of tax law due to technical difficulties, this concept has also been addressed by the science of finance, which has developed the resource and net increase theories to define *income* (Turhan, 1993: 116–117).

In tax laws, a separate definition of income from the economic concept of income is made by combining both the source and net increase theories. Tax laws determine income by explicitly counting or defining taxable income, taking into account temporary income in their definition of it. This approach in tax laws is characterized as the financial definition of income (Erginay, 1998: 88).

---

7 Conceptual Framework for Financial Reporting (2018). Paragraph 4.68. Retrieved at: https://www.kgk.gov.tr/Portalv2Uploads/files/Duyurular/v2/TMS/Finansal%20Raporlamaya%20%C4%B0li%C5%9Fkin%20Kavramsal%20%C3%87er%C3%A7eve%20(2018%20S%C3%BCr%C3%BCm%C3%BC).pdf

A generally accepted definition of income has not been made; however, various countries have created their own income tax legislations based on income theories. In the Turkish tax system, the first income tax in the modern sense was applied in 1950 (Arıkan & İnneci, 2016: 12). Today, the income tax regulation in the Turkish tax system is the Income Tax Act, NO. 193 (ITA)[8], which came into force in 1961 and has undergone many changes and regulations since then. In addition, the income elements regulated within the scope of this law are also used in the taxation of corporation earnings, if they are obtained by corporations. The legal regulation regarding the tax to be collected on corporation earnings is the Corporation Tax Act, No. 5520 (CTA)[9].

In the 1st article of the Income Tax Act, which regulates the subject of tax, income is defined as "the net amount of earnings and revenues earned by a natural person in a calendar year" and in the 2nd article, the elements of income are listed under seven headings. One of these earnings and revenues is commercial income.

According to the regulation in the Income Tax Act, commercial income is "*earnings arising from all kinds of commercial and industrial activities and commercial earnings is determined according to the provisions of the TPL and the actual (balance sheet or business account basis) or simplified procedures explained in this law*" (ITA, art. 37). Commercial income on balance sheet basis it is defined in ITA, art. 38 as "the positive difference between the values of the equity in the undertaking at the end and at the beginning of the accounting period". In addition, it is regulated that during this period "the values added to the enterprise will be deducted from this difference" and "values withdrawn from the enterprise will be added to this difference". During the determination of the commercial profit in this way, "*the valuation provisions of the TPL and the 40th and 41st articles of the ITA must be complied with*" (ITA, art. 38).

Balance sheet, financial balance sheet, prepared in line with the regulations in tax laws, as well as the balance sheet prepared in accordance with the provisions of the TCC, are the commercial balance sheets (Öncel et al., 2018: 266). While the tables created in accordance with the accounting and financial reporting standards are prepared on the basis of commercial profit (commercial balance sheet), the tables, books, records and documents prepared according to the TPL

---

8 https://www.mevzuat.gov.tr/mevzuat?MevzuatNo=193&MevzuatTur=1&MevzuatTertip=4.

9 https://www.mevzuat.gov.tr/mevzuat?MevzuatNo=5520&MevzuatTur=1&MevzuatTertip=5.

are based on the financial profit (financial balance sheet) (Hacıköylü, 2017: 10). The concept of profit calculated according to tax laws, the purpose of which is to secure tax receivables, and the concept of profit determined according to the flexible rules of commercial law often do not overlap (Öncel et al., 2018: 266). The tax law rules differ from commercial law rules mainly in deductible and non-deductible expenses, valuation and depreciation provisions, exemptions and exceptions. Therefore, such differences force taxpayers and responsible persons to prepare a tax balance sheet while preparing the balance sheet (Öncel et al., 2018: 266). As the provisions of the TPL contain mandatory provisions with a protective point of view trying to prevent the tax base from being eroded and leave little initiative to the taxpayer while determining the tax base, it is the accuracy of the tax base rather than the truthfulness that is emphasized in the financial statements (Uçan, 2015: 11). The concept of taxable profit, which is calculated for tax purposes other than the concept of commercial profit, prevents the establishment of a correct ratio between the commercial profit appearing in the income statements and the tax amount to be paid, which causes the commercial profit / loss amounts in the income statement to be reflected incorrectly (Balcı, 2012: 160).

TCC article 88 and temporary article 1 states that natural or legal person traders, who are obliged to keep books as per the laws to which they are subject, must prepare their individual or consolidated financial statements in accordance with the Turkish Accounting Standards (TAS) published by the Public Oversight Accounting and Auditing Standards Authority (POA). In addition, financial statements are urged to be prepared in accordance with International Financial Reporting Standards (IFRS) by stressing that POA is authorized to set special standards and regulations for various sectors and businesses. This regulation in the TCC is aimed at reflecting the financial statements in the most accurate way to meet the information needs of a large audience of the business (Uçan, 2015: 10).

4. National and International Regulations in Determining the True Income

In order to ensure that the activities and results of enterprises and enterprises that keep books in the balance sheet method in Türkiye are accounted in a healthy and reliable way, to ensure that the information presented to the relevant parties through financial statements reflect the real situation by preserving their consistency and comparability, and to facilitate auditing in enterprises, The Accounting System Implementation General Communiqué (ASIGC) Serial No.

1 by the Ministry of Treasury and Finance was published in the Official Gazette in 1992 and its implementation has been made mandatory since 1994.[10] The following are targeted with the ASIGC (Dinç & Atabay, 2019: 181):

- Delivering sufficient and correct accounting information to those who are in a decision-making position,
- Comparing different periods of the same business with different businesses,
- Ensuring that account names in the financial statements have the same meaning for all segments,
- Ensuring comprehensibility through the unity of terms in accounting, and
- Establishing an element of trust between businesses and those concerned.

In line with the purposes above, Uniform Chart of Accounts (UCA) has been implemented. The UCA appears as a system that has many deficiencies in today's accounting practices due to its association with the Turkish tax legislation rather than the truth principle (Dinç & Atabay, 2019: 180). The ASIGC states that "enterprises will carry out their accounting systems in accordance with the rules stipulated in the Communiqué and its Annex but will take into account the special provisions in tax laws during the determination of financial profit". Since there is insufficient explanation about the valuation of assets and liabilities in the communiqué, businesses inevitably use tax rules when valuing (Dinç & Atabay, 2019: 180).

The determination of the tax base is important for both businesses and tax administration. In order for a taxation system to function effectively in the legal sense, there must be clarity in accounting at every stage from recording transactions to reporting. Thus, financial statements in accounting have to be determined according to the generally accepted principles to reflect the truth. Erroneous and manipulative reporting practices were among the reasons for 1929 Economic Depression, and the effect of globalization and the existence of multinational companies brought the need for a common accounting system to be used worldwide.[11] For this purpose, the Financial Accounting Standards Board (FASB) was established in 1973 and internationally accepted accounting standards were established under the name of International Accounting Standards (IAS) and International Financial Reporting Standards (IFRS) (Erol & Aslan,

10 ASIGC (MSUGT) with serial number 1, Official Gazette dated 26.12.1992 and numbered 21447. https://www.resmigazete.gov.tr/arsiv/21447_1.pdf Erişim tarihi: 16.01.2021.

11 https://www.accounting.com/resources/gaap/#:~:text=Generally%20accepted%20accounting%20principles%2C%20or,approved%20accounting%20methods%20and%20practices Retrieved: 07.01.2021

2017: 55). In Türkiye, these standards have been translated and brought into national legislation since 2002 and implemented in publicly traded companies since 2005. The Public Oversight Accounting and Auditing Standards Authority was established in 2011 with the Turkish Commercial Code No. 6102 and determined the Turkish Financial Reporting Standards and Turkish Accounting Standards to ensure that financial reports are prepared and audited by complying with international standards (Ergin, 2016: V). The TASs and TFRSs published by POA are a translated version of the IAS and IFRS. The standards translated from IFRS and IFRS by POA and implemented as TASs and TFRSs in Türkiye, use the fair value basis based on market value in valuation.

There are some incompatibilities between the TAS/TFRS and the TPL. Since the provisions of the TPL contain mandatory provisions, organized with a protective point of view trying to prevent the tax base from being eroded and leave little initiative to the taxpayers when determining the tax base, the financial statements focus on the preparation of the tax base in line with the stipulated rules rather than compliance with the truth (Uçan, 2015: 10). In TAS/TFRS, the aim is to present the financial statements that will meet the information needs of the broad masses that make up the business environment in the most realistic way. Due to the incompatibility between TAS/TFRS and TPL, some problems are encountered in the process from accounting to taxation of corporation earnings.

5. Valuation Processes in Determining True Income

A number of accounting processes are carried out to determine of the truth income, which relate to the recording of economic events related to the enterprise and the valuation of economic assets (Üyümez, 1998: 73). To determine the tax base correctly, businesses should consider the basic concepts of accounting and valuation provisions for every transaction while making their accounting records (Tuna, 2010: 6). Valuation is a two-stage process. In the first stage, the amount of economic asset subject to valuation is determined through inventory. In the second stage, the economic asset whose amount is determined has a value in terms of a certain currency as of the valuation day (Küçük, 2018: 40). The purpose of the valuation is to determine the monetary value and profit-loss status of the economic assets and liabilities of the enterprises on the balance sheet date (Yiğit Şakar, 2020: 114). The valuation process is aimed at bringing the recorded values of the tangible and intangible goods and rights in the business to their fair values on the valuation day (Şimşek et al., 2016: 1).

Regulations regarding valuation are contained in the TPL and TCC. The provisions regarding valuation in the TPL are included in articles 258–298. In

TPL, valuation is defined as Art. 258). In the valuation, *"the values of the economic assets on the days a"appraisal and determination of economic assets related to the calculation of tax bases"* (TPL, *nd times indicated in the tax laws are taken into account"* (TPL, Art. 259). In the valuation, *"each of the economic assets is taken into account on its own"* (TPL, Art. 260). Unlike the TCC, the TPL has adopted different minimum valuation criteria according to the types of economic assets (Öncel et al., 2018: 267). In art. 261 of the TPL nine valuation measures are specified according to the type and nature of the economic asset, which comprise the *"cost value, stock exchange value, savings value, book value, nominal value, current value, value of equal, tax value and purchase price"*. In addition, it can be observed that the "inflation adjustment and revaluation rate regulation" and the regulations related to valuation in the repeated article 298 have much more extensive coverage than the TCC. However, with the reference to TAS/TFRS in the TCC, the framework regarding the valuation has become broader.

Article 69 of the TCC states that *"traders have to comply with and apply the interpretations that are an integral part of Turkish Accounting Standards, accounting principles in the conceptual framework and published by the POA"*. However, Article 64/5 of the TCC states that *"natural and legal persons subject to this Law, pursuant to the provisions of the Tax Procedure Law No. 213 regarding bookkeeping and timing and have to comply with the regulations made pursuant to the authority contained in the 175th and repeated 257th articles of the same Law."* For this reason, taxpayers subject to independent auditing, *have to calculate their corporation or income tax bases by adding and/or deducting the positive and negative effects of the different valuation provisions in the Tax Procedure Law, non-tax-deductable expenses and tax-exempt incomes to the commercial profit, based on the commercial profit generated in their uniform financial statements prepared according to TAS.*[12] During the determination of taxable corporation income, the balance sheets and income statements prepared in line with TAS should also be rearranged by the companies according to the TPL, and therefore ASIGC.

5.1. TFRS 13 fair value

One of the valuation principles in TFRS is "fair value". Fair value, which allows the presentation of actual information in financial statements. TFRS 13 is *"a financial reporting standard that defines fair value, regulates the framework for*

---

12 Communiqué on the Conceptual Framework of Financial Reporting No: 209. Retrieved at: https://www.mevzuat.gov.tr/File/GeneratePdf?mevzuatNo=14701&mevzuatTur=Teblig&mevzuatTertip=5, Accessed: 07.06.2022.

fair value measurement in a single TFRS and specifies disclosures regarding fair value measurement".[13] TFRS defines fair value as *"a market-based measurement that is not an entity-specific measurement"* and states that the definition of fair value focuses on assets and liabilities.[14]

TFRS 13 defines fair value as "*the price that would be received to sell an asset or paid to transfer a liability in an orderly transaction between market participants at the measurement date*". The purpose of fair value measurement is to *"estimate the price in an orderly transaction at the measurement date for the sale of an asset or the transfer of a liability between market participants under prevailing market conditions. This purpose is the same both for assets or liabilities for which market transactions or information are observable, and for assets or liabilities for which market transactions or information are not observable."*[15]

A fair value measurement is made for a particular asset or liability. Therefore, when measuring the fair value of an asset or liability, an entity *"takes into account features that market participants would consider pricing the asset or liability at the measurement date (for example, the condition and location of the asset and any restrictions on the sale or use of the asset)".*[16] *"When the price of an identical asset or liability is not observable, an entity measures fair value using another valuation method that maximizes the use of relevant observable inputs and minimizes the use of unobservable inputs".*[17]

Valuation methods commonly used in fair value measurement are market approach, cost approach and income approach (Sağlam & Yolcu, 2019: 105). An entity uses valuation methods that are consistent with one or more of these approaches to measure fair value. In some cases, a single valuation method may be appropriate (for example, when valuing an asset or liability using quote prices for identical assets or liabilities in an active market) and in others (for example, when valuing a cash-generating unit), more than one valuation method may be appropriate. (Sağlam & Yolcu, 2019: 106). If more than one valuation

13 https://kgk.gov.tr/Portalv2Uploads/files/Duyurular/v2/TMS_TFRS_Setleri/2021/K%C4%B1rm%C4%B1z%C4%B1_Kitap/TFRS%2013(1).pdf Accessed: 03.01.2021.

14 https://kgk.gov.tr/Portalv2Uploads/files/Duyurular/v2/TMS_TFRS_Setleri/2021/K%C4%B1rm%C4%B1z%C4%B1_Kitap/TFRS%2013(1).pdf Accesed: 03.01.2021.

15 https://kgk.gov.tr/Portalv2Uploads/files/Duyurular/v2/TMS_TFRS_Setleri/2021/K%C4%B1rm%C4%B1z%C4%B1_Kitap/TFRS%2013(1).pdf Erişim Tarihi: 03.01.2021.

16 https://kgk.gov.tr/Portalv2Uploads/files/Duyurular/v2/TMS_TFRS_Setleri/2021/K%C4%B1rm%C4%B1z%C4%B1_Kitap/TFRS%2013(1).pdf Erişim Tarihi: 03.01.2021.

17 https://kgk.gov.tr/Portalv2Uploads/files/Duyurular/v2/TMS_TFRS_Setleri/2021/K%C4%B1rm%C4%B1z%C4%B1_Kitap/TFRS%2013(1).pdf Retrieved: 03.01.2021.

method is used to measure fair value, the results (fair value indicators) are evaluated considering the acceptability of the value range they represent. Fair value measurement is the point that best reflects the fair value in the current conditions in the aforementioned range (Sağlam & Yolcu, 2019: 106).

5.2. Comparison of TFRS/TAS/TCC and TPL valuation provisions

Valuation refers to a process that directly affects the operating profit for the period. While the purpose of the valuation in line with the regulations made within the framework of international standards is to determine the financial status of the enterprises and the results of their activities accordingly (Duman & Yücenurşen, 2017: 1310), the purpose in terms of tax legislation is to determine the economic asset rate values for the determination of the tax base (Küçük, 2018: 47). There are some differences between TAS/TFR and TPL in terms of valuation criteria, since the valuation provisions in the TPL aim to determine tax receivables, and TAS/TFRSs aim to present the economic assets in the financial statements over their current and fair values (Ergin, 2016: 20). Tab. 1 (TPL; TFRS; Duman & Yücenurşen, 2017: 1323) shows a comparison of the standards and valuation provisions in the TPL.

Tab. 1: *Comparison of TFRS/TAS/TCC and TPL valuation provisions*

Asset Type	TPL Valuation Provisions	TFRS/TAS/TCC Valuation Provisions
Receivables and Payables	***Rediscount, prepaid value*** *Receivables and payables are valued at their book values. Debts and receivables based on deposit or loan agreements are considered together with the interest to be calculated until the valuation day. (TPL art. 281 and 285)*	*It is valued at "amortised cost."*
Cash (Turkish Lira)	***Nominal value*** *"The cash holdings are valued at their nominal values." (TPL art. 284)*	It is valued at *"nominal value using the fair value method".*
Cash (Foreign Currency)	***Stock exchange price, purchase price*** *Foreign currencies are valued at the stock exchange value. If it is understood that there is collusion in the stock exchange value, the purchase price is taken as the basis instead of this stock exchange value. If the foreign currency does not have a current value in the stock exchange, the rate to be applied to the valuation is determined by the Ministry of Treasury and Finance. (TPL art. 280)*	It is valued at *"period-end exchange rate using the fair value method".*

Tab. 1: Continued

Tangible and Intangible Assets	***Cost price*** *"All real estates included in commercial enterprises are valued at cost". (TPL art. 273)* *"Intangible rights are also valued like real estate". (TPL, art. 269)* *"Tools, equipment, furnishings and fixtures are valued at cost". (TPL art. 273)*	It is valued by "*deducting the accumulated depreciation and accumulated impairment losses from the cost value, if any*".
Doubtful	***Savings value*** *"For doubtful, provision can be made in liabilities according to the savings value of the valuation day." (TPL art. 323) (Optional.)*	*"Expense directly." (Required.)*
Securities	***Cost price, stock exchange value and purchase price*** *The* ***investment fund participation certificates****, which consist of shares and at least 51 % of the fund portfolio of companies established in Türkiye are valued at the* ***stock exchange value****. However,* ***securities*** *that do not have a stock market value, whose yield depends on the profit and loss of the issuer and cannot be calculated as of the valuation day, are valued at* ***the purchase price****. (TPL art. 279)*	It is valued at "*cost value amortised using the effective interest rate*".
İntentories	***Cost and precedent*** *Commodities are valued at cost. In cases where the sales prices on the valuation day show a decrease of 10 % or more compared to the cost value of the commodity, the taxpayer may apply the value of equal measure instead of the cost price, excluding the procedure in the second row of Article 267. (TPL art. 262)*	It is valued at "*the lower of cost or net realizable value*".

Source: (TPL; TFRS; Duman & Yücenurşen, 2017: 1323).

When the valuation differences between tax legislation and standards are examined as a whole (Duman & Yücenurşen, 2017: 1323);

- In the TPL, the assets are specified specifically and how they are valued one by one is explained. However, in the standards, the assets are evaluated in terms of the relevant group.
- While the standards aim to present the financial situation of the enterprises in accordance with the truth and needs by valuing assets and liabilities over their

fair values, it has been deemed sufficient to account for assets and liabilities at cost in TPL.

- While it is not allowed to set a provision before a financial transaction takes place in the TPL, the standards allow businesses to make provisions for some negative situation assumptions.
- Since the definitions of assets, resources, expenses and income in the standards differ according to TPL, some values that are considered as assets according to TPL regulations can be expensed without being evaluated in accordance with the standards.

The use of different valuation measures in standards and tax legislation makes it difficult to determine the fair value of business profitability, and this affects the truth of the tax base. When businesses that have prepared their financial statements according to TPL have to revise them according to TAS/TFRS, they have to re-correct many accounting records (Yücel, 2017: 88).

6. Conclusion

The determination of the tax base is crucial for both businesses and tax administration. There are differences between TAS/TFRS and TPL in terms of valuation criteria, since the valuation provisions in the TPL aim to determine tax receivables, and TAS/TFRSs aim to present the economic assets in the financial statements over their current and fair values. The use of different valuation criteria in standards and tax legislation complicates the process of determining the fair value of business profitability. Differences between the TAS/TFRS and TPL regulations result in differences in financial statement results.

Businesses that prepare their financial statements in accordance with TAS/TFRS, re-arrange their financial statements in accordance with the provisions of the TPL, also require the restatement of many accounting records. Financial statements created according to TAS/TFRS are more dynamic and up to date than the statements created according to the TPL. In transactions where the TPL does not allow the creation of records for some cases or allows registration under strict conditions, the creation of records according to the TAS is important to reveal the risks posed by the business resources and assets and show the opportunities more clearly. This is also important in reaching the truth in taxation.

In determining the fair value of an asset or liability, the zeitgeist must be captured by considering the economic changes in an up-to-date manner. To make a fair taxation, the actual nature (essence) of the taxable event should be considered within the context of its economic, legal and financial components.

The valuation measures set forth in the standards regarding assets and liabilities are more comprehensive and more in line with the spirit of the time than the measures set forth in line with the TPL. Compliance with the standards of TPL regulations is important both to ensure integration into the global system and truth in taxation. Therefore, tax legislation should be aligned with international standards and needs to be compatible with the TCC and other relevant laws. Harmonization with the regulations in the TAS/TFRS can be achieved by referring to the standards prepared by the POA in the valuation regulations both in the TCC and TLP.

References

Akkaya, M. (2002). *Vergi Hukukunda Ekonomik Yaklaşım* (2. Baskı), Ankara, Mali Akademi Yayınları.

Aksoy, Ş. (1994). *Kamu Maliyesi: Kamu Harcamaları – Kamu Gelirleri – Bütçe – Maliye Politikası* (2. Baskı), İstanbul, Filiz Kitabevi.

Arıkan, Z. & İnneci, A. (2016), "Vergilendirilebilir Gelir ve Gelir Vergisinde Üniter Yapıyı Bozan Uygulamalar", *Sosyoekonomi,* 24(30), pp. 11–28.

Balcı, B. R. (2012). "Yeni Muhasebe Düzeninde Mali Kâr Hesaplamaları", *Dokuz Eylül Üniversitesi İktisadi ve İdari Bilimler Fakültesi,* 27(1), pp. 159–179.

Dinç, E. & Atabay, E. (2019). "Tekdüzen Muhasebe Sisteminde Gerçekliği Bozan Hükümler ve Güncelleme İhtiyacı", *Uluslararası İktisadi ve İdari İncelemeler,* (22), pp. 179–192.

Duman, H. & Yücenurşen, M (2017). "TMS/TFRS ve VUK Çerçevesinde Değer, Değerleme ve Ölçüm", *Social Sciences Studies Journal*, 3(10), pp. 1310–1325.

Ergin, N. E. (2016). "Vergi Mevzuatı ile TMS/TFRS'nin Değerleme Ölçüleri Açısından Karşılaştırılması", *Vergi Dünyası,* (418), pp. 9–20.

Erginay, A. (1998). *Kamu Maliyesi: Kamu Gelirleri – Kamu Giderleri – Devlet Bütçesi – Kamu Borçları – Maliye Politikası* (16. baskı), Ankara, Savaş Yayınları.

Erol, M. & Aslan, M. (2017). "Uluslararası Muhasebe ve Denetim Standartlarının Gelişmesi", *Muhasebe ve Finans Tarihi Araştırmaları,* (12), pp. 55–86.

Hacıköylü, C. (2017). "Bağımsız denetim ve vergi hukuku" Proceedings EconWorld2017@Rome 25–27 January, 2017; Rome, Italy.

Hançerlioğlu, O. (2016). *Felsefe Sözlüğü* (23. Baskı), İstanbul, Remzi Kitabevi.

Küçük, M. (2018). *Değerleme*, İstanbul, Maliye Hesap Uzmanları Derneği.

Öncel, M., Kumrulu A. & Çağan, N. (2018). *Vergi Hukuku* (21. Baskı), Ankara, Turhan Kitabevi.

Özer, İ. (1975). *Gelir Vergisi Politikası*. Ankara, Maliye Bakanlığı Tetkik Kurulu Neşriyatı No:164–1975.

Sağlam, N. & Yolcu, M. (2019). *Uygulamalı UFRS TFRS Rehberi*, Bursa, Muhasebe Kitapları İnternet Yayıncılık Eğitim ve TİC. A.Ş.

Şimşek, A. Özkök, S. & Gündüz, N.K. (2016). *Vergi Muhasebesi* (6. Baskı), İstanbul, Huz Akademi Yayıncılık.

Taylar, Y. (2013). *Vergi Hukukunda Vergiyi Doğuran Olay*. Yayınlanmamış Doktora Tezi. İzmir: Dokuz Eylül Üniversitesi, Sosyal Bilimler Enstitüsü.

Tuna, S. (2010). *Vergi Muhasebesi ve Uygulamaları,* İstanbul, Türkmen Kitabevi.

Turhan, S. (1993). *Vergi Teorisi ve Politikası,* İstanbul, Filiz Kitabevi.

Uçan, R. (2015). "Dönem Sonunda Ticari Kârdan Mali Kâra Geçiş ve Özellikli Durumlar." *Vergi Raporu*, 2(2), pp. 9–28.

Üyümez, M. E. (1998). *Gelir Kavramı ve Türk Vergi Hukukunda Gerçek Gelir.* Yayınlanmamış Doktora Tezi. Eskişehir: Anadolu Üniversitesi, Sosyal Bilimler Enstitüsü.

Yücel, K. (2017). "Mali Kârdan Ticari Kâra Geçiş Uygulamasında Kayıt ve Raporlama Düzeni", *Anadolu Bil Meslek Yüksekokulu,* 12(47), pp. 77–91.

Yiğit Şakar, A. (2020). "*Değerleme/Amortisman*" *Vergi Usul Hukuku,* (Ed.) Üyümez, M. E. & Hacıköylü, C., Anadolu Üniversitesi Açıköğretim Yayınları, Eskişehir, pp. 113–138.

Oxford Learner's Dictionaries. https://www.oxfordlearnersdictionaries.com/definition/english/truth?q=truth (25.10.2022).

Public Oversight Accounting and Auditing Standards Authority. (2021). https://kgk.gov.tr/Portalv2Uploads/files/Duyurular/v2/TMS_TFRS_Setleri/2021/K%C4%B1rm%C4%B1z%C4%B1_Kitap/TFRS%2013(1).pdf (03.01.2021).

Turkish Commercial Code, No. 6102. https://www.mevzuat.gov.tr/mevzuat?MevzuatNo=6102&MevzuatTur=1&MevzuatTertip=5 (28.10.2022)

Turkish Corporation Tax Act, No, 5520. https://www.mevzuat.gov.tr/mevzuat?MevzuatNo=5520&MevzuatTur=1&MevzuatTertip=5 (28.10.2022).

Turkish Income Tax Act, No. 193. https://www.mevzuat.gov.tr/mevzuat?MevzuatNo=193&MevzuatTur=1&MevzuatTertip=4 (28.10.2022).

Turkish Language Association, Glossary of Philosophy Terms (1975). https://sozluk.gov.tr/ (25.10.2022).

Turkish Tax Procedure Act, No. 213. https://www.mevzuat.gov.tr/mevzuat?MevzuatNo=213&MevzuatTur=1&MevzuatTertip=4 (28.10.2022).

The Accounting System Implementation General Communiqué Serial No. 1, Official Gazette dated 26.12.1992 and numbered 21447. https://www.resmigazete.gov.tr/arsiv/21447_1.pdf (16.01.2021).

https://www.accounting.com/resources/gaap/#:~:text=Generally%20accepted%20accounting%20principles%2C%20or,approved%20accounting%20methods%20and%20practices (07.01.2021).

Ayşegül Yücel[1] & Burçin Bozdoğanoğlu[2]

Metaverse: Evaluation of the Alternative Virtual Universe in the Context of Taxation Power

1. Introduction

The metaverse is the final point in the digital world. It is defined as a decentralized and borderless universe where people interact with each other in a three-dimensional way, which is currently depicted as a twin of the real world. The Metaverse is built on 5G, augmented reality and edge computing, blockchain, and machine learning technologies. The metaverse, which is accessed through various platforms that offer different services to people, is a concept that is increasing in popularity day by day.

The Metaverse is not defined as a digital environment that people use only for socializing. In the Metaverse, people also engage in various economic and commercial activities. As a result of intense economic relations, value is created in this virtual universe. Recently, people in the metaverse have been using their digital wallets to carry out various trading transactions in the virtual universe with the digital currency of each platform and record them in their wallets in the form of NFTs. Under these circumstances, it seems clear that states will want to tax the metaverse, as it may generate huge profits that cannot be described as a mere socializing space. However, there has not yet been a legal arrangement for states to tax the metaverse.

In this study, firstly, the technical dimension of the metaverse concept will be explained, and then the taxation of the value chain created in the metaverse according to classical principles will be discussed. In the face of the inadequacy of the guidelines for the taxing authority of states in a digital universe, taxation in the metaverse will be evaluated within the framework OECD/BEPS project about taxation of digital economy.

---

1 Res. Asst., Bandirma Onyedi Eylül University, Faculty of Economics and Administrative Sciences, Department of Public Finance, ayucel@bandirma.edu.tr,

2 Prof. PhD., Bandirma Onyedi Eylul University Faculty of Economics and Administrative Sciences Department of Public Finance, bbozdoganoglu@bandirma.edu.tr,

2. Metaverse Concept

Metaverse is a combination of the Ancient Greek words meta, meaning beyond or after, and verse, meaning universe (Mystakidis, 2022: 486). In other words, the metaverse means the universe after reality. The first person to use the word metaverse was the writer, Neal Stephenson. In his 1992 novel Snow Crash, Stephenson defined the word as a three-dimensional place established by people trying to escape from the world that no longer attracts attention (Riva & Wiederhold, 2022: 3). This concept, which has recently been popularised by Facebook founder Mark Zuckerberg, is defined as a three-dimensional, decentralized and unlimited universe where people interact socially (Momtaz, 2022: 227,228). Metaverse does not only mean a single universe but includes countless and unlimited universes (Momtaz, 2022: 230).

Although the metaverse is a new concept, it has predecessors. For example, online games such as Second Life and World of Warcraft can be considered as primitive forms of the metaverse. In these games, people can socialize or play games with the help of a digital avatar. However, these games do not have enough equipment to explain the metaverse (Ball, 2022).

The metaverse should not be seen only as a game or social activity area. According to some predictions, the metaverse is depicted as an alternative life in the future that is unlimited, non-stop and progresses simultaneously with real life. This situation suggests that in the metaverse, every individual living in the real world can take place in the form of a digital entity, participate in social life in any way they want, and create economic value (having a job, investing, or being employed in any job) (Ball, 2022).

3. Basic Components of Metaverse

The metaverse is a digital reality that combines the features of social media, online games, Augmented Reality (AR), Virtual Reality (VR), Blockchain, and cryptocurrencies to allow users to interact virtually (Folger, 2022). In this way, the metaverse, which is an umbrella concept for a group of technologies, is also created by the use of all these technologies at different times. Metaverse is built on 5G, extended reality and edge computing, blockchain, and machine learning technologies (Cheng et.al., 2022: 2).

Blockchain technology is used in the metaverse. This technology is primarily important for data privacy and security in the metaverse. Metaverse platforms that have integrated blockchain and crypto assets into their infrastructure and economy are also called crypto metaverse. Examples include Decentraland,

Cryptovoxels, Alien Worlds, Axie Infinity, and The Sandbox platforms. Thanks to this integration, who can join the platforms and what they can do on the platforms are differentiated, and interaction and trade over economic values become possible. Metaverse digital objects are modeled as tokens, their ownership is recorded on the blockchain, and they can change hands on decentralized exchanges.

Extended reality used in the metaverse is an umbrella concept that includes the concepts of virtual reality, augmented reality, and mixed reality (Mystakidis, 2022: 487). People can partially or fully participate in digital environments created through these forms of reality.

Virtual reality is a completely fictionalized digital environment. In this reality, users move as if in another world with virtual reality headsets or glasses and mechanical devices that provide 360-degree mobility (Mystakidis, 2022: 487). These technological devices, which provide a connection with virtual reality, try to provide users with an experience in which all five sensory organs are active.

Augmented reality is defined as a live or indirect physical appearance created in the real world by enriching it with digital audio, video, graphics, and GPS data (Mystakidis, 2022: 487). Mixed reality is a more intricate concept consisting of a combination of virtual and augmented reality concepts. In augmented reality, users do not remain in a fixed position, but rather move their bodies in the real world and these movements are transferred into the virtual universe. The transfer of user movements is realized through virtual reality glasses, wireless in-ear sensors, and cameras monitoring the environment (Mystakidis, 2022: 488). Users can interact with the avatars of other users in the metaverse simultaneously (Riva & Wiederhold, 2022: 4).

4. Value Chain and Main Sectors in Metaverse

The reason why the metaverse has become so popular is not only the technological revolution but also the fact that people can perform certain transactions through the metaverse. Experts such as Jon Radoff state that the metaverse consists of a seven-layered value chain to attract the user. These seven layers are; (Radoff, 2021). (i) Experience, (ii) Discovery, (iii) Creative Economy, (iv) Spatial Computing, (v) Decentralisation, (vi) Human Interface, and (vii) Infrastructure. The convergence of various technological trends such as AR, VR, Artificial Intelligence, NFTs, cryptocurrency, blockchain, Internet of Things, 5G network, and haptic technology through the creation of Metaverse enables results to be achieved at different levels of the Metaverse (Nishith Desai, 2022). In other words, the value created by these technologies is differentiated in these seven layers. When the seven-layered Metaverse ecosystem is analyzed as a value chain; (Radoff, 2021):

1. Layer: Experience (Games, Social applications, e-sports, shopping)
2. Layer: Discovery (ad networks, stores, agencies)
3. Layer: Creative Economy (Design tools, Asset Markets, Workflow, Trade)
4. Layer: Spatial 3D Programming (3D Augmented Reality, Virtual Reality, Multitasking User Interfaces, Geospatial Mapping),
5. Layer: Decentralisation (Artificial Intelligence, Intelligent Agents, Blockchain)
6. Layer: Human Interface (Wearable Technologies, Smart Glasses, Mobile Technologies, Touch, Mimics, Voice, Nerves)
7. Layer: Infrastructure (5G, Cloud Computing, MicroEloctro Mechanical Systems)

Within the framework of these explanations, the metaverse, which can be considered a twin of people's daily life, is not just a socializing or gaming platform. The metaverse is a virtual world where people will establish intensive economic relations. Especially with the pandemic effect, an increase in corporate and sectoral digitalization has been observed and the use of digital reality applications has increased accordingly. The worldwide virtual reality and augmented reality market size was $ 12 billion in 2020 and is expected to reach $ 73 billion by 2024 with an average annual growth rate of 57 %.

5. Evaluation of Taxation Authority in the Metaverse

5.1. Evaluation of Metaverse in The Digitalization and Value Creation Process Within the Framework of Classical Taxation Authorization Principles

The metaverse is a new digital universe where people from all over the world can come together to socialize, play games, participate in various artistic and social activities, and maintain economic and commercial relations. The metaverse, which has the possibility of allocating an alternative resource for production factors that are limited in the face of the infinity of human needs, will be able to create a large-scale digital market with users producing value not only as consumers but also as producers (Ball, 2022). This situation shows that the factors of production listed as labor, capital, entrepreneurs, and natural resources will also change with digitalization.

On the other hand, considering the value created here and the possibility that users can earn high amounts of profit as a result of the rapid change process, it is inevitable that governments will demand taxes from these virtual universes to contribute to their national economies. It is clearly understood that governments will not remain indifferent to the metaverse in this scenario. Each state may want to control the economy of the metaverse and demand management rights. For example; South Korea has established the municipality of Seoul in the metaverse. Barbados is the first country to open an embassy in the metaverse (XR Today, 2022).

However, due to the unlimited and independent nature of the metaverse, the taxation of the metaverse is a matter of great uncertainty. This situation first raises questions as to whether the taxation authority in the metaverse will be used according to the classical classification or another classification. The fact that users in the metaverse create value or generate income as a result of their transactions suggests that the transactions will be subject to taxation. However, there is no regulation yet on the rules under which the value created will be included in the taxation jurisdiction of which country. Administrative authorities may have difficulty in identifying and taxing income in the metaverse. In addition to this, the question may arise as to which digital borders states have taxation authority in terms of taxation. The metaverse has an authority that extends beyond the legal borders of the state. Legitimate governments may have difficulty enforcing laws and regulations specific to the metaverse. Because the metaverse is not bound by national borders (Johan, 2022: 160). At this point, the strategic question in terms of taxing authority is whether local and national tax authorities around the world can assert tax authority over transactions that take place in a virtual arena devoid of provincial, state, and national borders that provide the framework for real-world tax administration.

On the other hand, in such a case, there may be people who can protect their legal rights and interests by having digital citizenship under any governance model in the metaverse. It is also envisaged that there will be a universal metaverse constitution that protects citizens (Qin, Wang & Hui, 2022: 4). It is unclear who will be the owner or, if not the owner, the operator of the metaverse. However, digital technology giants (Facebook, Microsoft, Amazon, etc.) want a share of the metaverse and desire to dominate it (Ball, 2022).

This situation shows that the digital economy, which is based on the concept of "value creation" emerging in the digitalization process, is gradually expanding, but the taxation problems experienced will be carried to different dimensions with the new applications that will develop in the metaverse and beyond. In this framework, how the taxation authority will be used in the Metaverse seems to be one of the most fundamental problems.

In this context, it is understood that the main change in taxation is the concepts of business models and value creation brought by increasingly digitalized trade. To tax digitalized trade and to ensure compliance with international taxation, the concepts of value addition and value creation are focused on in different business models. In other words, it is stated that taxation should be carried out at the stage and place where and where the added value is created, and tax responsibilities should be defined accordingly.

In digitalizing economies, taxation according to the stage at which the value is created and determining which country is within the scope of taxation jurisdiction of this value creates an important problem. It is possible to explain the problem in its most basic form as follows (Bozdoğanoğlu, 2020: 103):

Through an internet platform operating in country A, a seller in country B sells his goods to a buyer in country C. In such a case, who will be the tax responsibilities, and which country will tax? Again, through an internet platform operating in country A, a person in country B exhibits his/her talents with the videos he/she uploads, and a person in country C watches these videos by accessing the website. While the platform in country A generates advertising revenue, it partially shares it with the person in country B who exhibits his/her talents. In this case, at which stage the value and profit are created, how they are shared between them, and which country has the taxation authority. The existing principles in international tax law are insufficient to answer these questions.

At this point, the classical principles that dominate international tax law and are the determinants of taxing power;

- resource-based taxation
- residence-based taxation
- taxation based on nationality
- destination or place of departure.

In source-based taxation, whichever country is the country where the income arises and the value is created has the taxation authority. Residence-based taxation, on the other hand, is based on the principle that states tax the income of persons residing in their own countries, regardless of where these incomes are generated. Here, the place of residence for individuals and the legal center or business center for legal entities gain importance. States that adopt the principle of nationality tax the income earned all over the world by everyone who is bound to them by the bond of nationality. It does not matter where the income is generated or the residence of the taxpayers. In terms of taxes on expenditures, destination and origin principles are used. The destination principle gives the right of taxation to the country where the final consumption is made. On the contrary, the place of origin principle gives the right of taxation to the country where the seller is located. Therefore, in terms of taxation within the framework of these principles, the rates and locations at which multinational and technology-oriented companies should declare their profits constitute an important problem. In cases where there is no physical presence in a country, more complex and troublesome consequences may be encountered. This situation leads to tax planning practices in which digitalizing multinational companies shift their intangible assets and the income derived from them to lower-income countries.

5.2. Assessment of Taxation Authority in the Metaverse Within the Framework of OECD Recommendations on Taxation of the Digital Economy

The inadequacy of the classical principles on the limitation of taxing power to grasp the value created by digital assets has led countries to search for new ways to tax the digital economy. As a result of this search, the Base Erosion and Profit Shifting (BEPS) action plan prepared by the OECD was published in 2015. In Action Plan No. 1 of this project, which consists of 15 action plans, in the section on Combating the Tax Problems of the Digital Economy, the digital economy is defined as a result of the change process brought about by information and communication technology (ICT).

This action plan generally includes amending the concept of permanent establishment to be compatible with the digital economy, making relevant updates to the transfer pricing guidance, and making the necessary changes in the context of the problems in the taxation of controlled foreign corporate income in the digital economy. In the Addressing the Tax Challenges of the Digital Economy section of the BEPS Action Plan No. 1, there are three options recommended to countries. These are; (1) taxation within the scope of a digital permanent establishment in case of significant economic assets according to the nexus principle (2) withholding tax on certain digital transactions, (3) equalization tax (Bozdoğanoğlu, 2020: 306).

In this context, income-based factors, digital factors, and user-based factors are used as criteria in determining the existence of a significant economic asset (presence), in other words, in determining whether a workplace is established.

In this framework, the first proposed criterion for determining whether the activities of a non-resident organization will constitute a permanent establishment according to classical taxation principles is the income factor. If a significant level of income is generated as a result of the purchase and sale contracts concluded through digital platforms between an organization operating abroad and the citizens of the relevant country, this is presented as a criterion for determining the permanent establishment in the new nexus approach (Bozdoğanoğlu, 2020: 306).

The second criterion proposed in determining the permanent establishment approach based on a significant economic presence is to look at digital factors. Accordingly, if a foreign enterprise has local domain names, a website, and payment options in the local currency of the country, this will cause the activity to constitute a permanent establishment (Bozdoğanoğlu, 2020: 307).

The third approach is to look at user activities. In this context, it is proposed to make an evaluation based on the number of monthly active users, the number of contracts made, and the data collected. Assuming that a permanent establishment is established in the source country according to these criteria, the taxation authority will pass to the source country.

The other proposal is the application of an equalization tax. The equalization tax is based on the principle of calculating and declaring the tax by applying the determined rate on the revenues obtained by foreign sellers for long-distance sales, even if they do not have a workplace or permanent representatives in the source country (Bozdoğanoğlu, 2020: 309.)

While multinational companies are making tax plans and implementing them, especially after the increase in digitalization, countries are taking and increasing their measures against these plans. Examples include the Diverted Profits Tax (DPT) introduced by the UK and Australia, Italy's Voluntary Disclosure Regime for Permanent Establishment (PE), India's new linkage rules based on the concept of Significant Economic Presence (SEP), and the United States tax on base erosion and anti-abuse.

In 2020, the OECD published a report titled "Tax Challenges Arising From Digitalisation-Economic Impact Assessment: Inclusive Framework on BEPS,2020". In the report, a two pillars solution is emphasized for the solution of tax problems arising from digitalization through a multilateral instrument (MLI) (OECD, 2020). The first pillar focuses on nexus and profit allocation, while the second pillar focuses on a global minimum tax designed to address the remaining BEPS issues. In this framework, pillar one aims to adapt the international tax system to new business models through a consistent and simultaneous examination of profit allocation and nexus rules. The second pillar (pillar two) is designed to address the remaining BEPS challenges and ensure that businesses operating internationally pay the minimum level of tax, regardless of where they are headquartered or operating.

At the OECD meeting held on 8 October 2021, it was stated that 137 members of the OECD/G20 BEPS ("Base Erosion and Profit Shifting") Inclusive

Framework agreed on the Two-Pillar Solution (OECD, 2021a). In this meeting, it was agreed that 25 % of the residual profits of multinational enterprises (MNEs) with a global revenue of EUR 20 billion and a profitability exceeding 10 % would be allocated to market areas with a tax nexus using an income-based allocation key (Pillar One) (OECD, 2021b).

On the other hand, concerning Pillar Two, within the framework of the Global Anti-Base Erosion Rules (GloBE) and BEPS 13th Action Plan (Country by Country Reporting), it was agreed that the global minimum corporate tax rate for multinational enterprises (MNEs) with annual revenues exceeding EUR 750 million should be 15 % (OECD, 2021a).

In a multilateral agreement under the two-pillar solution, the parties commit to abolish all digital services taxes and other similar measures on companies and to refrain from adopting such measures in the future (OECD, 2021a).

On the other hand, it is unclear whether the unilateral measures taken by some countries for the taxation of the digital economy will be effective in taxing the value created in the metaverse. The implementation of these measures will continue until the global minimum corporate tax begins. As a matter of fact, India, which is one of the countries that try to act fast in the taxation of the digital economy, has different regulations such as SEP (significant economic presence), e-com EL (Equalisation Levy), VDA (Virtual Digital Asset) definition and taxation. However, there is neither a guide nor a clear application on the taxation of the value created in the metaverse with these regulations. The applicability of the provisions contained in different laws should be assessed based on the nature of each transaction. For example, if a person purchases e-suits, virtual land, etc. on Metaverse, the applicability of the E-com EL and SEP provisions will need to be examined. The SEP provisions will only come into play if the Metaverse platform is outside a country with which India does not have a tax treaty and the SEP thresholds are exceeded. E-com EL is applicable at the rate of 2 % on the consideration paid by the Indian resident for the purchase of e-articles on Metaverse. In case the Metaverse platform charges fees for such activities, the E-com EL provisions may also apply. Income from transactions involving VDAs on Metaverse may be subject to tax at the rate of 30 % under the Income Tax Act. Further, the Metaverse platform may be under an obligation to withhold tax at the rate of 1 % when Indian sellers make payments against the transfer of Virtual Digital assets on their platform. As a matter of fact, it is stated that local practices in India will be applied until the global minimum corporate tax provisions enter into force.

India seems to be an example of a country trying to adapt to the digitalization process with different regulations such as SEP, EL, and VDA in its tax legislation.

However, it is also seen that the regulations in the tax legislation may not always be sufficient to tax the value created. Therefore, international cooperation is critical in taxing the value created in the digitalization process.

6. Conclusion

It is known that there has been a significant increase in internet use, especially in the last ten years. It has become necessary to move this process to the next stage, now known as Web 3.0. The mentioned stage can also be considered as a version with more human contribution in terms of internet applications. In other words, it enables decentralized interactions between users and provides spatial experiences comparable to those that exist in the real world. On the other hand, with the development of these experiences, the boundaries between the digital and physical worlds may be blurred at the end point of Web 3.0.

Expressed as the next version of the Internet, Web3.0 has the potential to extend today's Internet in a decentralized way based on distributed ledger technology. With this technological expansion, Web 3.0 has leveraged artificial intelligence (AI) to spawn blockchain platforms for the public and private sectors, as well as new digital assets such as cryptocurrencies, NFTs, and smart contracts. As a result of the addition of virtual and/or augmented reality to these technological developments, everything necessary for the emergence of the metaverse becomes almost ready.

Augmented Reality, Virtual Reality, Extended Reality, Artificial Intelligence, Internet of Things, advanced network i.e. 5G, blockchains and machine learning are key elements in the digitization process mentioned here. These elements in Web 3.0 are about shaping the internet of the future. Metaverse focuses entirely on how we experience this new version of the internet. As a result of these developments in the digital world, governments and businesses are working to organize their tax policies in the axis of these new concepts. Currently, some states have begun to use Web3 technology to improve public services, protect personal data use, and deliver critical social services more efficiently. On the other hand, when evaluated in terms of the private sector, it is known that businesses are building an alternative reality in the metaverse by using Web3.0 infrastructure and multinational brands are taking action quickly to establish (virtual) stores.

The tax consequences of all these developments are expected to be quite comprehensive and staggering. As a matter of fact, since tax regulations are realized on the basis of the principle of legality, they cannot be updated in accordance with the speed of digitalization, in other words, they are always a few steps behind in catching up with technological developments. The OECD, one of the most active in international taxation, is in the process of creating a common crypto tax framework to build consensus on taxation authority. However, it is not clear how long this process will take and how many countries will be involved. However, each country continues to develop different tax policies, classify digital assets in different ways and apply different tax procedures to transactions with them in this rapid digital process. Such different tax practices make the situation more complex and riskier, especially for businesses operating in the international arena.

For solutions to the problem of taxing the value created in the metaverse, the use of Web3 infrastructure or metaverse-based applications can be offered as an alternative. It is possible to explain this solution with the technical features of Metaverse. Seen as a decentralized, largely disordered and anonymous environment, the metaverse; is transparent because of using blockchain infrastructure and it is possible to "see" transactions taking place in distributed ledger networks in real time. This means; It is possible that real-time tax reporting systems can be built on blockchain-based systems that automate transaction information with tax administrations, replacing the traditional reporting process. Although the Metaverse and its underlying Web3 technology pose significant tax challenges and uncertainties, it also has the potential to offer promising new tools to tax practitioners. If such a solution is implemented, it will be possible to ensure that the right amount of tax is collected at the right time, in a much more efficient and cost-effective manner for all parties involved.

On the other hand, the innovations of an alternative universe such as the metaverse require that countries design broad policy measures to protect businesses as well as citizens, with the assurance of government taking into account tax consequences. Many countries seem likely to find it easier and more advantageous to take advantage of a clear and globally harmonized set of tax rules associated with this latest version of the digital economy. As a matter of fact, in this process, tax policy makers in many countries in different parts of the world are working on cooperation on proposals to make significant changes in international tax rules in the context of the globalization and digitalization of the economy. In this context, the G20/OECD project BEPS, the foundation of which was laid in 2013 and which deals with the taxation of the digital economy, started a two-stage study on taxation of the digital economy in 2019 as BEPS 2.0 with various updates and revisions.

The first pillar of BEPS 2.0., which consists of two pillars, deals with the establishment of new linkage and profit allocation rules to allocate taxation entitlements to market countries proportionally higher than global business income. The second pillar includes the rules on a new global minimum tax, approved in December 2021 by the 137 jurisdictions (approximately 90 % of the global economy) participating in the BEPS 2.0 project. The second pillar model rules include providing a global minimum tax of 15 % applied to multinational enterprise (MNE) groups with global turnover of €750 million ($760 million) or more.

In particular, the success of the global minimum corporate tax reform under the second pillar depends not only on cooperation between tax administrations and agreement on the details of the new rules. It is also linked to coordination in how these rules are applied, which appear to be a barrier to cross-border investments, to avoid claims of tax authorities' conflicting taxation rights on the income of globally operating businesses.

The perspectives of doing business in the Metaverse, a new and almost infinite space for economic transactions, clearly require harmonization efforts from the law. Both tax administrations and taxpayers should be particularly careful when it comes to taxation. Digital assets with economic value can be traded and thus taxed. In the absence of specific legislation specific to digital assets, as in the case of India, general tax rules will apply. Since these rules are based on physical presence such as source, residence, nationality, etc., they are insufficient to capture the value created in the digital economy and the exchange of digital assets. Therefore, it is seen that international cooperation has been established and tax reporting mechanisms have been established on a global scale in the face of the difficulty of renewing the legislation in line with the speed of digitalization in the short term. In this framework, steps are being taken to expand existing legal frameworks with practices such as the OECD Crypto Asset Reporting Framework (CARF) and Common Reporting Standard (CRS), Directive on Administrative Cooperation (DAC-8), and the United States Foreign Account Tax Compliance Act.

References

Ball, M. (2022). The Metaverse: What It Is, Where to Find It, and Who Will Build It, https://www.matthewball.vc/all/themetaverse, (22.12.2022).

Bozdoğanoğlu, B. (2020). Digitalization and Taxation, Ankara, Gazi Bookstore.

Cheng, R., Wu, N., Chen, S., & Han, B. (2022). Will Metaverse be the Next Internet? Vision, Hype, and Reality, *IEEE Network*, *99*, pp. 1–9.

Folger, J. (2022). Metaverse Definition, https://www.investopedia.com/metaverse-definition-5206578, (17.02.2022).

Johan, S. (2022). "Metaverse and Its Implication in Law and Business," *Jurnal Hukum Progresif, 10*(2), pp. 153–166.

Momtaz, P. P. (2022). "Some Very Simple Economics of Web3 and the Metaverse", *FinTech*, 1, pp. 225–234.

Mystakidis, S. (2022). "Metaverse", *Encyclopedia*, 2, pp. 486–497.

Nishith Desai. (2022). A Metaverse New Universe: Legal, Regulatory and Tax Issues, July 2022, https://www.nishithdesai.com/fileadmin/user_upload/pdfs/Research_Papers/Metaverse_A_New_Universe.pdf, (25.12.2022).

OECD. (2020). Tax Challenges Arising from Digitalisation – Economic Impact Assessment: Inclusive Framework on BEPS, https://www.oecd-ilibrary.org/docserver/0e3cc2d4-en.pdf?expires=1673789172&id=id&accname=guest&checksum=08B14FE83A8F7949E861685368BE4F53, (21.12.2021).

OECD. (2021a). Members of the OECD/G20 Inclusive Framework on BEPS joining the October 2021 Statement on a Two-Pillar Solution to Address the Tax Challenges Arising from the Digitalisation of the Economy, https://www.oecd.org/tax/beps/oecd-g20-inclusive-framework-members-joining-statement-on-two-pillar-solution-to-address-tax-challenges-arising-from-digitalisation-october-2021.pdf , (10.01.2023)

OECD. (2021b). Statement on a Two-Pillar Solution to Address the Tax Challenges Arising From The Digitalisation of the Economy, 08.10.2021, https://www.oecd.org/tax/beps/statement-on-a-two-pillar-solution-to-address-the-tax-challenges-arising-from-the-digitalisation-of-the-economy-october-2021.pdf, (16.12.2022)

Qin, H. X., Wang, Y., Hui, P. (2022). Identity, Crimes, and Law Enforcement in the Metaverse, https://arxiv.org/abs/2210.06134, (27.12.2022).

Radoff, J. (2021). The Metaverse Value Chain, https://medium.com/building-the-metaverse/the-metaverse-value-chain-afcf9e09e3a7, (30.12.2022).

Riva, G., Wiederhold, B. K. (2022). "What the Metaverse is (Really) and Why We Need to Know About It", *Cyberpsychology Behavior, and Social Networking, 25*(6), pp. 355–359.

XR Today. (2022). Who Will Govern the Metaverse? (No, It Won't Be Facebook), https://www.xrtoday.com/virtual-reality/who-will-govern-the-metaverse-no-it-wont-be-facebook/, 10.01.2023.

Ali Osman Yilmaz[1] & Mustafa Erkan Üyümez[2]

Effects of Artificial Intelligence on Tax Inspections

1. Introduction

Our organization and activities are changing because of developments in information technologies (IT) and the effects of these developments on areas such as health, education, security, transportation, economy, agriculture and industry. As a result of all these developments, the need for a deeper and more effective analysis of different types and large amounts of data arises to monitor, manage, and control business processes. The data produced with technological developments continues to grow increasingly.

sThe taxation problems of tax administrations on digitalized economic activities and their ability to audit these economic activities are discussed. It is seen that the tax inspection method is in a change from the classical inspection model to the risk-based inspection form because of changing economic conditions and technological advances.

In the past, information technologies, which were used in the process of auditing, were almost non-existent, but nowadays, it is seen that the examination activities that make use of information technologies have increased. The inspection process, which started with record checks on paper in the past, now includes data warehouses that include e-applications such as e-ledger and e-invoice. Big data, which will be audited and analyzed within the framework of developing and digitalizing economic activities, continues to increase day by day. Using data analytics and technologies, it becomes possible to reveal relationships that cannot be discovered with classical methods from the data owned by institutions or companies. It can be said that with the help of artificial intelligence applications such as big data analysis technologies, artificial learning (machine learning), deep learning and natural language processing, it has the potential to provide much more insight into tax inspection activities and increase the

---

1 Karabük University, Safranbolu Ş.Y.D. Vocational School, Department of Accounting and Tax, aliyilmaz@karabuk.edu.tr

2 Anadolu University, Faculty of Economics and Administrative Sciences, Department of Public Finance, meuyumez@anadolu.edu.tr

accuracy of tax inspections. In tax examinations, it can be said that it is inevitable that the importance of artificial intelligence applications will increase in the near future.

The aim of this research is to determine the contribution and impact of the developments in the field of artificial intelligence and data analytics on tax inspections. Considering that tax inspection rates in Turkey are around 2 %; It can be said that it is inevitable to use artificial intelligence and data analytics to increase the scope and effectiveness of tax inspection. In a digitalized economy, suggestions for artificial intelligence and data analytics will be presented for the tax administration to reduce tax loss and evasion, increase taxpayer compliance, and increase the efficiency and efficiency of tax inspections. Within the scope of the research a literature review on big data, data analytics and artificial intelligence will be presented. Afterwards, foreign country applications on tax analytics and artificial intelligence will be discussed. Within the scope of the study, evaluations and results regarding the possible contribution and reflection of artificial intelligence to tax inspections will be presented to the beneficiaries.

2. Literature Research

2.1. Artificial Intelligence

Artificial intelligence is a broad concept used to describe technologies that make machines "intelligent" (IIA, 2017: 5). It is seen that artificial intelligence is defined differently in the literature. Say (2018: 83) defines artificial intelligence as "the branch of science that examines how natural systems can do every cognitive activity that artificial systems can do at even higher levels of success". Artificial intelligence is a science that deals with intelligent algorithms whether it learns from data or not (Husain, 2019: 18).

Regarding the term artificial intelligence.

- Deep learning,
- Machine learning (artificial learning)
- Image identification,
- Natural language processing,
- Conceptual informatics,
- Intelligence upgrade,
- Conceptual increase,
- Machine-enhanced intelligence concepts are also used (Özdemir, 2019: 46).

Research companies conduct artificial intelligence research and development activities to automate and copy human analytical intelligence, decision-making ability. Artificial intelligence applications are widely used in many sectors and fields. Ordinary daily tasks such as data analysis, loss modeling, credit analysis, valuation transactions, transaction processing, and many other tasks that have been done for years can be done more effectively and easily with artificial intelligence.

Artificial intelligence mainly relies on algorithms. An algorithm is a way designed to solve a particular problem or achieve a particular goal. Algorithms can be expressed as a set of rules that machines can follow. Machine (artificial) learning is a sub-branch of artificial intelligence and relies on algorithms that learn from data. Artificial learning can be generally classified as supervised learning, unsupervised learning, semi-supervised learning and deep learning. In supervised learning, it is expected that the audit experience and methodology will be transferred to the system and that it will learn about the inspection activity. In unsupervised learning, artificial intelligence is expected to perform its own learning and analysis activities by making use of big data (Husain, 2019: 19–20, IIA, 2017: 5). Deep learning is a set of algorithms in machine learning that tries to learn at multiple levels, corresponding to different levels of abstraction. Deep learning is designed by taking advantage of the way the human brain works with neurons. Deep learning has achieved very high success by working on the data that occurs in pictures and videos (Demirhan & Doğan Demirhan, 2022: 52).

Narrow artificial intelligence is machine-based systems that can only perform tasks for example, robot miles from Boston Dynamics, drones with programmed navigation skills. Broad AI is machine-based systems that can learn and solve innovative problems (Husain, 2019: 31–33). In addition to this classification, it is seen that the types of artificial intelligence are also classified as follows.

Type I AI : Reactive machines

The most basic form of artificial intelligence is reactive machines. Reactive machines give the same reaction to a given situation every time. These machines are not capable of using past experiences and cannot create memories. An example of this is machines that can beat world-renowned chess players. Deep Blue is the best example of such machines. Deep Blue can identify the pieces on a chessboard and know how each one moves. They are programmed to predict the next move of both players.

Type II AI: Limited memory

Limited-memory AI machines can look into the past. However, memories are not recorded in these machines. Therefore, such machines cannot accumulate memories. For example, driverless vehicles that can stop at a red light in traffic. Limited-memory AI machines cannot save experience like humans.

Type III AI: Theory of mind

The theory of mind is based on the idea that a machine can understand that the people it communicates with have feelings, thoughts, and expectations. Therefore, a machine equipped with Type III Artificial Intelligence can adjust its behavior in accordance with the feelings, thoughts, and expectations of the other person.

Machines with Type III AI can be expressed as the place where machines included in Broad Artificial Intelligence begin. This is where the AI-based machines currently in use and future AI-based machines diverge.

Type IV AI: Self-awareness

The final point of AI development is to build systems that can form representations about themselves. A machine equipped with Type IV Artificial Intelligence identifies machines that are aware of their own existence (Hintze, 2016).

Type III AI and Type IV AI show the points that artificial intelligence-based machines need to reach in the future. The first two types of artificial intelligence include the artificial intelligence-based machines that we are currently using. The last two types of AI classifications cover the broad AI-based machines that ongoing research and development projects are expected to reach in the future.

2.2. Big Data

Big data is expressed as "conversion of all kinds of corporate data digitally coded by both humans and machines, and personal data generated through internet and social media sharing, into a meaningful and workable form" (Tellan, 2014: 42). Every transaction made in the digitalized world creates data. However, these data need to form meaningful clusters to be processed and analyzed. These datasets are called Big Data. Big data for inspection; It can be said that it refers to large amounts of financial and non-financial data, accounting and non-accounting data, all quantitative and qualitative data in different formats.

Artificial intelligence processes the information in these meaningful datasets within the framework of the relationships between trends, behaviors, and makes decisions (Brands & Smith, 2016). The increase in the volume, variety and speed of data day by day has led to the emergence of big data (Diebold, 2012: 2–3). The term volume indicates how large the generated data is. The term Velocity describes the rate at which the data is produced. Data produced faster results in an increase in the number and variety of transactions at the same rate. Also, this component indicates high speed connection and broadband size. The term diversity describes data types. Data can be classified as structural, semi-structural and unstructured. Veracity states that the data must be watched and seen by the right people so that it does not change during the flow (Özdemir & Sağiroğlu, 2018: 472–473).

The reliability, accuracy, and completeness of the data on which artificial intelligence algorithms are based is very important. In practice, it is very common for data to be inconsistent and insufficiently defined. Often, systems do not communicate with each other, or they communicate through complex plug-ins or custom settings. Therefore, the way the data is gathered, combined, and validated is critical (IIA, 2017: 11). The data warehouse of the Turkish Tax Inspection Board (TTIB) contains data arising from e-applications within the Revenue Administration (e-invoice, e-ledger, e-waybill, e-declaration, etc.), notifications of all financial institutions, all data transmitted by institutions and organizations, especially the Ministry of Commerce, especially banks, constitute.

2.3. Data Analytics

The typical data analysis concept is used to reveal patterns in data and relationships between them. Data analytics is the process of gathering and analyzing data to discover and visualize information using statistical science and modern numerical computation methods (Özdemir, 2019: 41). According to KPMG (2012: 2), data analytics is "the process by which insights are obtained from operational, financial and other forms of electronic data within or outside the organization." Data analytics can also be described as a set of tools developed to make sense of big data (Salijeni).

Big data analytics is at the forefront of technological developments that change businesses and transactions. (Nadas, 2021: 19). For tax inspections to be accurate, meaningful, and useful, big data must be properly analyzed. Data analysis is used to identify patterns in data and relationships between them. In data analytics, algorithms are designed by humans. Errors in algorithms will affect data analytics results (IIA, 2018: 4). Therefore, the design of algorithms is vital in data analytics. However, data analytics, combined with the judgment of the inspectors, make the forecasts and valuations of the inspectors better equipped to formulate the audits. Auditors' qualifications are among the challenges that auditors face in using data analytics (Earley, 2015: 496–498). Therefore, an auditor who does not have sufficient knowledge and competence in data analysis technologies may have difficulty in understanding the area he is auditing. Therefore, it is necessary to increase the equipment of the inspectors in data analysis technologies.

Turkish Tax Inspection Board has been using data analysis in its audits for a long time. While data analysis was initially done with manual methods, these methods have started to be replaced by data analysis technologies with the developments in information systems. Such technologies are used to increase the efficiency and effectiveness of the tax inspection process. therefore, tax inspectors use data analytics technologies to process the detection of tax losses and evasion more quickly and easily.

3. Artificial Intelligence Applications

Many countries such as Switzerland, France, Belgium, Canada, USA, England and Australia use big data analytics to determine tax evasion (İlgün 2020: 14).

The Chinese Government is trying to develop its big data analysis capacity with the "Golden Tax Phase III Project". In this context, On March 1, 2019, the national and local tax systems were combined. However, real estate, household registration and data of some government offices have not yet been included in the database. Therefore, there is a risk of tax evasion. Therefore, "big data" and "cloud platform" functions still need to be developed. (Zhou, 2019: 202).

With the "British Connect system" used by HM Revenue and Customs Office in England, it has enabled the determination of the professions with the highest probability of tax irregularities and tax evasion. It tries to estimate the total income of taxpayers by working on data obtained from many different sources such as real estate records, bank accounts, loans, vehicle licenses, employment records, insurance policies, local government, and hospital records. The British Connect System has enabled the detection of activities with a high risk of tax evasion and irregularities (Maciejewski, 2017: 125).

An artificial intelligence assisted simulation model (Simulating Tax Evasion and Law through Heuristics, STEALTH) developed by Massachusetts Institute of Technology for tax evasion prediction has been developed. In this model, potential tax evasion methods were determined by using different methods and layers such as tax regulations, expert reports, tax evasion decision tree models, audit scores, optimization process for audit risk. The results of the model were found to be successful.

In addition to governments, artificial intelligence-based applications are also used by private companies for auditing. Artificial intelligence-based applications were first used by PwC in audit activities. PwC Halo is a data auditing tool that analyzes vast amounts of data and provides advanced risk assessment (PwC, 2016: 11–13). EY Helix is data analytics driven auditing technology using artificial intelligence tools. Helix GLAD technology of the same company can catch risky entries in ledger accounts by using artificial intelligence technologies. Deloitte's first cognitive control application is Argus. Apart from this, there are also technologies called Optix and Cortex. These technologies are artificial intelligence development technologies with hardware such as smart automation and machine learning.

CognitiveSpend collects complex transactional data. on these data uses natural language processing processes and machine learning technologies. CognitivePersonnel uses machine learning to help accelerate staff insights. Exploring alternative organizational structures helps create an interactive environment for modeling optimal staff configurations. MissionGraph integrates seamlessly with existing enterprise infrastructures, providing an end-to-end data analytics solution powered by machine learning. With the support of artificial intelligence technologies. CogniSteward ensures data management, rapid data relations and data readiness for insights (Nadas, 2021: 47–49).

4. Electronic Applications and Activities in Turkey

Many electronic applications related to tax business and transactions are used by the Ministry of Treasury and Finance in Turkey. There is a Risk Analysis Evaluation and Research System (RADAR) under the Risk Analysis General Directorate of the Ministry of Treasury and Finance. RADAR System can be expressed as an analysis tool that allows working and cross-checking on big data. It is aimed to carry out analyzes by transferring cluster analysis results created by machine learning method to this system (MTF, 2022: 119).

36 applications and activities are carried out electronically by the Revenue Administration. Among these applications, E-Declaration, E-Invoice, E-Ledger, New Generation Payment Recorder, E-Archive, E-Polling System, E-Notification, E-Ticket, E-Waybill, E-Producer Receipt, E- Self Employment Receipt, Prepared Declaration System, VAT Refund Risk Analysis System, Revenue Institutions Standard Return System, False Document Risk Analysis Program (SARP) are included. When these electronic applications are examined, it is understood that artificial intelligence-based applications have not been used yet (AR, 2022: 111–125).

The unit responsible for tax inspection in Turkey is the Tax Inspection Board. Within the VDK, tax inspections are carried out on a risk-based basis. In this context, Risk Analysis System (VDK-RAS) is one of the most basic applications. The Risk Analysis System data warehouse consists of information collected continuously and periodically from public institutions, professional organizations, real and legal persons. Tax Inspection Board analyzes taxpayer activities, sectors, and scales of taxpayers through big data, and risky areas are identified (TIB, 2022: 26–27). Apart from the Risk Analysis System.

- VDK-RAS (Risk Analysis System)
- MBR (Taxpayer Information Report) application
- VDK-VEDAS (Tax Inspection Analysis System)
- VDK-SIGMA (Continuous Surveillance and Control Network)
- E-Inspection
- VDK-EID (Electronic Inspection File)
- VDK Taxpayer Portal electronic applications are also used (TIB, 2022: 27–33).

It is understood that e-applications in Turkey are not yet artificial intelligence-based applications.

5. Use of Artificial Intelligence based applications in Tax inspections

In this part of the research, evaluations on the possible contributions of artificial intelligence-based applications to tax inspections will be presented. In many countries, artificial intelligence-based applications are used in tax transactions. However, it has been determined that the use of artificial intelligence technologies in data analytics is limited except for certain developed countries.

Big data analytics has the potential to improve the quality of tax inspection activities. Many benefits can be achieved because of supporting data analytics with artificial intelligence-based applications.

- With artificial intelligence-based applications, the whole population can be examined instead of sampling,
- The probability of detecting errors, omissions and anomalies in the inspection universe can be increased,
- The effectiveness of tax inspections can be increased through data analysis to be made by using data sources such as video, image and social media,
- Tax inspectors can look at the whole organization from a different perspective, thanks to artificial intelligence-based data analysis tools,

- By means of these data analysis tools, faster control mechanisms can be developed for analysis results,
- Areas of critical risky areas that cannot be audited can be revealed.

As a matter of fact, because of the analysis studies of the Risk Analysis Evaluation and Research System (RADAR-non-artificial intelligence-based) of the Risk Analysis General Directorate of the Ministry of Treasury and Finance, it was determined that 28,845 taxpayers out of 200 thousand taxpayers did not declare their rental income at all or did not declare incompletely. Similarly, in another analysis study over the RADAR System, 5 thousand 589 real estate agents who did not partially or completely fulfill their tax obligations were analyzed and tax inspections were initiated for 683 of these taxpayers (Anatolian Agency, 2022).

Artificial intelligence can help taxpayers identify potential fraud risks. In addition, it can contribute to taxpayers in identifying clues to tax evasion. AI-based applications can detect tax evasion cases in advance that could be missed by tax inspectors. Risky taxpayers identified using artificial intelligence can be subject to immediate audit. Therefore, tax collection amounts can be increased.

As a result of further increasing the efficiency of tax inspections, the areas of informal work can be narrowed. It can also help taxpayers improve their tax compliance. It can contribute to the full and accurate determination of the real income of taxpayers through artificial intelligence-based applications. As a result, taxpayers' activities to hide their income can be reduced.

Very large data sets, which are impossible for tax inspectors to examine effectively and in a timely manner, can be analyzed with artificial intelligence in a short time. As a result, it can contribute to revealing the income movements of taxpayers. Taxpayers are aware of the low probability of their detection due to low tax inspection rates (Üyümez et al., 2021: 436). That's why AI applications can help make tax inspections continuous and more effective. As a result of increasing the probability of being inspected, taxpayers' behaviors against tax legislation can be reduced.

The fact that companies hide their earnings through the transfer pricing process distorts competition among companies and reduces the tax revenues of the state. By using artificial intelligence applications, the factors that cause such tax loss can be detected quickly. In addition, it can provide measures to be taken by analyzing the legal gaps in the tax legislation (Turan, 2020: 60–61).

6. Conclusion

Today, where the volume of big data continues to increase rapidly, not day by day, it has been determined that there is a need to develop data analysis methods primarily by using artificial intelligence-based applications.

For tax inspectors to perform more effective, high quality, accurate and comprehensive audits on existing e-applications and for the Tax Inspection Board to perform its duties more effectively, data analysis technologies should be utilized. In addition, it is considered critical to implement artificial intelligence applications in order to increase the efficiency and productivity of tax inspections.

It has been determined that in the developing and changing economic conjuncture, it is necessary to increase the knowledge of tax inspectors in artificial intelligence-based applications and data analytics, and to adapt both organizational and corporate culture to the new situation.

Tax audits are changing all over the world. It can be said that the number of governments that did not switch from the classical audit methods to the risk-based audit model is quite low. However, some difficulties occur in tax inspections as a result of current technologies such as big data, cloud computing and electronic commerce changing the audit universe. In today's world, where economic activities and other applications are rapidly digitalizing and becoming much more complex, it is very necessary to switch to policies and practices for artificial intelligence-based applications.

As a result, studies on artificial intelligence-based applications should be started in order to reduce tax losses in the developing and rapidly digitalizing world and in Turkey. tax inspectors should be supported with artificial intelligence-based applications. In this framework, it will be beneficial to develop the institutional and individual inspection perspective in a way that will comprehend the new audit universe. It has been determined that there is a need to give priority to research and development studies on artificial intelligence-based data analytics and tax auditing.

References

Anatolian Agency, (2022). Economy News Bulletin. https://www.aa.com.tr/tr/ekonomi/hazine-ve-maliye-bakanligi-gayrimenkul-sektorundeki-vergi-kayip-kacagini-onleme-calismalarini-genisletti/2708025 (11.10.2022).

Brands, K., & Smith, P. (2016). Ready or not, here comes accounting automation. Strategic Finance. https://sfmagazine.com/post-entry/march-2016-ready-or-not-here-comes-accounting-automation/ (05.03.2022).

Demirhan, H., & Dogan Demirhan, G. (2022). "Öğrenmenin Yaşı Yok Makinesi Var". *Rehber Zeka,* 2, pp. 50–53.

Diebold, F. X. (2012). "A Personal Perspective on the Origin(s) and Development of 'Big Data': The Phenomenon, the Term, and the Discipline". https://papers.ssrn.com/sol3/papers.cfm?abstract_id=2202843 (02.02.2022).

Earley, C. E. (2015). "Data Analytics in Auditing: Opportunities and Challenges". *Business Horizons,* 58(5), pp. 493–500.

Hintze, A. (2016). Understanding the Four Types of AI, from Reactive Robots to Self-Aware Beings. https://theconversation.com/understanding-the-four-types-of-ai-from-reactive-robots-to-self-aware-beings-67616 (07.04.2022).

Husain, A. (2019). *The Sentient Machine the Coming Age of Artificial Intelligence.* (Trans. Dalgakıran, D.). İstanbul: Siyah Kitap.

İlgün, M. F. (2020), "Big Data Analytics in Tax Audit". *SEYAD,* 8(1), pp. 1–23.

KPMG (2012). Leveraging data analytics and continuous auditing within internal audit. https://assets.kpmg/content/dam/kpmg/pdf/2016/05/Leveraging-Data-Analytics.pdf (07.09.2022).

Maciejewski, M. (2017). "To do More, Better, Faster and More Cheaply: Using Big Data in Public Administration". *International Review of Administrative Sciences,* 83(1), pp. 120–135.

Ministry of Treasury and Finance. (2022). MTF 2021 Annual Report. https://ms.hmb.gov.tr/uploads/2022/03/Hazine-ve-Maliye-Bakanligi-2021-Yili-Faaliyet-Raporu.pdf (08.10.2022).

Nadas, E. (2021). " Artificial Intelligence Applications in Accounting and Auditing", (M.Sc. Thesis), İstanbul Bilgi University, İstanbul.

Özdemir, İ. and Sağıroğlu, Ş. (2018). "Use of Big Data in Audits and An Evaluation on It". *Gazi University Journal of Science Design and Technology,* 6(2), pp. 470–480.

Özdemir, İ. (2019). "Roadmap For The Use of Big Data Analytics in Auditing", (M.Sc. Thesis), Gazi University, Ankara.

PwC. (2016). Technology in the PWC audit: Driving innovation. https://www.pwchk.com/en/audit-assurance/technology-in-pwc-audit.pdf (03.07.2022).

Revenue Administration. (2022). RA 2021 Annual Report. https://www.gib.gov.tr/sites/default/files/fileadmin/faaliyetraporlari/2021/2021_faaliyet_raporu_4.pdf (09.10.2022).

Say, C. (2018). 50 Soruda Yapay Zeka. İstanbul: 7 Renk Basım Yayın ve Filmcilik Ltd. Şti.

Tax Inspection Board. (2022). TIB 2021 Annual Report. https://ms.hmb.gov.tr/uploads/2022/04/VDK-2021-Birim-Faaliyet-Raporu.pdf (10.10.2022).

Tellan, D. (2014). "*Büyük Veri Türbülansını Yönetmek*", Türkiye Bilişim Derneği, TBD 31. Ulusal Bilişim Kurultayı Bildiri Kitabı, pp. 41–42.

The Institute of Internal Auditors. (2017). Küresel Bakış Açıları ve Anlayışlar. https://www.tide.org.tr/file/documents/pdf/GPAI-Artificial-Intelligence-Part-I-Revised.pdf (10.01.2022).

The Institute of Internal Auditors. (2018). Küresel Bakış Açıları ve Anlayışlar, IIA'nın Yapay Zekâ Denetim Çerçevesi. https://www.tide.org.tr/file/documents/pdf/Artificial-Intelligence-Part-III-15-02-2018.pdf (10.01.2022).

Turan, D. (2020). "Artificial Intelligence and Its Effects on Tax Applications". *Anadolu Akademi Sosyal Bilimler Dergisi*, *2*(1), pp. 55–70.

Üyümez, M. E., Yılmaz, A. O., & Ünlüer, S. (2021). "What Are the Objectives of the Tax Inspection?: A Case Study of Turkey". *Journal of Economics Business and Political Researches*, *6*(16), pp. 432–452.

Zhou, L. (2019). Opportunities and Challenges of Artificial Intelligence in the Application of Taxation System. https://www.atlantis-press.com/proceedings/icemci-19/125927534 (03.03.2022).